>>>>>>>>>>>>>>>>>>>>

Acknowledgments

We thank Clare Holmes and Darren Hedley for assistance with literature searching and notation, and Nicole McCallum for referencing assistance.

Quote on p.7 reproduced with permission from Benjamin Wallace/New York Magazine.

First published in 2015
by Jessica Kingsley Publishers
73 Collier Street
London N1 9BE, UK
and
400 Market Street, Suite 400
Philadelphia, PA 19106, USA

www.jkp.com

Library of Congress Cataloging in Publication Data
Brewer, Neil.
Crime and autism spectrum disorder : myths and mechanisms
/ Neil Brewer and Robyn L. Young.
pages cm
Includes bibliographical references and index.
ISBN 978-1-84905-404-1 (alk. paper)
1. People with mental disabilities and crime. 2. Autism
spectrum disorders. I. Young, Robyn (Robyn
Louise) II. Title.
HV6133.B74 2015
364.3'8--dc23
2014048579

British Library Cataloguing in Publication Data
A CIP catalogue record for this book is available from the British Library

ISBN 978 1 84905 404 1
eISBN 978 0 85700 773 5

Printed and bound in Great Britain

Crime and Autism Spectrum Disorder

Myths and Mechanisms

Neil Brewer and Robyn L. Young

Jessica Kingsley *Publishers*
London and Philadelphia

>>>>>>>>>>>>>>>>>>>>>

Contents

Chapter 1

>>>>>>>>>>>>>>>>>>>>

SOME BAD GUYS

Every generation has its defining psychiatric malady, confidently diagnosed from afar by armchair non-psychiatrists. In the fifties, all those gray-suited organization men were married to 'frigid' women. Until a few years ago, the country of self-obsessed boomers and reality-TV fame-seekers and vain politicians and bubble-riding Ponzi schemers made narcissistic personality disorder—diagnosis code 301.81 in the American Psychiatric Association's Diagnostic and Statistical Manual of Mental Disorders, fourth edition—the craziness of the moment. And who among us has not proudly copped to our own 'OCD' or 'ADD,' deemed a mercurial sibling 'seriously bipolar,' written off an erratic ex as 'obviously borderline,' or nodded as a laid-off friend pronounced his former boss a 'textbook sociopath'? Lately, a new kind of head case stalks the land—staring past us, blurting gaucheries, droning on about the technical minutiae of his boring hobby. And we are ready with our DSM codes: 299.00 (autistic disorder) and 299.80 (Asperger's disorder). (Wallace 2012).

Wallace's piece highlights that almost any high-profile person who might have displayed some form of social distinctiveness or awkwardness may have been loosely labelled as being *on the spectrum*. Identities listed by Wallace and others include Mitt Romney, Barack Obama, Bill Gates, Mark Zuckerberg, Warren Buffett, Dennis Rodman, Jim Carrey, Daryl Hannah, Slash, Billy Joel, J. K. Rowling, Adam Carolla, Kanye West, Dan Harmon, Clay Marzo, Gary Numan, Abraham Lincoln, Albert Einstein, Alexander Graham Bell, Béla Bartók, Benjamin Franklin, Bobby Fischer, Carl Jung, Emily Dickinson, George Bernard Shaw,

George Washington, Marilyn Monroe, Henry Ford, Isaac Newton, Jane Austen, Ludwig van Beethoven, Mark Twain, Michelangelo, Thomas Edison, Thomas Jefferson, Vincent van Gogh, Virginia Woolf, Wolfgang Amadeus Mozart, Alfred Hitchcock, Andy Warhol, Charles Schulz, Howard Hughes, Jim Henson, John Denver, Al Gore, Bob Dylan, Charles Dickinson, David Helfgott, James Taylor, John Motson, Oliver Sacks, Robin Williams, Napoleon Bonaparte, Teddy Roosevelt, Leonardo da Vinci, Elvis Presley, Tom Hanks, Shakespeare, Goethe and even Hans Asperger. The suggestion that any or all of the above artists, inventors, musicians, politicians, authors, actors and other well-known individuals may be on the spectrum has occurred despite the fact that few of these people have been formally diagnosed; indeed, some have even been labelled posthumously. Clearly the suggestion that these individuals may be on the spectrum has sometimes been made in jest. Nevertheless, the tendency to apply the label in the absence of any clinical diagnosis indicates a preparedness to connect the label autism spectrum disorder (ASD) with displays of any behaviour that are out of the ordinary.

The application of the *on the spectrum* tag has not, however, been restricted to off-the-cuff labelling of high-profile achievers. It has also been applied to individuals such as Nicky Reilly, Robert Napper, William Cottrell, Jeffrey Dahmer, Ted Kaczynski, Adam Lanza, Martin Bryant and Anders Breivik – all men who have committed brutal crimes such as rape, arson and mass murder – and computer hackers such as: Adrian Lamo and Gary McKinnon. It is of course possible that this diverse array of individuals shares a single pathology that explains their criminal behaviour. But the tendency to invoke the *on the spectrum* tag when discussing all manner of unusual behaviours highlights just how common the use of this diagnostic term has become and the diversity of the individuals to whom it has been applied.

When people's behaviour significantly violates social norms it is not uncommon for observers to seek a label that purports to provide some sort of psychological explanation for their behaviour. Often these labels emerge not on the basis of any formal diagnostic procedure but rather from suggestions made by onlookers. The following three case studies describe the behaviour of men for whom the ASD label was applied by onlookers, media or professionals, apparently in an attempt to provide a meaningful and unitary explanation for their extreme criminal behaviour. For each of these cases we (a) outline the criminal event, (b) indicate how the application of the ASD label arose (i.e., the 'diagnosis') and (c) highlight the involvement of other intertwined and likely causal factors.

Some Major Crimes Linked to ASD
The Crimes of Martin Bryant, Gary McKinnon and Adam Lanza
The Crimes
Martin Bryant was responsible for the largest mass killing by a single individual in Australia. In a shooting spree in 1996, he shot and killed 35 holidaymakers and diners, and injured 21 others, at Port Arthur in the Australian state of Tasmania. He is currently serving 35 life sentences plus 1035 years without parole in the psychiatric wing of a prison hospital. Gary McKinnon, a UK citizen and resident, was arrested in 2002 for hacking into the computer systems of the US Government and was indicted on multiple charges. After ten years of legal wrangling, including attempts to extradite him to the US for trial, the Department of Public Prosecutions has elected not to bring criminal charges against him. In 2012 Adam Lanza shot and killed his mother, 20 students and 6 teachers at Sandy Hook Elementary School in Connecticut, USA, before shooting himself.

The 'Diagnosis'
Following the Port Arthur massacre Martin Bryant was described as a loner who was bullied at school; soon after, the diagnosis of Asperger's syndrome (AS) emerged, with one psychiatrist noting he was grossly disturbed from childhood, suffering the *semi-autistic Asperger Syndrome*. This conclusion appeared to be shaped by some of Martin Bryant's mannerisms: his high-pitched, toneless voice, his inability to empathise with others, his odd gestures and postures, his apparently obsessive interest in certain topics, all characteristics consistent with the AS profile. Notably, however, other experts concluded that he did not display various central features of the condition. Gary McKinnon was arrested for computer hacking in 2002 but his AS diagnosis appeared not to eventuate until 2008 when appealing his extradition to the US. Consideration of the diagnosis was

prompted following appearances on television and calls to the family by concerned viewers. Until his arrest in 2002 Gary McKinnon was just an 'inoffensive computer nerd' with an obsessive interest in UFOs. His diagnosis was at least confirmed by a highly respected professional in the field (Simon Baron-Cohen) rather than being conducted by the media. Like Gary McKinnon, Adam Lanza had not been diagnosed prior to the mass shooting at Sandy Hook Elementary School. But within hours of the massacre, Adam Lanza had been posthumously diagnosed – in the media – with autism, or at least *a bit of autism,* by laypeople. This diagnosis appears to have been based on reports of his apparent discomfort in social situations and his flat affect or lack of emotion.

Other Causal Factors
Gary McKinnon was formally diagnosed with AS subsequent to his crimes. Martin Bryant and Adam Lanza appear not to have been formally diagnosed, but – as with Gary McKinnon – media accounts have implicated the disorder as a potential contributing factor. AS is a relatively common disorder, with prevalence rates cited at about 1 in 160 persons. Persons with the disorder are not *freaks of nature* but everyday citizens who experience difficulties in certain areas. It seems unlikely, therefore, that the presence of the disorder either turns a person into a mass murderer or, conversely, makes them immune to criminal involvement. In two of the three cases just described, the presence of AS may have been one of the critical components within a network of interacting causal variables. We do not know to what extent the disorder – even if definitely present – was influential. We do, however, know that there is abundant evidence to suggest (in each of these cases) an array of other factors that may have shaped their antisocial behaviour.

In the case of Martin Bryant, some behaviours consistent with a diagnosis of AS were apparent, but his presentation was atypical. For example, he had previously been involved in acts of explosive violence. He lacked core features of the disorder such as repetitive behaviours and absorbing interests. Further, he had positive symptomatology such as low IQ and a marked delay in the acquisition of language, which would preclude a diagnosis of AS. Moreover, other behaviours observed in Martin Bryant – such as disinhibition, inappropriate sexual advances (as well as limited empathy) – can be found in persons within the typical population as well as within many other known disorders such as psychopathy, schizophrenia, head trauma, dementia, Alzheimer's, reactive attachment disorder, attention deficit hyperactivity disorder (ADHD), conduct disorder and all personality disorders. Some diagnostic features point to the possibility of autistic disorder (AD) but his history strongly suggests other environmental influences and comorbid conditions that provide a better explanation for his behaviour. For example, he had often responded to frustrations with aggression towards other people and property. From an early age his behaviour was characterised by a tendency to torment others. He had also experienced the death of a close friend followed shortly afterward by the suicide of his father. He had been bullied and socially isolated and had developed grudges against people. Taken together, his presentation and history suggests a diagnosis somewhat more complicated or multidimensional than AS or AD.

For Gary McKinnon, a similarly complex story emerges. While he was formally diagnosed with AS some years after his arrest, and while many of his supporters during the protracted legal wranglings argued that his condition engendered a naiveté that called into question whether he was a criminal, it seems likely that he was cognisant of the potential damage of his hacking activities. This perspective is reinforced by his alleged leaving of cyber notes warning the US Government of their poor security, as well as a message comparing US foreign policy to state-sponsored terrorism. And importantly, based on first-hand accounts of his behaviour provided by his mother, it seems there may have been relevant psychological factors over and above any obsessive interests and social naiveté associated with ASD. For example, signs of paranoia and delusional thought (e.g., he was convinced UFOs were invading) were mentioned, both of which suggest the possibility of other potentially significant psychopathology.

Finally, examination of Adam Lanza's background suggests a combination of factors that likely contributed to his involvement in the mass shooting. He was allegedly raised in a dysfunctional domestic environment involving guns and violence. He was a social misfit who was entertained by violent video games. He was struggling to forge a career or any close relationships and he was bullied, angry and resentful. Again, his case points to a troubled life history regardless of any presence of AS, a history that seems likely to have shaped his criminal behaviour.

While Gary McKinnon has a formal diagnosis of AS, the available evidence does not resolve whether Martin Bryant and Adam Lanza had ASD. Nor does the evidence provide a definitive indication as to whether some characteristics of the disorder may have contributed to their crimes. Regardless, the nature of the crimes – all of which were well planned and designed to cause mayhem – and the background histories of the three individuals suggest to us that it is most unlikely that an ASD was the key contributing factor.

We are not suggesting that ASD, or some of the key social and cognitive characteristics thereof, cannot underpin involvement in criminal activity. Indeed, later in the chapter we present some case studies that strongly suggest how criminality may be linked to such characteristics and, in subsequent chapters, we examine those characteristics in detail. Before doing so, however, we consider some of the unfortunate consequences that may flow from the application of the ASD label in an attempt to explain extreme cases of criminal behaviour such as those described above.

Implications of Attributing Criminal Behaviour to ASD

It is perhaps unsurprising that ASD should be considered as a possible contributing factor when we seek explanations for extremely serious and deeply puzzling cases. Not only are such cases difficult to comprehend but the culprits are clearly very unusual – and, of course, ASD is a label that people will often associate with unusual social behaviour. For example, following the Colorado movie theatre massacre (July 2012), Joe Scarborough said the following on MSNBC's Morning Joe programme.

> As soon as I heard about this shooting, I knew who it was. I knew it was a young, white male, probably from an affluent neighborhood, disconnected from society – it happens time and time again. Most of it has to do with mental health; you have these people that are somewhere, I believe, on the autism scale...I don't know if that's the case here, but it happens more often than not. People that can walk around in society, they can function on college campuses – they can even excel on college campuses – but are socially disconnected.

I have a son who has Asperger's who is loved by everyone in his family and who is wonderful, but it is for those that may not have a loving family and a support group and may be a bit further along on the autism spectrum, an extraordinarily frustrating, terrible challenge day in and day out, and so, I do think, again, I don't know the specifics about this young man, but we see too many shooters in these type of tragedies bearing the same characteristics mentally.

While in reality many perpetrators of mass shootings may – just like many other people – display some autistic-like symptoms, the situation is far more complex in the sense that a wide array of other risk factors can be identified (e.g., comorbid psychopathology, numerous socio-environmental risk factors).

It is also unsurprising that extreme cases such as those discussed thus far attract widespread and long-running media attention, thereby often ensuring that people are constantly reminded of the possible connection between ASD and criminality. While inferences about the causal role of ASD and the extent of any associated media attention may be predictable, such speculation generally offers little insight into any cognitive or social characteristics associated with the disorder that might underpin any predisposition towards criminality. Nor does an explanation reliant on a single diagnostic classification help elucidate the likely complex psychological and environmental determinants of an individual's involvement in serious criminal activity. Even worse, however, such speculation potentially has significant consequences for the way in which adults who have been diagnosed with ASD are perceived and treated, especially if they should come into contact with the criminal justice system. In the following section we consider some of these possible consequences.

Effects of Media Publicity on Formation of Social Schema or Stereotypes

The social psychological literature is replete with examples of how people's perceptions or judgements of others may be shaped by schemas (or stereotypes) they hold that are associated with categorising or labelling of people (cf. Fiske and Taylor 2013). Schemas can have a profound influence not only on our encoding of incoming information but also on our memory for information. It is not guaranteed that a label that *assigns* someone to a category ensures that our processing of information is driven by schemas we may hold about that category. Indeed, people are responsive to schema-inconsistent information and they do show individual differences in the degree to which schemas drive processing of information about other people. Nevertheless, there is abundant evidence indicating how social schemas – cued by a label or categorisation based on some trait – can bias our perceptions or judgements of people.

Applied to the present context, what if extensive media publicity implicating ASD as a causal factor for certain types of major crimes cues a schema we hold about adults with ASD as *socially undesirable individuals with a propensity for committing violent or other serious crimes?* At a minimum, such judgements may have negative implications for the capacity of individuals with ASD to assimilate within the community. At worst, they could prove to be highly prejudicial should, for example, an adult with ASD become involved in interactions with the criminal justice system in which their credibility is being assessed by police, jurors or the judiciary.

Although, to our knowledge, there is no direct empirical evidence available that points to the stigmatising effects of such publicity on adults with ASD, there is evidence from contexts involving other psychiatric diagnoses to suggest this is clearly a possibility. For example, Angermeyer *et al.* (2005) interviewed more than 5000 adults about their print and television media consumption. Desire for social distance from people with schizophrenia (i.e., the extent to which they would like to interact in social, familial and professional contexts) was also evaluated. Among the variables correlated with social distancing were reading tabloid and regional newspapers and television viewing time. In another study, Angermeyer and Matschinger (1996) presented over 12,000 adults with a written vignette that described an individual with schizophrenia, depression or alcoholism and measured desire for social distance in relation to this individual. Participants were recruited in six waves from April 1990 to November 1992. Two waves of data collection in 1990 occurred after extensive media coverage about violent crimes that had been committed by individuals labelled as having schizophrenia. The percentage of participants who desired greater social distance increased progressively throughout the study, especially after the media reports.

For example, 19 per cent of the people surveyed in April 1990 did not want the person with schizophrenia described in the vignette to be their neighbour while 36 per cent of the people surveyed in December 1990 felt this way. The December 1990 survey point occurred two months after the second media report and approximately eight months after the first media report. Similarly, the percentage of participants who rated someone with schizophrenia as dangerous and unpredictable was greater for the waves of data collection following the media reports. While it is impossible to draw causal conclusions from studies using such methodologies, the findings are at least consistent with those of carefully controlled experimental studies. Whether similar patterns would emerge if ASD were substituted for schizophrenia is unknown, but it is possible. Should such stereotyping occur we also have grounds for anticipating the likely effects on perceptions of adults with ASD.

Effects of Labelling and Stereotyping

We know that behaviours that are characteristic of the presentation of mental disorders influence societal perceptions or reactions. We also know that stereotypes invoked by the label *mentally ill* have an impact on such perceptions (e.g., Link *et al.* 1987). Both the label and the knowledge of mental illness have been shown to activate numerous negative stereotypes held by police and members of the general public about people with mental disorders (Angermeyer and Matschinger 2003; Link *et al.* 1987; Wright, Jorm and Mackinnon 2011). Similarly, more specific labels such as schizophrenia, psychosis (Angermeyer and Matschinger 2003; Link *et al.* 1999; Watson, Corrigan and Ottati 2004a; Watson *et al.* 2004b; Wright *et al.* 2011), major depression and drug and alcohol dependence (Link *et al.* 1999) arouse stigmatising views of labelled individuals, more so than occurs in response to an identically behaving person with a label of a physical disorder or no label at all. Individuals labelled with mental illness are often judged negatively (e.g., Stone and Colella 1996) and sometimes as lacking credibility (Finn and Stalans 1995; Watson *et al.* 2004a). Indeed, it has been argued that the stereotype of low credibility is an important mediator of the relationship between the label and a variety of discriminatory behaviours. So, for example, witnesses labelled as mentally ill may be judged as lacking credibility and, in turn, they are perceived to be unreliable as witnesses, their information is often not acted upon immediately, they are more likely to be perceived as being responsible when a crime is committed, and they are more likely to be wrongly charged for violent crimes (Finn and Stalans 1995; Steadman 1981; Watson *et al.* 2004a, 2004b).

Similar patterns of findings have emerged from studies involving other psychological conditions. For example, attributions made by children, adolescents and adults without an intellectual disability about the likeability and employment outcomes of a person labelled mentally retarded, and about their desire to interact with them, have been shown to be more negative than for an identical unlabelled individual (Gibbons and Kassin 1982; Gottlieb 1975). Research into the effects of labelling people with ASD is scarce and primarily focuses on children's perceptions and judgements. However, a recent study found that vignettes describing an adult with the social symptoms of ASD lead to an increased desire for social distance when the vignette disclosed that the individual had AS, and even when it did not (Butler and Gillis 2011). Finally, there is also evidence to suggest that an awareness of behaviours that are commonly associated with the label of AS may be stigmatising. Penn, Kohlmaier and Corrigan (2000) invited adults with mild schizophrenia to engage in a filmed three-minute conversation with a confederate and were told either that the social skills of the confederate or themselves were under evaluation. Observers blind to diagnosis then made ratings using a social distance scale about the individuals depicted. Characteristics such as flattened affect, emotional distancing and motor retardation correlated with a greater desire for social distance. Difficulty engaging in reciprocal conversation, poorer social skill and *strangeness* also related to greater desire for social distance. Interestingly, these are behavioural characteristics that, for many, would be associated with their stereotype of ASD.

Some Crimes More Justifiably Linked to ASD

Our focus earlier in the chapter was on particularly nasty or complex crimes where (a) there appears to have been a complex network of interacting, and difficult to disentangle, causal factors and (b) ASD appears to have been implicated almost as if to provide a convenient handle when no other single causal factor leapt to mind. By way of contrast, we now present three examples of cases where ASD – or the social and cognitive characteristics thereof – appear to have been at the core of the criminal events that unfolded.

The Crimes of Darius McCollum, AB and AP

The Crimes

Darius McCollum, AB (see Murrie *et al.* 2002) and AP (see Chen *et al.* 2003) were all charged with crimes that might be most easily understood within the context of AS. Darius McCollum first attracted media attention at the age of 15 when he drove a New York City subway train. He has since been charged and jailed for a series of similar offences in which he presented himself as a transit employee – typically a bus or subway driver (Tietz 2002). Darius McCollum is now listed as one of *Time* magazine's top ten imposters of all time, reflecting his extensive record of being arrested and charged on more than 25 different occasions. All crimes were in the pursuit of his restricted interest or obsession.

In contrast, AB apparently developed an interest in fires after seeing a fire on the news, although he was not obsessed with fires. After becoming preoccupied with the persons who had wronged him in his earlier years, he decided to use his interest in fires to exact revenge on bullies who had tormented him throughout his school years. The houses burned were not, however, directly connected to the bullies. Rather, AB fastidiously identified tiny details of the homes that reminded him of the bullies with whom he had become obsessed. AB was charged with setting fire to 11 neighbourhood homes, each of which he had systematically doused in petrol before setting it alight; no one was physically harmed in these incidents.

AP came to the attention of the criminal justice system due to repeated stealing. He stole paper, boxes, cups and plastic bags from schools and, later, a university. His illegal behaviours led to his expulsion from school and university and subsequent institutionalisation. AP would position his stolen goods throughout his living room and would become very upset if these objects were touched or moved. If this occurred he would return the objects to their original position. He made no apparent attempt to hide these goods and, thus, was easily caught. Given his inability to stop his collecting, his mother would lock him in their apartment, but he would climb out of the window to steal letters from mailboxes in the neighbourhood. Once again, these crimes were not targeted at any specific person, nor were they designed to cause mayhem. Instead, they appear to be based on a desire to pursue an obsession.

The 'Diagnosis'

Darius McCollum, AB and AP have been formally diagnosed with AS by relevant professionals. It is unclear when Darius McCollum first received his diagnosis, although his early development has all the characteristics of a child with AS. By the time he was eight he could visualise the entire New York City subway system. He would spend hours watching trains to the exclusion of everything else. AB and AP, as often appears to be the case, were not formally diagnosed until they were arrested. AB had no criminal or psychiatric history until the age of 31 when he commenced his arson spree. He was described as shy and quiet by his parents yet considered *peculiar* by teachers. Behaviours consistent with the diagnosis of ASD were evident in school and included attention to detail, a series of well-researched interests, strict adherence to routines, resistance to change and limited friendships. AB met *DSM-IV* diagnostic criteria for pyromania and for AS.

AP was diagnosed initially with schizophrenia and treated with medication for more than two years following expulsion from school and, later, university. The diagnosis of AS disorder was finally given when alternative diagnoses were explored given his continued recidivism and lack of response to medication. Although other disorders were considered (e.g., kleptomania, conduct disorder and schizophrenia), these were later dismissed and AS was considered the most appropriate. These other diagnoses, including schizophrenia, were later dismissed. AP's eventual diagnosis seemed somewhat unsurprising given his early developmental history, which included difficulty with interpersonal relationships, reluctance to go to public places, social naiveté and using toys in repetitive ways.

Other Causal Factors

Despite the apparent link with ASD in these cases, additional factors may well have contributed in all of them. For example, all three had been socially excluded and bullied when younger. None of these men had received intervention for ASD. Unlike Martin Bryant, Gary McKinnon and Adam Lanza, however, Darius McCollum, AB and AP did not seem intent on causing mayhem. The crimes did not appear to have been designed to hurt people and there was no intended victim. Darius McCollum and AP were clearly acting in a self-absorbed manner in pursuit of their restricted interest or obsession. While Darius McCollum's crimes had the potential to cause serious harm, the relevant history suggests that this was not a consideration. Similarly, while AB's fires may have easily caused human tragedy, the homes targeted were selected based on some aspect of their appearance rather than because of their occupants.

Unlike the first three cases reviewed, the latter three cases may be characterised as extremely quirky and odd rather than as malicious and vexatious in intent – even though two of them had the potential to produce catastrophic outcomes. It is these types of *peculiar* crimes that seem to be more consistent with AS. Of course, this does not mean that the legal outcomes for the offender will differ systematically. Although the presence of ASD has often been advanced in the case for the defence, there is certainly no guarantee that this tactic will be effective. In the Darius McCollum case it has been argued that his condition meant he was unable to control his behaviour due to his condition, an argument that has been rejected. For example, in one court appearance the judge disagreed with expert testimony regarding the diagnosis of AS and was reported in *The New York Times* (Murphy 2001) as saying: 'He could stop doing this if his family and friends would stop telling him "Isn't this amusing."' But, in other cases the court has been more sympathetic. For example, Schwartz-Watts (2005) reports a case of the acquittal of a 35-year-old person with AS who shot and killed a man who had entered his house, touched his glasses and punched him – the perpetrator had a hypersensitivity to sensory stimuli, which was judged to be one of several ASD-related contributing factors that justified the decision that he had acted in self-defence.

The Plan From Here

The case studies discussed in this chapter set the scene for the rest of the book by hinting at how certain characteristics of ASD are likely to be pivotal factors contributing to criminality, or criminal vulnerability, in *some* individuals with ASD. First, in Chapter 2, we examine whether there is any firm evidential basis for believing that individuals with ASD are particularly prone to involvement in criminal activity. We review existing prevalence research on the relationship between ASD and criminal offending, including both large-scale prevalence studies and small-scale studies that have focused specifically on the presence of individuals with ASD in specific forensic settings. Our review addresses the limitations of these studies and how these constrain our understanding of actual prevalence rates. This analysis of prevalence studies – combined with a close examination of many individual case studies – led us to the view that (in the absence of other contributing comorbid conditions) only a sub-group of adults with ASD – those possessing a particular combination of psychological characteristics – are likely to become involved in criminal activity.

Second, we examine those specific cognitive and behavioural characteristics unique to ASD, and other characteristics that are often associated with ASD, that may contribute to adults becoming involved in criminal activity. In Chapter 3 we examine the diagnostic criteria for ASD, highlighting those adaptive behaviour deficits that, while defining the condition, may exist in varying degrees of severity. In subsequent chapters we argue that it is the intensity of these deficits and, especially the interaction between them and prevailing environmental or situational characteristics, that shape the likelihood of criminal involvement. In Chapter 4 we consider possible links between criminality and (a) comorbid disorders and (b) socio-environmental influences commonly associated with ASD. Chapter 5 outlines our position that some of the core characteristics of ASD – Theory of Mind (ToM), strong restricted interests and sensory sensitivities – interact with specific environmental conditions to influence criminal vulnerability. We argue that significant deficits or problems in these areas are pivotal in heightening criminal vulnerability. We review the scientific evidence on the nature of these deficits in ASD and demonstrate the general behavioural or adaptation consequences of such deficits. In Chapter 6 we illustrate our position with a number of case studies from the authors' own criminal justice system cases.

Third, we show how these core deficits may be prejudicial to the outcomes of interactions people with ASD have with criminal justice system personnel. In Chapter 7, we suggest that the resultant behaviours may sometimes result in police (inappropriately) judging them unfavourably in situations such as police interviews. Similarly, we argue that the impressions such individuals create in legal interviews and courtroom interactions are also likely to prejudice their outcomes and increase the likelihood of conviction. Further, the lack of skills required to successfully minimise their risk of conviction is also addressed. Again, our arguments are illustrated with relevant examples.

Chapter 8 then addresses two significant applied issues: the implications of these core deficits of ASD for (a) forensic assessment and (b) intervention programmes, not only for adults with an ASD but also for criminal justice professionals. We consider the types of assessment instruments that need to be developed and the psychometric evidential support they will require. The chapters leading up to Chapter 8 make a strong (implicit) case for the development of intervention programmes that could minimise the criminal vulnerability of adults with ASD as well as preparing them for interactions with the criminal justice system. Chapter 8 outlines the desirable nature and focus of these programmes, including consideration of programmes that can prepare criminal justice system professionals for dealing with adults with ASD in ways that ensure those interactions are not prejudicial. In the final chapter we focus primarily on major limitations in our knowledge base and suggest priorities for future scientific research, including research on assessment and intervention.

Chapter 2

PREVALENCE OF CRIME

In Chapter 1 we presented brief overviews of several cases in which links have been suggested between ASD and the commission of serious crimes. For some of these cases we suggested that there appears to have been a complex network of interacting causal factors, with the presence of an ASD perhaps being only a very minor component of that network. For others, the characteristics of the crimes, and especially the offender's behaviour, led us to suggest that some characteristics associated with the perpetrator's ASD were likely to have been major contributing factors. However, these are case studies only. While these – and the numerous other case studies that have been reported in the literature – may be a source of interesting, and ultimately even fruitful, hypotheses about the link between ASD and the commission of crime, they cannot provide answers to a number of important questions. For example, they tell us nothing about the prevalence of criminality among individuals with an ASD, nor how it compares with that of other psychiatric samples or indeed the non-ASD population. Moreover, while each individual case study obviously focuses on a particular crime, and may suggest possible causal mechanisms, case studies do not permit generalisations about the likely involvement in specific types of crime of individuals with ASD. And, while in some cases the perpetrator's behaviour may look like a classic example of ASD-related behaviour, case study evidence alone cannot answer the question of whether the presence of an ASD was a causal factor.

Answers to some of these questions can come from studies of prevalence of criminality in individuals with an ASD. Well-designed and well-conducted prevalence studies are potentially informative about the extent of criminal involvement of individuals with an ASD, relative to other sectors of the population, and about any idiosyncratic features of the nature of that criminal involvement. Like case studies, prevalence studies cannot speak directly to the causal role of ASD in crime commission, although some prevalence data patterns may be strongly suggestive of causal influences. However, depending on the characteristics and scope of these studies, they may highlight contributory individual difference and environmental variables, and even prove informative about the influence of criminal justice system practices and case management on the criminal involvement of individuals with ASD.

Prevalence Studies of Criminality and ASD

So what sorts of studies are available to provide guidance regarding the likely involvement in crime of individuals with an ASD? Various types of studies have been reported, including studies of individuals who:

> › are incarcerated in psychiatric hospitals or prison

> › have had a known involvement with the criminal justice system but were not incarcerated at the reference point for data collection

> › are living in the community, where the focus is on rates of involvement in criminal offending

> › have committed particular types of crimes.

A number of these studies were not actually designed to provide prevalence estimates of criminality in association with ASD. Nevertheless, they represent the available empirical evidence on the extent and nature of the involvement of individuals with an ASD in criminal activity. As will become clear, however, they fall well short of providing a detailed understanding of actual prevalence rates.

Studies of Individuals Incarcerated in Prisons or Psychiatric Hospital

One strategy for exploring the involvement in criminal activity of adults with an ASD has been to examine prevalence in prison or secure psychiatric hospital populations. Although a number of studies have reported such data, some do not address this question at all because, for example, attempts to screen and diagnose inmates were not comprehensive (e.g., Myers 2004) or comprehensive screening had been undertaken with a clearly inadequate psychometric instrument (e.g., Robinson *et al.* 2012).

There are, however, several studies that have provided what might be considered to be converging evidence, although it will shortly become clear that the interpretation of this evidence is complex. Scragg and Shah (1994) probed the prevalence of AS in a maximum-security UK hospital where the majority (proportion unspecified) of patients had been placed as a result of their criminal behaviour. Patients' files were checked for reference to specific behaviours, with those patients presenting with certain criterion behaviours then screened for autistic behaviour via an interview with nursing staff and the patients themselves. Six out of 392 patients were classified as AS, and the prevalence rate of 1.5 per cent (95% Confidence Intervals = 0.6%, 3.3%) exceeded their best estimate (0.55%) for the general male population. Although the authors suggested a criminality prevalence rate around three times that of the community prevalence of AS, this conclusion is clearly clouded by the 95 per cent Confidence Interval data, the relatively subjective nature of the assessment protocol and the comorbid neurological pathologies found in all six AS patients identified. A similar type of study sampled from the same hospital and two other UK hospitals (Hare *et al.* 1999). From a screening of over 1300 patients, a total of 31 – or 2.4 per cent – were identified with ASD, again a rate that appears higher than their population prevalence estimate of 0.71 per cent for ASD. An even higher criminality prevalence estimate emerged from a study of a maximum-security prison sample (Fabio, Pietz and Denny 2012). Just over 20 per cent of 1800 non-randomly sampled prisoners agreed to complete the *Autism Spectrum Quotient* (Baron-Cohen *et al.* 2001b), with 4.4 per cent exceeding the typically used screening cut-off score. The apparent higher criminality prevalence for ASD prisoners in this study must, however, be interpreted against the backdrop of an absence of both any formal diagnosis and any detail on potential comorbid contributing conditions.

Evidence from such studies is sometimes used to suggest greater likelihood of criminality in ASD individuals – and that may well turn out to be the case. But, as we foreshadowed above, the interpretative difficulties associated with these data are considerable. We have already noted the absence in some studies of the application of formal diagnostic procedures as well any data on comorbid psychopathologies that might underpin criminality. There are additional broader interpretative difficulties that apply to all of these studies. For example, the data relate to serious crimes that led to placement in high-security detention but do not speak to prevalence of offending in general. These studies provide no information or control for potentially crucial background socio-environmental factors. Nor do they allow for possible differences between ASD and non-ASD individuals in terms of factors such as ease of detection and apprehension, the ease of procuring evidence associated with a successful prosecution, the likelihood of conviction and the likelihood and nature of sentence applied. We return to a consideration of such issues later in this chapter.

Studies of Individuals with a History of Involvement with the Criminal Justice System

Various studies have examined the psychiatric profiles of individuals who have come to the attention of the criminal justice system but were not incarcerated in prison or hospital settings at the time the relevant data were recorded. Several of these have attempted to explore the extent and nature of the involvement of individuals with ASD, focusing primarily on adolescents and young adults. We discuss four of these studies, which differ in terms of the method of identification of the ASD sample, sample size and location, and the nature of the data used to index criminal offending.

One of these studies (Allen *et al.* 2008) purported to study prevalence of offending by adults with AS in Wales (UK). Contact was made with a variety of services considered likely to interact with adults with AS and criminal offenders to identify individuals who had been diagnosed with AS and been involved in criminal offending that had (or could have) placed them in contact with the criminal justice system. Of 126 adults identified with ASD, 33 met these criteria and 16 of these contributed to the data on the frequency and types of offending behaviour. However, the small sample size, coupled with the absence of any matched comparison sample, again precludes any meaningful generalisations from this study about the likely extent and nature of offending behaviour in adults with ASD.

Kumagami and Matsuura (2009) report prevalence data for individuals with pervasive developmental disorder (PDD) obtained via an examination of juvenile court cases in four Japanese courts over a one-year interval. Unfortunately, the number of juvenile crime cases in each jurisdiction was small, ranging from 67 to 149. The offending (excluding traffic violations and accidents) prevalence rates for PDD in the four settings were 1.4 per cent, 1.3 per cent, 6.7 per cent and 18.2 per cent, with this last figure coming from a court that only examined unique crimes (e.g., arson or sex offences) that had been specifically investigated from a psychiatric perspective. The first two estimates were reportedly similar to or perhaps in excess of PDD prevalence in the general population; the latter two were clearly higher. Again, however, it is impossible to determine the extent to which these prevalence rates reflected the contributions of factors such as other comorbid conditions, negative familial and environmental influences or sample-related biases in the disposition of cases.

A study that was similar in some respects to the previous one, but involved retrospective classification of child neuro-psychiatric disorders, was reported by Siponmaa et al. (2001). The diagnoses of 126 young (15–22 years) Swedish offenders who had undergone a forensic psychiatric assessment after committing a serious offence were revisited and retrospectively examined for a definite or probable child neuro-psychiatric disorder. Of the classifiable cases, 4 per cent were classified as definite AS cases and another 8 per cent as possible cases. These data also suggest prevalence rates well above the population prevalence of AS. In this case, just some of the problematic factors clouding interpretation are (a) the reliability of the retrospective diagnosis, (b) the fact that only a very small proportion of offenders were referred for such an examination, with the likelihood of such a referral perhaps increased by unusual behavioural characteristics of AS, and (c) the absence of any control comparison group.

Apparently high rates of involvement in offending by individuals with ASD were also identified in another much larger Swedish epidemiological study (Fazel et al. 2008). The focus of this study was on the comparative prevalence of psychopathology in adolescent, young adult and older offenders who had been referred for pre-sentencing forensic psychiatric evaluation over a five-year period. Data from over 3000 cases showed a diagnosis of ASD for 8.3 per cent of 15–17-year-olds, 7.4 per cent of 18–21-year-olds and 2.6 per cent of individuals 22 years and older. Although these rates are clearly in excess of the prevalence of ASD, a key confounding factor is again a referral bias. In Sweden, forensic assessment referral was determined by the courts on the basis of the unusual behaviour or apparent mental state of the offender; some of the behavioural characteristics of offenders with ASD likely increased the chances of such referral.

Studies such as these seem to suggest that individuals with ASD are likely to be over-represented in young offender populations. But the evidence is, at best, suggestive. Meaningful conclusions about prevalence of offending are clouded by sample size limitations, the absence of any controls for other potential causal factors such as comorbid conditions or socio-environmental variables, and the very real possibility that the sometimes unusual behavioural characteristics of ASD individuals will increase the likelihood of referral for forensic psychiatric assessment.

Studies of Criminal Involvement of Individuals Living in the Community

A number of studies have been conducted in which individuals with ASD living in the community have been identified and any associated patterns of criminal offending explored. Similar to the studies described in the previous section, they again vary in terms of the identification, size and origin of the ASD sample, and the nature of the offence statistics. Here we again review four such studies to provide a flavour of the nature of the evidence base they provide.

Woodbury-Smith *et al.* (2006) contrasted offending in a sample of 25 adults with an ASD and a comparison group of 20 local adults. The former were a subset of 102 individuals – located through a variety of service delivery agencies and media requests within one UK health district – who were prepared to participate, met diagnostic criteria for ASD and had measured IQ in the normal range. Offending characteristics were assessed by self-report and a UK Home Office Offenders Index and data analysis focused on the number of individuals reporting one or more offence category and on variations in offence category across the two groups. Forty-eight per cent of the ASD sample and a staggering 80 per cent of the comparison group reported criminal offending, although only 7 per cent of the former had ever been convicted (conviction rates for the latter were unknown). Are we to conclude from this that one in two adults with ASD are criminal offenders and that most non-ASD adults are likewise? Both seem extremely unlikely. Rather, these data likely reflect peculiarities of the sampling. For example, although background information on age, IQ and gender was reported for both samples, no data were reported that permit any examination of, or control for, any other personal background or socio-environmental variables. And, perhaps the ASD individuals targeted in the study had attracted the attention of the reporting agencies because of their experience with the criminal justice system.

Cheely *et al.* (2011) reported a study of considerably greater scope that examined the extent of offending in youths aged 12–18 years sampled in South Carolina (US). Individuals with an ASD diagnosis were identified via a large-scale project designed to track all eight-year-old children with ASD and then their contact with the criminal justice system at age 12–18 years was logged via juvenile justice department records. In sharp contrast with the Woodbury-Smith *et al.* (2006) statistics, only 32 of 609 youths, or 5 per cent, with ASD had been charged with an offence. A comparison group (N=99) matched on age, sex, race and county recorded more charges per person than the ASD sample, a different profile of charges and a different pattern of judicial outcomes (e.g., case diverted, case prosecuted). Unlike the ASD sample, however, this comparison group was selected exclusively from youth already involved in the juvenile justice system. Consequently, no conclusions about comparative prevalence rates can be drawn, nor are the between-group data on differences in offence profiles and judicial outcomes amenable to any meaningful comparative interpretation.

Data for older samples of individuals with AS and AD have been reported in separate studies by Cederlund *et al.* (2008), and Mouridsen *et al.* (2008). Cederlund *et al.* (2008) conducted a broad examination of adult adaptation of individuals aged 16–38 years and diagnosed with either AS (N=76) or AD (N=70) in Sweden at least five years earlier.

Parental reports about these samples' involvement with the police and the law revealed that 10 per cent of the AS sample had some form of offending history, an involvement rate considered not atypical given their age and context. For the autism sample there were no reports of offending history.

Mouridsen *et al's*. (2008) study was much more comprehensive. Children initially seen from 1960–1984 as in-patients at clinics serving most Danish children with PDD were followed up within the age range of 25–59 years. They were reclassified in 1985 based on then current diagnostic criteria (a procedure probably associated with some degree of classification error), with the resulting sample including cases classified as childhood autism (*N*=113), atypical autism (*N*=86) and AS (*N*=114). Each of these 313 individuals was matched by sex, time of birth, region of birth and social group with three individuals listed on a Danish register for the population as a whole. Offending statistics were then taken from a national criminal register that logs all convictions in Denmark. The conviction prevalence rates for the various PDD categories and their respective control samples were 0.9 per cent and 18.9 per cent (childhood autism and control), 8.1 per cent and 14.7 per cent (atypical autistic and control) and 18.4 per cent and 19.6 per cent (AS and control). These statistics do not suggest any markedly higher frequency of criminal convictions in the ASD samples although, of course, we are unable to assess whether these frequencies were moderated by differences within the Danish justice system in terms of disposition to convict individuals with and without an ASD.

Studies of Particular Types of Offenders

Another approach to understanding prevalence involves an examination of the extent to which individuals with ASD are involved – and possibly over-represented – in particular types of crimes. The primary focus has tended to be on whether adults with AS are over-represented in arson, sex or violent crimes. Here, hard evidence is even thinner on the ground, with one striking exception. Several of the studies reviewed earlier in this chapter reported the possibility of over-representation of individuals with AS or ASD in arson crimes. For example, in the study already discussed by Siponmaa *et al.* (2001) the more frequent involvement in arson crimes of individuals with ASD compared with the other diagnostic groups examined (e.g., ADHD, mental retardation) was noted. But the interpretative issues already discussed in relation to that study (e.g., issues of diagnosis, very small sample size) are again pertinent and the data are insufficient to sustain the broad conclusion that individuals with ASD are over-represented in arson offences. In their study of secure hospital patients Hare *et al.* (1999) also drew attention to the fact that a higher proportion of patients with ASD than other patients had been involved in arson crimes (16% vs. 5%), but the number of cases is again so small (5 vs. 8) as to be uninterpretable. Mouridsen *et al.* (2008) also noted significantly more frequent arson convictions in the AS sample. However, when cases were disaggregated into type of offence, the number of cases was very low (5 vs. 0 for AS vs. control, respectively) and it would be bold to conclude that this difference is a reliable one. Perhaps the most persuasive evidence comes from Enayati *et al.* (2008), who contrasted diagnostic information on 214 arsonists who had received forensic psychiatric assessments in Sweden with that for over 2000 violent offenders assessed in the same way. These assessments were conducted based on the suspicion that the offender had a mental disorder. Unlike most of the other *DSM-IV* disorders identified, individuals with AS were significantly more prevalent in arsonists than other offenders (7.1% vs. 2.5%). While this difference looks telling, it is impossible to determine if there may have been referral biases operating. For example, a stereotype amongst referrers that AS is likely to be associated with arson, coupled with an offender presenting with AS-type behaviours, may have biased the referrer towards requesting an assessment.

Empirical evidence on the relative prevalence of sex and violent crimes among individuals with and without an ASD is even sparser. The patterns for sex crimes are inconsistent. While Kumagami and Matsuura's (2009) Japanese juvenile court data suggested that involvement in sex offences was significantly higher for individuals with PDD than for non-PDD offenders (17.8% vs. 5.5%), Hare *et al.* (1999) reported the opposite pattern in their secure-hospital patients (3% vs. 20%) while finding no differences for (non-sexual) violent offences and homicide. Again, however, such comparisons are extremely difficult to interpret, not only because of the confounding factors already identified earlier in the chapter but also because of the very low frequencies when the data were split by crime. Woodbury-Smith *et al.* (2006) also highlighted what they referred to as some striking differences between the ASD and non-ASD samples in the pattern of offences, with the histories of the former more likely to include criminal damage and violence and the latter, drug offences. As we noted earlier in the chapter, however, this study is beset with problems; moreover, the reliability of the reported between-group contrasts of criminal offence patterns is again called into question by the extremely small sample sizes and low frequencies within the various criminal categories.

A valuable study from the perspective of interpreting violence prevalence data is Långström *et al.*'s (2009) examination of Swedish individuals discharged from psychiatric hospitals over more than a decade. Thirty-one of 422 individuals (7%) diagnosed with autism or AS had been convicted of (non-sexual) violent crimes; a statistic that doesn't speak to the prevalence of violent offending. Importantly, however, the co-existence of comorbid psychiatric disorders (38.7%), personality disorders (9.7%) or substance abuse (16.1%) was high, as is typically found in violent offenders without an ASD. These patterns reinforce the difficulties associated with linking ASD to violent offending and, most likely, any offending.

Even more valuable is a substantial recent Swedish study (Lundström *et al.* 2014), which examined the risk of violent offending in over 3000 individuals born between 1994 and 2004 and diagnosed with various neuro-developmental disorders by child and adolescent mental health services. It included over 950 individuals with ASD. The study incorporated elaborate and large control group conditions including full and half siblings and random population controls. Violent crime encompassed homicide, assault, arson, robbery and sexual and other relevant crimes logged on the National Crime Register. Whereas ADHD emerged as a substantial risk factor for violent criminal behaviour, there was no evidence that a diagnosis of ASD elevated risk for violent offending.

In sum, much of the limited body of evidence on the possibility of heightened involvement in particular types of offending is inconclusive. The one very significant exception is the large-scale Swedish study on violent crime (Lundström *et al.* 2014). Generally, there is insufficient information on the involvement and role of comorbid psychopathology and socio-environmental factors. Consequently, any contribution of ASD per se is impossible to determine. Moreover, there has been no systematic controlled investigation of the mechanisms by which characteristics specific to ASD might render a person vulnerable to involvement in specific types of criminal activity. Nor has any such investigation addressed how adverse socio-environmental influences (e.g., bullying, ostracism, drug and alcohol use) might interact with ASD to heighten such vulnerability.

Overview of Prevalence Findings

In sum, we have a collection of studies (i) conducted in different countries, (ii) with different criteria for identifying samples and criminal involvement, (iii) with generally, at best, relatively small sample sizes, especially from the perspective of making prevalence estimates and (iv) questionable or, at best, less than perfect control samples, which have produced – not surprisingly given the above – quite varied prevalence estimates. Taken purely at face value, the general impression provided by the data from these studies is that individuals with an ASD are over-represented in crime – and perhaps particularly (though certainly not definitely) in arson crimes – when assessed against the prevalence of ASD in the population. To what degree they might be over-represented in criminal activity is impossible to specify given the many variations in sampling protocols, skimpy sample sizes, less than ideal diagnostic methods, possible referral biases and so forth.

However, when the study methodologies and data are subjected to close scrutiny, it is apparent that the data do not provide compelling evidence for a conclusion that a diagnosis of ASD – by itself – means a greater likelihood of involvement in crime relative to that of individuals without an ASD. Simply put, there are just too many interpretative problems arising from the wide array of potential moderating variables. In the next section we outline the sort of study and data needed to resolve these issues.

Characteristics of Informative Prevalence Studies

What might an ideal prevalence study look like? First, it would be prospective in nature. It would involve tracking a cohort of individuals with a formal diagnosis of ASD at least from early adolescence well into adulthood. In addition to the availability of an ASD diagnosis, objective data would be crucial for variables such as the following: educational background and IQ; family and socio-environmental background; psychiatric and/or neuro-psychological history that identified any comorbid psychiatric conditions that may increase criminal vulnerability (cf. Chapter 4). Regular updating of any components of these data likely to vary significantly over time (e.g., addiction patterns) would be necessary. The ideal prevalence study would also track a similarly large cohort of individuals without an ASD diagnosis – but matched on the key individual difference and socio-environmental variables listed above.

There is a wide range of other data that needs to be obtained in relation to both ASD and non-ASD samples that is crucial for distinguishing between (a) *true* prevalence of criminality associated with ASD and (b) prevalence statistics that reflect differences between individuals with and without ASD along variables that may be correlated with the presence of ASD but are not the actual causes of criminal involvement. For example, there may be particular cognitive, behavioural and social characteristics of people with ASD that shape the likelihood that they will be apprehended if they have committed a crime. There may be other characteristics associated with ASD that contribute to the admission of involvement in criminal activity under questioning by the police. In a similar vein, the likelihood of an individual with ASD being prosecuted for perpetrating a crime, referred for a forensic psychiatric assessment or being convicted and receiving a punitive sentence may also all owe something to characteristics associated with the condition that are independent of those characteristics that underpinned their involvement in criminal activity.

It important to distinguish the impact of such factors because if there are behavioural characteristics of individuals with ASD that, independent of committing crime, are likely to affect such outcomes, then estimates of prevalence gleaned, for example, from data on arrests, prosecution, assessment referrals, convictions or custodial sentences, are likely to provide a spurious indication of *true* prevalence (i.e., prevalence uniquely related to characteristics of ASD). Such behaviours may include a variety of unusual behaviours that draw attention to the individual (e.g., speech, gaze aversion), but also characteristics such as failing to remain silent or to seek appropriate legal assistance during police investigations, or interpreting everything said by other people quite literally. We address a range of these behaviours in depth in Chapter 7, showing how they may influence the course of an individual's interactions with the criminal justice system. Suffice it to say at this stage that such behaviours may prejudice the outcomes that individuals with ASD experience in their interactions with the police, legal representatives and even judges and jurors. Some behaviours may inflate some indices commonly used to assess prevalence of criminality (e.g., arrests) while others may have the opposite effect by diverting individuals from outcomes used to denote criminality (e.g., custodial sentences). Again, regular updating of those components of these data that are likely to vary significantly over time would be necessary as these factors may exert different degrees of influence in the context of youth versus adult offending.

Clearly, a prospective prevalence study that accommodated the dimensions just outlined and provided meaningful and stable estimates of likely criminality across these dimensions would require not only an extremely large sample but also a very substantial measurement exercise. These are, of course, critical components of effective prevalence studies, as illustrated by the following example taken from a related area. Murray *et al.* (2010) sampled 16,401 only-children born in Britain in 1970 recruited as part of an ongoing longitudinal study to examine early childhood risk factors for the development of conduct problems and criminal behaviour. Participants were followed from birth to 34 years of age, with data collected using medical records, self- and parent- report interviews, questionnaires and various psychometric instruments for assessing ability, psychological well-being and conduct problems. The potential risk factors for conduct problems and criminality that were explored included smoking during pregnancy, birth complications and weight, congenital abnormalities, parental style, death of a parent, marital status, maternal age, maternal depression, family size, family deprivation, neighbourhood wealth, hyper-activity, visual-motor skills and IQ. Parent reports when their child was five and ten years of age assessed conduct problems, and criminality was measured by exploring the participants' self-reported convictions at 30 or 34 years of age, which were compared to national registers of offending. This background information provides a flavour of the enormous scope and complexity of large-scale prevalence studies. Yet, seldom is it possible to conduct the ideal applied study. Unfortunately, as we have seen earlier in this chapter, in the area of criminality and ASD there is not even a close approximation, despite the existence of some more-specific, high-quality studies (e.g., Lundström *et al.* 2014).

Does the Field Need a High-quality Prospective Prevalence Study?

Studying the possible contributions of ASD to criminality appears to be inherently more difficult than many other types of prevalence studies, purely because ASD is a relatively low-frequency condition. Would the time, effort and expense required to deliver an adequate data set be worthwhile? We think the answer to this question is 'No', even though it is crucial to understand many of those factors listed above that have the potential to shape the nature and outcomes of interactions with the criminal justice system.

We suggest the following broad research strategy as an alternative. First, simply assume that prevalence of criminality in association with ASD is as high as in the non-ASD population, or maybe even assume it is significantly higher. Second, accept that we do not have detailed data that permit a determination as to whether it is some combination of cognitive and behavioural characteristics of ASD, comorbid psychopathology, socio-environmental influences or the complex interactions between some or all of these variables that are pivotal in shaping criminal behaviour. Perhaps there are some characteristics of ASD that, by themselves, render the individual vulnerable to certain types of criminal involvement. Perhaps these same (or other) characteristics of ASD interact with other influences such as those listed above to enhance criminality. Third, as an alternative to case study documentation and various types of epidemiological studies, use a combination of theoretical analysis and identification of consistencies across case presentations to develop specific hypotheses about causal mechanisms underlying criminality that can then be subjected to rigorous formal testing. Similarly, just as behavioural characteristics such as uncontrolled verbal or physical aggression can shape the nature and outcomes of any individual's interactions with the police and the legal system, assume that there may be particular cognitive and behavioural characteristics associated with ASD that can do likewise, and (again) develop and systematically test formal hypotheses about how they might shape interactions with the criminal justice system. Such approaches are certainly not the norm in this area of research but they provide a way of focusing research and advancing knowledge. In Chapters 5 and 7 we have tried to justify and detail a variety of hypotheses that could be subjected to rigorous testing.

Chapter 3

BEHAVIOURAL
CHARACTERISTICS OF ASD

Not all persons with ASD commit crime. Indeed, our examination of prevalence studies in Chapter 2 clearly indicates that – regardless of whether the prevalence of criminality is similar or higher for individuals with ASD than for the non-ASD population – only a small percentage of individuals with ASD commit crime. Yet, there are strong grounds for believing that there are some specific characteristics of ASD that contribute – whether it be in isolation, in interaction with other characteristics or situational variables, or both – to crime commission by some individuals. Some of the crimes may be committed knowingly, others naively, and some may even result from coercion or entrapment. There are also specific characteristics of ASD that may contribute to becoming a victim of crime and to being disadvantaged in interactions with the criminal justice system, but these are issues we take up in subsequent chapters.

Clearly, some individuals with ASD may be very much like other *bad* people in that they commit controlled acts of violent or non-violent crime not only with intent but also with insight as to likely consequences of the crime. What drives people like this to such criminal activity is beyond the scope of this book. Our concern is with understanding those specific cognitive, social and behavioural characteristics of people with ASD that, given appropriate situational conditions, can contribute to involvement in criminal activity. In this chapter we take the first steps towards answering this question by examining the diagnostic criteria for ASD. This allows us to characterise the way in which individuals – especially adults – with ASD present cognitively, behaviourally and socially. We focus on the substantial variability in autistic symptomatology that is observed both between and within individuals with ASD, especially with regard to the severity of the associated deficits. Given that such a small percentage of people with ASD become involved in criminal activity, it seems most unlikely that any of the characteristics identified in this chapter would, in isolation, explain criminality (unless of course it is simply reaching some threshold level of severity that is the critical factor). But, an understanding of the nature and variability of the various deficits associated with the disorder provides crucial background for the detailed hypotheses we develop in subsequent chapters regarding determinants of criminality in association with ASD.

What is Autism Spectrum Disorder?

The fourth edition of the *Diagnostic and Statistical Manual of Mental Disorders* (4th edition, text revision (*DSM-IV-TR*); American Psychiatric Association (APA) 2000) described autistic disorder (AD), Asperger's syndrome (AS), Rett's disorder, childhood disintegrative disorder and pervasive developmental disorder – not otherwise specified (PDD-NOS) under the umbrella term of pervasive developmental disorder (PDD). With the exception of Rett's disorder (subsequently removed from this grouping due to its aetiology now being known), these disorders have become collectively referred to as autism spectrum disorder (ASD) in the latest edition of the *Diagnostic and Statistical Manual of Mental Disorders* (5th edition (*DSM-5*); APA 2013).

In the *DSM-IV-TR*, PDDs were characterised by a triad of impairment that included (a) impairments in social reciprocity, (b) communication deficits and (c) repetitive and ritualistic patterns of behaviour and interests (APA 2000). In order to meet criteria for AD a person needed to meet a total of six or more criteria from each of domains (1), (2) and (3), with at least two from domain (1) and one each from domains (2) and (3). In Table 3.1 we provide an overview of the key criteria that are described fully in the *DSM-IV-TR*. The same criteria applied for the diagnosis of AS, but with the exclusion of the communication criteria.

Individuals who did not meet sufficient criteria may have been diagnosed with PDD-NOS or 'atypical autism' using the *International Classification System of Diseases-10* (*ICD-10*; World Health Organization 1994).

Table 3.1 Overview of DSM-IV-TR (APA 2000) Criteria for Autistic Disorder and Asperger's Disorder

Autistic Disorder
A. Six (or more) items from domains (1), (2) and (3), at least two from domain (1), and one each from domains (2) and (3):
1. Impaired social interaction, including two or more of: • impairments in nonverbal interaction behaviours (e.g., eye contact, facial expressions, gestures) • peer relationships not matching developmental level • absence of spontaneous sharing interests, achievements or enjoyment with others • failure to reciprocate socially or emotionally.
2. Impaired communication, including one or more of: • delayed language development • limited ability to initiate or sustain conversation • stereotyped, repetitive or idiosyncratic language • spontaneous or imitative play not matching developmental level.
3. Repetitive and stereotyped behaviours and interests, including one or more of: • restricted and abnormally intense interests • non-functional rituals • repetitive motor behaviours • preoccupation with object parts.
B. Abnormal or delayed functioning detected prior to age three in one or more of social interaction, social language or symbolic play.

cont.

Asperger's Disorder
A. *Qualitative impairment in social interaction, as manifested by at least two of the following:* <ul><li>impairments in nonverbal interaction behaviours (e.g., eye contact, facial expressions, gestures)</li><li>peer relationships not matching developmental level</li><li>absence of spontaneous sharing interests, achievements or enjoyment with others</li><li>failure to reciprocate socially or emotionally.</li></ul>
B. *Repetitive and stereotyped behaviours and interests, including one or more of:* <ul><li>restricted and abnormally intense interests</li><li>non-functional rituals</li><li>repetitive motor behaviours</li><li>preoccupation with object parts.</li></ul>
C. *Clinically significant impairment in key areas of functioning (e.g., social, occupational).*
D. *No clinically significant language delay.*
E. *No clinically significant delay cognitively or in self-help skills, adaptive behaviour (except social) etc.*

Under the *DSM-IV-TR*, not all criteria had to be met for a diagnosis and, thus, the diagnosis alone did not indicate the pervasiveness of the disorder. Further, the presence of any comorbid conditions, including intellectual disability, was not specified. Importantly, as will become evident later in the chapter, individuals diagnosed with ASD varied markedly in their presentation within each of these criterion domains and across domains. Likewise, the impact the disorder had on each individual's adaptive behaviours varied substantially. Some diagnosed individuals required permanent care and even institutionalisation, while others with the same diagnosis required minimal support. Persons with AD could have a severe intellectual disability coupled with a significant language delay, rendering them severely disabled. Alternatively, they might have no intellectual disability and develop speech, thereby presenting more akin to a person with AS as they aged. Given persons with AS could not (by definition) have either an intellectual disability or language delay, there was more homogeneity within that diagnostic category.

The overlap across diagnostic sub-categories formed part of the rationale for the *DSM-5* revision (APA 2013). The criteria outlined in this revision were finalised by a 13-person working group from medicine, psychiatry and psychology, guided by clinical experience, literature reviews, analyses of pre-existing data and public and professional consultation from the wider community (APA 2012; Clarke *et al.* 2013). We include this detail on the *committee* approach to formalising a diagnostic classification scheme only because it helps understanding of what will become a recurring theme in this book: namely, the disorder is not amenable to a straightforward empirically justified definition, but rather encompasses incredible diversity in behaviour and adaptive functioning.

Although the rationale for the *DSM-5* revision was complex, it stemmed in part from the fact that, when allowances were made for differences in ability levels, there was very little difference between AD and AS, other than severity. Thus, the *DSM-5* demonstrates a significant change in the conceptualisation of ASD. It discontinues the trend followed by classification systems such as the earlier *DSM*s and the *ICD* in which distinct behaviours provided the basis for discrete diagnostic labels. Instead, the *DSM-5* considers ASD as representing a dyad of impairment with severity represented on a continuum or spectrum. The two domains forming this dyad in the *DSM-5* are (i) social and communication interaction and (ii) restricted and repetitive behaviours and interests. Language is now included within the social communication domain because language delays may occur across the spectrum. Moreover, for those who develop language, language has defining features that are mostly related to its use in a social context. Nonverbal communication is typically awkward and verbal communication can be echolalic, literal, one-sided, repetitive and ritualistic. Language has thus been allocated to both the social-communication domain and ritualistic domains. Table 3.2 provides an overview of the key *DSM-5* diagnostic criteria for ASD.

Given that, in the *DSM-5*, ASD is no longer viewed as comprising a number of discrete diagnostic sub-categories, but rather a spectrum, it makes sense that a severity rating has been introduced to capture the individual's presentation more effectively – or at least the impact the condition is having on their daily life. Three levels of severity ratings are used in the *DSM-5* (see Table 3.3 for an overview). As an aside, however, the classification of each severity level, and the distinctions between them, are highly subjective for both the social communication and restricted interests and repetitive behaviours domains. For example, it would be interesting to see inter-observer reliability data for classification into the three severity levels of the restricted and repetitive behaviours distinguished in Table 3.3. Further, precisely how these severity ratings should be assigned is not yet fully understood as few diagnostic tools provide any information about severity – and those that do so often provide cumulative evaluations of performance against criteria that do not map readily onto DSM-5 criteria.

Table 3.2 Overview of DSM-5 Criteria for Autism Spectrum Disorder

A. Sustained and widespread deficits in social communication and interaction, spanning the areas of:
• social-emotional reciprocity • nonverbal social communicative behaviours • developing and maintaining relationships.
B. Repetitive and stereotyped behaviours and interests, including at least two of the following:
• repetitive motor behaviours, use of objects or speech • insistence on sameness, adherence to routines or ritualised patterns of behaviour • restricted and abnormally intense interest • hyper- or hyposensitivity to or unusual interest in, sensory stimuli.
C. Symptoms emerged early in development.
D. Clinically significant impairment in key areas of functioning (e.g., social, occupational).
E. Impairments not better explained by intellectual disability or global developmental delay. Individuals who previously met *DSM-IV* diagnosis of autistic disorder, Asperger's disorder or pervasive developmental disorder not otherwise specified should receive diagnosis of autism spectrum disorder.

Table 3.3 Overview of DSM-5 Severity Criteria for Autism Spectrum Disorder

Severity level	Social communication	Restricted and repetitive behaviours
Needs very substantial support *(Level 3)*	Severe social communication skill deficits cause severe impairments in functioning, limited initiation of and response to others' social interaction attempts.	Functioning markedly impaired by rigid behaviour patterns, restricted or repetitive behaviours or inability to cope with change. Redirecting these behaviours is very difficult and produces great distress.
Needs substantial support *(Level 2)*	Social communication skill deficits cause marked impairments in functioning, limited initiation of and response to others' social interaction attempts, even when there are supports available.	Functioning in various contexts undermined by obvious rigid behaviour patterns, restricted or repetitive behaviours or inability to cope with change. Redirecting these behaviours is difficult and produces distress.
Needs support *(Level 1)*	When no supports are available, social communication skill deficits cause discernible impairments, with difficulty initiating and responding to others' social interaction attempts.	Functioning in one or more contexts undermined by inflexible behaviour, with switching of activities difficult. Independence compromised by organisational problems.

It is clear, however, that at least in children and adolescents, severity can vary markedly not only across individuals but also across and within domains within an individual. Greaves-Lord *et al.* (2013) documented phenotypic severity profiles emerging from the *Children's Social Behavior Questionnaire* (Luteijn *et al.* 1998) of a large sample ranging in age from 6 to 18 years. Some showed low severity of symptoms across all behavioural domains, some were uniformly severely impaired, while others varied considerably even within domains. For example, in some individuals with various social communication impairments, stereotypies are severe, whereas this is only a minor issue in other individuals. In some individuals resistance to change is prominent. And, obsessive interests, long considered to be a hallmark of the disorder, can be absent provided other behaviours are prominent. Although the Greaves-Lord *et al.* study of severity profiles did not extend to adulthood, it will become apparent later in this chapter that behavioural patterns of adults are also characterised by marked variations.

In sum, it is clear that a diagnosis of ASD does not equate to homogeneity of presentation. It is also important to recognise that diagnostic outcomes may vary across clinicians (Regier *et al.* 2013) and diagnostic sites (Lord *et al.* 2012a). Moreover, the classification performance of the *DSM-5* criteria has been shown to vary markedly across studies. For example, sensitivity (i.e., the percentage of true cases correctly identified) has ranged from 36 per cent to 91 per cent and specificity (i.e., the percentage of non-cases correctly identified) from 53 per cent to 100 per cent (Huerta *et al.* 2012; Mattila *et al.* 2011; McPartland, Reichow and Volkmar 2012; Young and Rodi 2014). In other words, diagnosis is by no means an exact science.

ASD from Childhood to Adulthood

Autism was initially considered to be a disorder of childhood. Indeed, the diagnostic label *infantile autism* was given to the condition when it was first listed in the *Diagnostic and Statistical Manual of Mental Disorders* (3rd edition (*DSM-III*); APA 1980). The introduction of AS as a PDD in the *DSM-IV* in 1994 (APA) – a diagnosis that required that there be no intellectual disability – led professionals to appreciate the variability across these disorders. But, with AS positioned under the umbrella term of PDD, the perception of autism as a disorder of childhood was reinforced. Possibly as a result of these origins, research into the presentation of the disorder in adulthood is much less extensive than research on autism in childhood. In fact, the first nationwide study on the epidemiology of ASDs in adults in the UK was only published in 2011 (Brugha *et al.* 2011). This study found that, even with the increase in prevalence of diagnoses among children, prevalence rates among adults were consistent with those found among children, leading the researchers to propose that adults with ASD are living in the community, most likely socially disadvantaged and also undiagnosed. As a result, the clinical picture of autism in adulthood is not well understood.

What we do know, however, is that the behavioural presentation of adults with ASD varies dramatically between individuals and within individuals across the life span. Further, life outcomes vary markedly. Some individuals will require lifetime support and care due to limited intellectual capacity and severity of symptoms. For others, the disorder may have limited impact on their daily life and their ability to blend into the community, hold down a job, maintain a relationship – in other words, the disorder may be largely unnoticed (Brugha *et al.* 2011). Nevertheless, research investigating outcomes for adults with ASD has consistently reported outcomes (using a variety of measures) that are far from universally positive (e.g., Ballaban-Gil *et al.* 1996). Although many people with autism are able to hold down jobs, their employment rates are typically low and the positions held are often reported as menial (Ballaban-Gill *et al.* 1996). Only 11 per cent of the participants in Ballaban-Gill *et al.*'s study (N=5) were in open employment, consistent with trends reported in other studies conducted in the US and Sweden (DeMyer *et al.* 1973; Gillberg and Steffenburg 1987), although slightly lower than employment rates for people with ASD in Japan (Kobayashi, Murata and Yoshinaga 1992). Independent living is also for the select few, with most studies indicating the majority of participants were either in residential facilities or residing with family (e.g., Ballaban-Gill *et al.* 1996; Howlin *et al.* 2004). These studies likely provide an overly pessimistic picture, given that the diagnosis available at the time using the *DSM-III* did not include AS. Future research using higher-functioning individuals may well suggest more positive outcomes. The varying outcomes possibly reflect the heterogeneity of different samples studied and the neglect of severity in prior diagnostic endeavours.

Research into how specific behaviours, either in isolation or in combination with others, change over time within an individual is limited. Data from some studies do point to changes in symptom patterns with age, with these observed across the domains of communication, social interaction, and restricted and repetitive behaviours and interests. In these domains some abatement of symptoms has been reported from childhood to adulthood, although the patterns, again not surprisingly, vary across samples (Seltzer *et al.* 2003; Shattuck *et al.* 2007). However, the reported patterns of symptom abatement were not uniform across different domains of symptomatology, with improvements more common in the communication domain than in the other two areas of functioning. There was also substantial variation within each of these domains. For example, in the restricted and repetitive behaviours and interests domain, substantial improvement was detected for the repetitive use of objects, whereas individuals were much less likely to show meaningful improvement in areas such as unusual preoccupations, unusual sensory interests, verbal rituals and circumscribed interests (Seltzer *et al.* 2003). Of course, the extent to which these changes reflect a genuine decline of symptoms or perhaps sample characteristics or reporting biases (e.g., reporters become used to the behaviours or the behaviours are displayed in a more socially appropriate manner) is difficult to ascertain.

In sum, we have only a limited understanding of the predictors of longer-term outcomes. Perhaps, not surprisingly, one predictor of positive outcome is ability level. For example, Shattuck *et al.* (2007) noted a general improvement in autistic symptomatology at a steady rate from childhood to adulthood, with the most robust predictors of better social adjustment being intellectual ability and verbal skills. Other studies have also linked variables such as autism symptoms, maladaptive behaviours, functional independence and comorbid psychiatric disorders to outcome (Eaves and Ho 2008; Farley *et al.* 2009; Gillberg and Steffenburg 1987; Howlin *et al.* 2004; Klin 2006). But we do not have sound empirical evidence that links the severity of specific autistic characteristics within an adult to the behaviours of that same individual when they were younger. At best we can state that, with age, some behaviours may ameliorate while others continue to cause difficulties. The determinants of these changes are likely to be multivariate in nature, and hence complex, and likely involve influences outside the autism spectrum such as comorbid conditions and contextual variables. Given our limited understanding of the presentation and progress of the disorder, recognition and diagnosis of adults not surprisingly remains problematic. Indeed, our clinical observations suggest that many adults may be misdiagnosed or remain undiagnosed until after they have become involved in the criminal justice system. Ideally, clinicians should be aware of whether the absence or presence of some behaviours may have more diagnostic salience at particular ages and, moreover, contribute to criminal vulnerability. In the remainder of this chapter we expand on the information provided by the various *DSM* criteria to provide a very broad-brush picture of salient characteristics of adults with ASD. In subsequent chapters we explore in much more detail how some of these characteristics may contribute to criminality in ASD.

The Characteristics of Adults with ASD

The preceding section highlights that the transition from childhood to adulthood for individuals with ASD is neither well defined nor understood. But what can we expect in terms of the characteristics of adults with ASD? Under the (new) *DSM-5* criteria, adults with ASD can range from severely intellectually disabled to cognitively very able. In other words, measured IQ may span the entire range. Historically, estimates of the prevalence of intellectual disability in ASD samples have been as high as 55–80 per cent (e.g., Fombonne 2001); current estimates tend to be somewhat lower (e.g., 26% in Chakrabarti and Fombonne, 2001). Obvious sources of the substantial variability in these estimates are variables such as when the study was done and whether IQ measures or adaptive behaviour measures were taken. Persons with ASD but not a comorbid intellectual disability who have a language delay have been referred to as having high-functioning autism (HFA), thus distinguishing them from AS for which there is no language disorder. It has been suggested that AS and HFA individuals have different IQ profiles, with AS characterised by an advantage of verbal over performance IQ and the pattern reversed for those with HFA. But, while there is some evidence of such patterns, the sample sizes are such that the data are certainly not robust, and clear exceptions to these conclusions have been reported, although it is clear that variations in IQ profiles across individuals are to be expected (e.g., Ghaziuddin and Mountain-Kimchi 2004; Ozonoff, South and Miller 2000). Although we acknowledge there may be overlapping symptomatology between ASD and intellectual disability that may be associated with involvement in crime, the focus of our discussions in later chapters will be primarily on ASD individuals within the normal range of intelligence (i.e., spanning borderline to superior intelligence).

Despite potentially massive IQ differences between individuals with ASD, those with ASD will be unified by an inability to approach other people and engage in a socially appropriate manner. Social communication will generally be awkward, and conversation (when possible) will often be one-sided, as persons with ASD tend to engage in lengthy monologues or fail to reciprocate conversation. They will also often interpret information literally; for example, instead of interpreting, 'Do you really think I'm a fool?' as a rhetorical question, they may respond by stating, 'I don't know you well enough to decide.' Similarly, they may not recognise the nonverbal behaviours demonstrated by others (e.g., expressions of boredom, anger or annoyance), thereby sometimes evoking frustration and confrontation. While some individuals with ASD may appear aloof and disinterested, others will actively, though often unsuccessfully, seek out companionship. Friendships may exist but these are typically maintained because the other person tolerates the quirky and often inappropriate behaviour of the person with ASD. They will accept the person with ASD despite the relationship often being one-sided and the person with ASD appearing self-absorbed. Persons with autism may sometimes appear to have learned to read the emotions of others and modify their behaviour to address issues such as those outlined above, but the behaviour often appears scripted rather than intuitive. Intervention may enable some adults to camouflage many of the above behaviours. For example, adults may learn scripts to deal with social interaction. These scripts may enable them to function socially, although the social interaction is likely to remain hard work or cognitively demanding. This learning of social skills can perhaps be likened to learning a foreign language in adulthood: metaphorically speaking, the social skills will always have an accent.

In addition to the social and communication difficulties outlined above, adults with ASD will also display what are referred to as restricted and repetitive behaviours. Given that all criteria for this domain need not be met for a diagnosis, not surprisingly there is more heterogeneity associated with the expression of this domain. Persons with ASD may display stereotypical speech or movement patterns and other patterns of behaviour that are rigid and inflexible. This is often but not necessarily accompanied by an obsessive but narrow interest in something or someone. The *DSM-5* has also recognised the longstanding belief that sensitivity to environmental stimuli can also cause immense distress for this population. Once again, contextual variables (e.g., range and degree of educational, family, social and financial support) may enable some adults to minimise the impact these behaviours have on their lives through access to vital support and services. For others, however, the impact may be debilitating.

Although, the introduction of the ASD classification served to make the disorder more homogenous by requiring individuals to meet all three of the social and communication criteria, the broad range of behaviours covered by each of these criteria, together with the range of possible severity levels, dictate that heterogeneity will remain. Similarly, given only two of the four criteria in the ritualistic domain are required to meet diagnosis, some individuals may present as resistant to change and having obsessive interests, while others diagnosed with the same disorder may be quite flexible and have no obsessions but engage in excessive stereotypical behaviours and have some sensory sensitivity. Thus, although people with ASD share the core features of social impairments and restricted repetitive behaviours and interests, there is considerable heterogeneity in the presentation of this disorder across individuals.

For some persons diagnosed with an ASD, the attendant behavioural characteristics can significantly affect daily life; for others their presentation may fall just outside the normal range of variability. For some individuals the behaviours may be clearly atypical and attract immediate attention. Such behaviours may include lengthy monologues about areas of interest with little attempt to engage the listener, ritualistic and stereotypical behaviours, self-talk, limited reciprocity in relationships, contextually inappropriate nonverbal communication and outbursts when confronted with dealing with change. It is possible that non-ASD people may be more understanding when dealing with individuals whose disability is quite apparent, as the presence of a disorder is clearly recognisable. For others, however, the presence of a disorder may not be so easily recognisable and the individual's unusual behavioural characteristics may, for example, be attributed to their being narcissistic, unempathic, rude or unintelligent. In such cases, the appropriate diagnosis may be overlooked and, consequently, the person may remain unsupported.

What exactly underpins this behavioural variability remains unknown, as a comprehensive understanding of the core deficits of ASD, and how they translate into behavioural outcomes, does not exist. In the final section of the chapter we draw attention to case study information to introduce some of the possible links between the diverse behavioural characteristics of adults with ASD and involvement in criminal activity.

Possible Links Between Characteristics of ASD and Criminal Activity

A number of cases suggestive of an apparent connection between ASD and crime commission have been reported in some detail in the forensic or psychiatric literatures (e.g., Baron-Cohen 1988; Eltman and Goldman 2013; Griffin-Shelley 2010; Katz and Zemishlany 2006; Kibbie 2012; Lewis 2010; Murrie *et al.* 2002; Tietz 2002). The crimes span arson, assault, attempted murder, fraud, larceny and various sexual offences. Close scrutiny of these cases reveals an array of ASD-related characteristics that appear to have been influential in many of these cases. These include characteristics such as anxiety associated with social contact, lack of social and emotional reciprocity, deficits in maintaining relationships, difficulty following social rules and conventions, inability to read the intentions of others from their verbal or nonverbal behaviour, failure to appreciate the impact of one's behaviour on others, anxiety created by a change in routine, and the pursuit of a strong interest, obsession or fixation. Note, however, that there are many potential confounding factors evident in these case studies. In some cases it is clear that ASD is confounded with either low intellectual functioning or a prior psychiatric history or perhaps both. In others, it is not clear if the possibility of other psychiatric disorders has even been systematically evaluated, although their presence and contribution seem likely based on the case details. Nevertheless, these cases reported in the literature do provide pointers regarding patterns of behaviour that may help us understand criminality in individuals with ASD.

The following detailed case study is based on one of the author's files and highlights the complex array of factors associated with the disorder that may, given particular situational or environmental circumstances, be linked to criminal activity.

YB was accused of sexually assaulting a minor. He had been sitting on a couch talking to the alleged victim, her boyfriend and two other acquaintances when they all fell asleep. He reportedly later told the boyfriend and the other friends that, while the victim was sleeping, he had digitally penetrated her vagina. The girl was unaware of the alleged incident until a week later when her boyfriend recounted YB's story. She then called the police.

YB is a 27-year-old man with an IQ in the normal range but limited schooling. At the time of his arrest he met the *DSM-IV* criteria for AS with three independent psychologists confirming an ASD diagnosis, although he had not been formally diagnosed with a disorder prior to becoming involved with the criminal judicial system. Following his arrest he did not appear to show an understanding of the impact his behaviour had on others. Nor did he show empathy for the victim. Indeed, YB expressed surprise that his victim had called the police because he thought he had apologised to her and even bought her a packet of lollies, suggesting that he believed justice had been restored. The legal discussions in the courtroom centred on whether YB appreciated the wrongfulness of his behaviour in relation to the criteria for AS and ASD. The defence argued that the disorder contributed to YB's actions.

YB always struggled with developing and maintaining friendships, gravitating towards younger peers who were closer to his developmental level. This is often the case for persons with ASD, who may find relationships more comfortable with persons outside their peer group preferring to interact with persons older or younger than themselves (Lord and Hopkins 1986). YB's friendships were mostly with individuals in their early teens. He had no age-appropriate peers and saw nothing unusual with this. Although a problem with forming relationships is a diagnostic criterion for ASD, difficulties in engaging in effective social communication, both verbal and nonverbal, may affect the ability to form relationships. Difficulties in these areas, coupled with a lack of peer groups for appropriate social referencing and feedback, thus likely contributed to his inappropriate social behaviour. YB saw his 15-year-old friends experimenting sexually with other 15-year-olds. At the time of the offence he did not know that having sex with a 15-year-old was wrong and, even when this was explained to him, he was at a loss to see why as a 27-year-old he would be considered more at fault than his 15-year-old friend who was the boyfriend of the victim. YB had never had an appropriate sexual relationship or peers to educate him in appropriate behaviour. His knowledge of sexual matters revealed upon interrogation was understandably minimal due to this lack of exposure. It could be argued that his social and communication difficulties led to his behaviour and thus ASD was a contributing factor. Further, persons with ASD often have obsessive behaviours that can be reflected in an intense interest in something or someone. YB had an interest in his victim's sexual experiences, which was not discouraged by the victim in Facebook conversations. In these conversations the victim responded to questions about her sexual experiences and other sexual matters, but only in relation to her boyfriend (who was also under the age of consent). It is likely that a person with ASD may misinterpret these conversations due to their inability to interpret the emotions or intentions of others. For example, the victim had previously joked about group sex on Facebook – although this did not include YB's involvement. YB's misinterpretation of these comments, which, in context, were clearly jocular was evident when asked if she had given permission and he responded that she had previously suggested group sex. It is clear YB did not think his behaviour was inappropriate or that a sexual relationship between two minors was any different to that between a man of 27 and a minor. Further, he did not appreciate that, even had she not been asleep, she was in a relationship with someone – in fact, the person to whom he relayed the account of his deviant behaviour. Finally, the qualitative impairments in social interaction and adherence to literal interpretations may have led YB to misinterpret the verbal behaviour of his victim.

A close examination of the details of this case points to a number of aspects of YB's behaviour that (a) quite likely contributed to his involvement in this offence and (b) are consistent with ASD criteria. These include:

> social immaturity, naive social awareness and a misinterpretation of friendships

> misreading of social signals and a lack of knowledge of social rules that may underlie accusations of sexual misconduct

> lack of empathy or lack of insight into the effects of behaviour

> lack of awareness of likely outcomes, hence a willingness to initiate outcomes with unforeseen consequences.

> obsessions and preoccupations.

In sum, similar themes emerge from this case study as were noted in relation to the published case studies that we mentioned above – specifically, an array of salient social-cognitive deficits appear to be implicated, thus providing a background for our exploration in the ensuing chapters of the likely central mechanisms underpinning criminality in ASD. These social-cognitive deficits are clearly consistent with what are considered to be deficits in Theory of Mind (ToM), generally considered to be one of the core deficits of ASD. But, although it appears that deficits in ToM may render people more vulnerable to involvement in criminal activity, the fact that most people with ASD likely have ToM deficits suggests that a ToM deficit alone cannot explain criminal behaviour. Indeed, leaving aside the possible contribution of comorbid conditions, a detailed examination of cases such as those referenced in this chapter highlights other consistent behavioural themes, suggesting potentially important interactions between variables that may shape criminality. In a number of cases, for example, other pronounced ASD symptomatology involving obsessive interests in a person or thing and sensory (hyper or hypo) sensitivity is prominent. Moreover, as we will argue in Chapter 5, such symptomatology may only turn out to be significant given specific enabling environmental conditions.

These issues are explored in detail in subsequent chapters. In Chapter 4 we focus on the potential contributions of comorbid conditions and socio-environmental variables to criminality in adults with ASD. Chapter 5 is concerned with what we hypothesise are the critical characteristics of ASD – namely ToM deficits, strong restricted interests and unusual sensory sensitivity – which may interact with each other and with specific situational or environmental characteristics to increase the likelihood of criminality.

Chapter 4

>>>>>>>>>>>>>>>>>>>>>>>>>>>>>>

COMORBID AND
SOCIO-ENVIRONMENTAL INFLUENCES

In previous chapters we have distinguished between criminal acts committed by individuals with ASD that may be attributable to particular characteristics of ASD and criminal acts that may reflect, at least in part, the contribution of comorbid conditions that may sometimes be associated with ASD. The former will be addressed at length in Chapters 5 and 6. In this chapter we focus on the evidence for the proposition that persons with ASD may have comorbid psychopathology (typically understood as co-occurrence of independent psychiatric disorders) that increases the risk of criminal offending.

In an attempt to assess the prevalence of comorbid conditions in criminals with an ASD, Newman and Ghaziuddin (2008) conducted a computer-assisted search of databases linking AS and violent crime. They identified 72 published papers addressing the presence of comorbid psychiatric conditions among individuals with AS who had been involved in a violent crime. Fifty-four papers were excluded, however, as they did not meet their inclusion criteria and another was rejected because of the use of overlapping cases. This left the sum total of 37 individual cases (not papers) for review. Newman and Ghaziuddin concluded that (a) 29.7 per cent of the reviewed cases (N=11) involving individuals with AS provided evidence of a definite comorbid psychiatric disorder (i.e., a psychiatric diagnosis had been made or symptoms were sufficiently described to permit a diagnosis) and (b) for another 54.0 per cent (N=20) there was a probable psychiatric disorder (i.e., a definite diagnosis was not possible because insufficient details were available). These were the data underpinning the conclusion that most individuals with AS who commit violent crimes have an additional psychiatric disorder that likely raises the risk of offending. Yet, this conclusion was based on a tiny sample ($N=37$) that met the inclusion criteria for diagnosis and criminal behaviour. Moreover, the validity of the diagnosis for a large chunk (i.e., 54%) of the cases was unknown. Regardless of whether the patterns suggested by these data are reliable, this study illustrates the type of evidential base that sometimes underpins claims of significantly high rates of comorbidity among offenders with ASD.

Other researchers have also expressed reservations about the reliability of comorbidity prevalence estimates for offenders with an ASD. For example, Simonoff *et al.* (2008) highlighted the lack of standardised tools with which to corroborate comorbid diagnoses and the sometimes inadequate formal assessment of ASD that may contribute to biased and incomplete clinical ascertainment. There are additional problems associated with drawing comparisons between comorbidity prevalence in offenders and community samples. For example, as the former are invariably referred samples, sometimes from centres specialising in differential diagnosis, comorbidities may be overestimated. Yet, underestimates of comorbidity may also result due to factors such as the use of insensitive assessment tools, limited professional training in the presentation of adults with an ASD and hierarchical diagnostic coding systems that prevent dual diagnoses. These issues create difficulty in drawing clear-cut conclusions about the extent of the contribution of comorbidities in the criminal offending of individuals with an ASD.

Chromosomal abnormalities have been implicated as causal factors in ASD, as have defective genes and environmental triggers. Given this complex and varied aetiology, it is to be expected that presentations will vary greatly between individuals. In addition to this diversity in presentation, aetiology associated with ASD may underpin and contribute to the development of other disorders. Further, because deficits associated with ASD occur broadly across social, communication and behavioural domains, the likelihood that the symptoms will overlap with those that characterise other disorders is high. Persons with ASD may thus present with symptomatology found in other disorders and, in some cases, meet diagnostic criteria for a disorder in addition to ASD. However, given the hierarchical rules of the *DSM-IV*, for people diagnosed under those guidelines a primary diagnosis was often required because exclusion criteria that existed prior to the *DSM-5* did not allow a second diagnosis if it was thought to result from another disorder. Adding to the potential diagnostic confusion, these rules differed between the two major diagnostic classification systems. For example, in accordance with the hierarchical rule in *DSM-IV*, a person meeting the criteria for a PDD could not be diagnosed as having ADHD, yet this is permissible under the *ICD-10* classification system. Thus, while professionals may sometimes allude to comorbid conditions in their notes, these conditions are often not formally diagnosed. Diagnoses of comorbid conditions may also be lacking because of the use of non-specific and invalid assessment tools. All of these considerations simply reinforce our earlier observation that, despite claims of significant rates of comorbid psychopathology among persons with ASD, and more specifically among criminal offenders, the evidence is often difficult to interpret and prevalence rate estimates must be treated with caution.

Given the difficulties associated with determining the relative prevalence of comorbid conditions in criminal offenders and community samples with ASD, we have adopted the following strategy in this chapter. We examine whether there are particular psychopathologies that co-exist with ASD, and whether there appears to be a risk of criminal behaviour associated with those conditions. This approach is certainly not a substitute for knowing the true prevalence of comorbidities, but the information it provides can alert us to potentially important causal influences that may be unrelated to the presence of ASD. This is obviously critical for understanding any possible causal link between ASD and criminal activity. Understanding such comorbidities is also of clinical and theoretical importance in understanding the relationship between a disorder and crime, given the complex relationships between various disorders (Tyrer *et al.* 1997). We also examine the likelihood that there may be socio-environmental risk factors for criminality that are particularly prevalent among persons with ASD – or at least among those who offend. Distinguishing the possible contributions of socio-environmental risk factors that may be present in association with ASD from contributory characteristics of ASD per se is also obviously crucial for understanding any possible causal role of ASD.

Comorbid Intellectual Disability

Although Kanner's (1943) original description of AD did not include persons with an intellectual disability, the spectrum has come to include persons encompassing the full range of the IQ distribution. And, although the introduction of AS to the *DSM-IV* in 1994 directed attention to the more cognitively able end of the spectrum (because by definition persons with AS could not have an intellectual disability), there is obviously a strong link between autism and intellectual disability.

With an intellectual disability comes a greater potential for mental health problems and a heightened risk of adverse socio-environmental conditions. These include, but are not limited to, poverty, poor family functioning, poor maternal health and institutional care, disadvantaged lifestyles, exposure to abuse, social stigmatisation, drug use, poor self-esteem, and limited coping skills, social networks and ability to control their own destiny (Moss *et al.* 1998; Emerson and Hatton 2007). Many of these may contribute to an increased vulnerability to involvement in crime (Dickson, Emerson and Hatton 2005). Research investigating criminality among persons with intellectual disabilities overwhelmingly suggests vulnerability to criminal engagement is associated with these risk factors rather than the disorder per se (Dickson *et al.* 2005).

Given, as outlined in Chapter 3, our focus is on risk factors for criminality associated with ASD – rather than with intellectual disability or the aforementioned socio-environmental conditions – we concentrate in this chapter on research using samples with ASD that purportedly do not have a comorbid intellectual disability.

Comorbid Psychopathology and ASD

Although it is extremely difficult to assess the prevalence of comorbid psychopathology in offenders with ASD, we are able to examine whether some comorbid conditions occur with some regularity within the ASD population. By examining evidence for links between those conditions and criminality, we are also able to speculate about whether having any of these comorbid conditions – either alone or in combination with ASD – might contribute to or increase the likelihood of criminality.

Common Comorbid Conditions

The available evidence does suggest that individuals with ASD may be vulnerable to specific psychiatric disorders. In this section we provide an overview of comorbidity estimates of the more frequently reported comorbid conditions among adult samples. The data we report are from studies that *generally* meet the following criteria: (a) the samples comprise adults, (b) IQ screening was conducted and the individuals are in the normal range of intelligence, and (c) the comorbid conditions were diagnosed through formal assessment involving interview and recognised classification systems (i.e., *ICD* or *DSM*), a criterion that markedly reduces the number of eligible studies. There are a number of features of these samples that need to be considered when evaluating the data. Despite the above statement about IQ, some of the samples appear to include a small proportion of adolescents and individuals on the borderline or in the range of mild intellectual disability, and it is not possible to determine from the data provided what the exact proportions are. The samples are referred samples, typically referred to some kind of centre for assessing behaviour problems, though it is often difficult to determine the exact basis for the referrals. The screening for comorbid conditions ranges from a very specific screening (e.g., for mood disorders) to a more comprehensive evaluation. Finally, there is not a great deal of consistency across studies in terms of the way comorbidities are described. In some studies data are presented in terms of frequencies and percentages of the key diagnostic categories; in others these breakdowns are provided for different patterns of symptomatology within the various diagnostic categories. Moreover, some studies record individuals as having multiple disorders within the same category (i.e., the person counts twice). It is difficult, therefore, to report the data from different studies in a standardised way.

In Table 4.1 we provide our overview of comorbidity estimates of the more frequently reported comorbid conditions among these samples. Although the particular format we provide does not capture the detail of each study, it provides an economical characterisation of the limited range of studies, the small sample sizes and the sometimes substantial variability in comorbidity estimates across studies. In other words, these data have to be interpreted with extreme caution as they clearly provide only the crudest guide. Nevertheless, while this imprecision may be unsatisfactory for many purposes, it does not prevent us highlighting comorbid influences that at least deserve consideration as potential detrimental influences on the behaviour of some individuals with ASD.

Table 4.1 Overview of Studies[1] of Comorbid Psychopathologies in Adults with ASD

Comorbid condition	Number of samples	Sample size range	Percentage with comorbid diagnosis (range)
Affective disorders: mood (e.g., major depression)	6	39–122	36–77%
Affective disorders: anxiety (any)	4	54–122	28–59%
ADHD	4	39–122	28–68%
Oppositional defiant disorder	1	63	53%
Conduct disorder	1	63	11%
Personality disorder	2	63–122	10–62%
Psychotic disorders	3	22–63	2–13%
Obsessive-compulsive disorder	3	39–122	3–24%
Substance/alcohol abuse	4	56–122	0–33%

[1] *Ghaziuddin, Weidmer-Mikhail and Ghaziuddin (1998); Hofvander et al. (2009); Joshi et al. (2013); Lugnegård, Hallerbäck and Gillberg (2011); Munesue et al. (2008); Tani et al. (2012).*

The comorbid disorders that are prominent and emerge consistently across samples are the affective disorders of mood and anxiety, and ADHD. Also prominent – though not as consistently reported – are disorders such as conduct disorder, oppositional defiant disorder or some variety of personality disorder. We believe it is important to highlight these, regardless of whether they are represented any more strongly in ASD than non-ASD samples, because – as will become apparent later in this chapter – they are often discussed in connection to crime causation. For the same reason we have highlighted data for substance abuse and psychotic disorders such as schizophrenia.

Comorbidity in Childhood

Evidence from large-scale longitudinal research with non-ASD samples (Costello *et al.* 2003) shows a high degree of continuity from childhood to adolescence for diagnoses of many psychiatric disorders. However, it also indicates the possibility of a progression from one diagnosis to another (e.g., a progression from depression to anxiety or from ADHD to oppositional defiant disorder). Given that later psychiatric disturbance may be predicted and anticipated from childhood presentation, we briefly examine here evidence for comorbidities in samples of children with ASD.

Depression and anxiety-related disorders are also two of the more commonly reported comorbid disorders among children with ASD (e.g., Kim *et al.* 2000; Leyfer *et al.* 2006), while ADHD also features prominently among children (e.g., Leyfer *et al.* 2006). A particularly comprehensive comorbidity study among 10–14-year-old children is that reported by Simonoff *et al.* (2008), despite the fact they did not screen for all possible comorbid disorders. Notable features of the study are that it used a population-based sample, a standardised parent interview measure to examine rates of *DSM-IV* disorders in children with ASD and a statistical approach that generated population prevalence estimates. Some comorbid disorder was implicated in approximately 70 per cent of cases, with an anxiety disorder noted in more than 40 per cent of cases and ADHD in 28 per cent of cases. Also interesting was the prevalence of oppositional defiant disorder, detected in 28 per cent of cases. As we discuss later in this chapter, to the extent that oppositional defiant disorder in adolescents progresses to conduct disorder or antisocial personality disorder in adults, this comorbidity is potentially extremely important for understanding the involvement of individuals with ASD in certain types of crime given the over-representation of those disorders among criminals.

The Links Between Comorbid Psychopathology and Criminality

Here we investigate the relationship between criminal activity and those comorbid disorders that, despite the limitations of the available evidence, appear to be more common among persons with ASD. This investigation should provide some pointers to the possible contributions of comorbid conditions to offending in individuals with ASD. As one might imagine, disentangling the roles of these various individual difference characteristics, as well as teasing out environmental influences and interactions, is extremely difficult. And, our ability to do so is constrained by the fact that there is limited research investigating the direct link between these disorders and crime.

Mood Disorders, Anxiety and Other Affective Disorders

In studies where the presence of affective disorders has been examined among male criminal samples, prevalence estimates cannot be easily or reliably interpreted. This is due to the nature of the sample, the crime committed, whether it was the first offence, whether the person was ultimately convicted and whether other potentially influential comorbidities (e.g., drug use) were excluded. Further, what constitutes an affective disorder differs between papers due to the differences in diagnostic tools used and categorisation. In addition, a variety of factors conspire to complicate any evaluation of the contributions of affective disorders towards criminal activity. Samples are often selected because psychiatric disorders are suspected. Some individuals within a sample may have multiple disorders; this is important because, given particular combination of comorbid disorders, the risk of offending and recidivism appears to increase – at least for those whose condition is severe enough to warrant hospitalisation (Modestin, Hug and Ammann 1997). Some individuals within a sample may have committed multiple crimes. Different affective disorders are sometimes lumped together in one category. Diagnosis of disorders may have been determined by self-report rather than clinical interview, and there is considerable variability in the operationalisation of criminal activity, with offences as diverse as speeding and murder sometimes combined. So even in studies where the type of crime has been categorised separately, estimates vary substantially.

Moreover, other potentially important contributing factors are often implicated. Not surprisingly, therefore, interpretation of the data is often messy. By way of illustration, when comparing persons with major affective disorders with persons with schizophrenia in a sample of persons who had undergone rehabilitation, Hodgins, Lapalme and Toupin (1999) reported that persons with major affective disorders were twice as likely to offend following discharge as persons with schizophrenia – but three times as likely to offend when more violent crimes were considered. Yet, those with major affective disorders had a higher lifetime prevalence of drug abuse or dependence than those with schizophrenia, with 88 per cent of those convicted returning positive samples for drug use during the two-year post-release follow-up compared with only 21 per cent for those who had not offended. Thus, the contribution the affective disorder makes to the crime is clouded by the involvement of drug use and, possibly, the impact of the rehabilitation programme.

There are numerous examples of findings such as these which highlight that the relationship between criminality and affective disorders is not straightforward. There is some evidence to suggest that affective disorders, in isolation, do not predict an increased likelihood of criminal activity. For example, Eronen, Hakola and Tiihonen (1996) found that major depressive episodes and anxiety disorders had minimal impact in terms of increasing the statistical risk for homicide among 693 homicide offenders, arguing that, when other criminological risk factors were considered (e.g., juvenile delinquency, underprivileged social standing), affective disorders appeared to contribute little to predicting criminal activity. Copeland *et al.*'s (2007) findings suggest a middle ground. They acknowledge that having an anxiety disorder may increase criminal vulnerability, but its influence is intertwined with substance abuse and it is, therefore, extremely difficult to disentangle the two factors. Others have argued for a different position. Oakley, Hynes and Clark (2009) point to forensic psychiatrists' apparent lack of appreciation of potentially important connections between mood disorders and violent behaviour. They argue that the diminished inhibition that may accompany extreme affective states is likely to underlie the expression of aggressive or violent behaviour, supporting their argument with data from very large-scale community studies that point to similar connections between violence and affective disorders such as depression as for schizophrenia (e.g., Brennan, Mednick and Hodgins 2000; Swanson *et al,* 1990). But, they also note the moderating effects of variables such as substance abuse, leaving us again with uncertain conclusions. Finally, while some (e.g., White *et al.* 2012) have argued that social anxiety may contribute to aggressive behaviour and, in turn, increase the likelihood of criminal behaviour, it has also been suggested that anxiety may be a protective factor that reduces the likelihood of criminal behaviour by inhibiting peer relationships that may prove to be antisocial in nature (C.F. Kuhn and Laird 2013). As we suggested at the outset, the picture is very confusing.

One affective disorder that we have not discussed thus far – but, because of overlapping symptomatology, always comes readily to mind when considering ASD – is obsessive-compulsive disorder (OCD). The obvious apparent commonalities between the two disorders are the rituals and the circumscribed interests seen in persons with ASD and the obsessions and compulsions typically seen in persons with OCD. It is these obsessive interests or obsessions that some have hypothesised may be closely related to specific types of criminal offending such as stalking, compulsive theft (cf. Berney 2004) or perhaps arson. Moreover, in speculation about causal links between OCD symptomatology and crime, others have pointed to intrusive thoughts that may be sexual or aggressive in nature as possible contributory factors in criminal activity (e.g., Veale *et al.* 2009). In Chapter 5 we discuss the possible role of intense restricted interests in criminal involvement of people with ASD but, as will become apparent there, the mechanism posited does not rely on the impact of intrusive thoughts. Whether there is a link between specific obsessions, such as those seen in OCD, and particular types of criminal activity is unknown. At present we do not have empirical data on the issue and we often cannot be sure from case study reports linking obsessions to crime whether the particular individuals involved have OCD, ASD or simply an obsessive behaviour or interest. Thus, while OCD is sometimes comorbid with ASD, hard evidence for its role in crime causation is lacking. Further, there is no evidence to suggest that co-existing OCD and ASD increases criminal vulnerability. Of course, this does not rule out the possibility that there may be specific types of obsessions that could produce problematic consequences in particular individuals who are unable to control their engagement in those obsessions or, perhaps, their reactions to any interruption to their engagement with them.

What then are we to make of the relationship between affective disorders and violent or other criminal behaviour? We are not sure. The evidence is not only difficult to interpret (for a variety of reasons) but it is also equivocal. It is difficult, therefore, to argue strongly that the likely relatively high comorbidity of affective disorders and ASD either can or cannot explain any involvement of individuals with ASD in crime. Thus, given the current state of knowledge in this area, it seems unwise to attribute automatically the crime of an offender with diagnoses of ASD and a comorbid affective disorder to some unique characteristics of ASD. Perhaps what is a little more certain is that the presence of such disorders may render the individual more susceptible to the negative influence of other adverse socio-environmental variables (e.g., substance abuse) that do appear to increase the risk of criminality.

Psychotic Disorders: Schizophrenia

As shown in Table 4.1, there is a likely comorbidity of schizophrenia and ASD. And indeed, schizophrenia has a special relationship with ASD, the nature of which we discuss at the end of this section. First, however, we explore the links between schizophrenia and criminality. There is now a body of converging evidence from studies using different methodologies to suggest a relationship between engagement in criminal activity, especially violent crime, and the presence of a lifetime psychotic disorder such as schizophrenia. Although the absolute risk of violence by such individuals is low, the prevalence is higher than in samples without this diagnosis (cf. Walsh, Buchanan and Fahy 2002). For example, in a study of male prisoners on remand, Taylor and Gunn (1984) found that 9 per cent of those later convicted of non-fatal violent crimes had schizophrenia, with estimates increasing to 11 per cent for those convicted of fatal crimes – prevalence rates that were higher than those reported in community samples. Using data from the Danish offender register, Munkner *et al.* (2003) reported that 41 per cent of persons with schizophrenia had committed offences ranging from traffic to violent offences. Although no prevalence data were provided, a large population-based study (*N*=538) in London of persons diagnosed with schizophrenia between 1964 and 1984 also reported an increased risk of criminal behaviour among females and an increased risk of convictions for violence in males (Wessely 1998). Studies such as these have led to the overarching conclusion that persons with schizophrenia are over-represented in the criminal judicial system and more so when violent crimes are involved (e.g., Lindqvist and Allebeck 1990; Tiihonen *et al.* 1997). There is also widespread agreement that the relationship between schizophrenia and violence is significantly shaped, possibly explained or at least exacerbated by substance abuse problems (e.g., Fukunaga and Lysaker 2013; Monahan 1983; Mullen 2006; Wallace, Mullen and Burgess 2004).

The mechanisms underpinning the schizophrenia–violence nexus are not well understood but – as we will see in the next paragraph when we discuss the schizophrenia–ASD relation – could be very important in understanding some of the criminal involvement of individuals with ASD. Recent studies offer some possible candidate mechanisms that are worth bearing in mind, even if far from conclusive. These include disorganised thinking or cognition that might undermine the individual's capacity to react appropriately in complex social interactions (Fukunaga and Lysaker 2013) and a suggested, and possibly causal, pathway involving common delusional beliefs (specifically, persecution, being spied on and conspiracy) producing anger and, in turn, violent behaviour (Coid *et al.* 2013).

The Relationship Between Schizophrenia and ASD
As noted earlier, schizophrenia has a special relationship with ASD, a relationship that has the potential to produce diagnostic confusion and obfuscate the relationship between ASD, or schizophrenia, and criminal behaviour. To understand the schizophrenia–ASD relationship, one needs to understand the historical development of these two diagnostic labels.

The clinical and biological link between the two disorders has been debated in the literature since Kanner first described autism in 1943 and debate arose as to whether there was a phenotypic overlap between the two disorders. When AD was introduced to the *DSM-II* in 1971, it was under the diagnostic umbrella of schizophrenia. In response to the work of Kolvin (1971), the *DSM-III* revisions separated autism and schizophrenia. Although schizophrenia is thought to occur with equal probability in the ASD population and the wider community, studies of child-onset schizophrenia indicate the disorder is often either preceded by or comorbid with ASD, with more than 30 per cent of the participants with childhood schizophrenia having a comorbid ASD (e.g., Rapoport *et al.* 2009).

Importantly, some individuals with ASD may respond poorly to stress, which may in turn evoke psychotic symptoms (Jansen *et al.* 2000). Further, ASD symptomatology, including confusion regarding social rules, may also lead to increased paranoia (Blackshaw *et al.* 2001). Other behaviours seen in persons with ASD, such as social withdrawal, poor communication and reduced eye contact, may also be misdiagnosed and considered negative symptomatology as part of the schizophrenia diagnosis. And, another complicating factor for our understanding of these disorders is the varying nomenclature used to describe these individuals. For example, the term multiple complex developmental disorders (MCDD) has been used to describe children who met criteria for ASD and also exhibited affect dysregulation and disordered thinking (Cohen, Paul and Volkmar 1986). Given van der Gaag et *al.*'s (2005) observation that significant numbers of children with MCDD developed psychosis in adulthood, it is clear that further opportunity for diagnostic confusion may arise. It remains unclear whether there is a genuine comorbidity, phenotypic overlap or simply diagnostic uncertainty surrounding ASD and schizophrenia. Yet, although delineating these disorders is not easy for clinicians, it is important not only for enhancing our understanding of the disorders and providing effective intervention but also for identifying risk factors within each of these disorders that independently or in combination may be associated with criminal behaviour.

Attention Deficit Hyperactivity Disorder
ADHD is one of the most common psychiatric disorders, affecting approximately 5–10 per cent of children and adolescents (Taylor and Sonuga-Barke 2008). A comprehensive review of 102 studies published worldwide (Polanczyk *et al.* 2007) reported a pooled prevalence rate of 5.3 per cent in children and adolescents among the general population. Similar prevalence rates ranging from 5.9 per cent to 7.1 per cent were reported by Willcutt (2012) from 86 studies, again involving children

and adolescents. Estimates appear to be slightly lower among adults, with a large US nationally representative sample producing a 4.4 per cent estimated prevalence rate of ADHD in adults aged 18–44 years (Kessler *et al.* 2006).

Importantly, ADHD is commonly linked to additional disruptive behaviours such as aggression and antisocial behaviour, illustrated by the *ICD-10* inclusion of a category called hyperactive conduct disorder (von Polier, Vloet and Herpetz-Dahlmann 2012). Thapar, Harrington and McGuffin (2001); reported that approximately half of the persons with ADHD have conduct disorder. Both ADHD and conduct disorder are predictors of adult disruptive behaviours, including criminal activity (Gunter *et al.* 2006). In addition, they are also linked to personality disorders in adulthood (Fischer *et al.* 2002) – possibly the most common condition among offenders – with Young *et al.* (2003) noting that up to 78 per cent of offenders with a personality disorder diagnosis likely met ADHD criteria as children.

The exact nature of the link(s) between ADHD and criminal behaviour is difficult to unravel. Whether ADHD directly increases the likelihood of criminal activity, and whether its link to criminality is related to comorbid psychiatric diagnoses such as conduct disorder and antisocial behaviours or to environmental risk factors, which may even contribute to the likelihood of developing the disorder, is debated. Nevertheless, the body of evidence suggesting a relationship with crime is somewhat stronger than for some other comorbidities. Studies of the presence of ADHD in offender samples yield relatively consistent results. In a US sample, Teplin *et al.* (2002) reported that 17 per cent of males and 21 per cent of females among 1829 juveniles in temporary detention had ADHD. Similarly high estimates have been reported in other countries, including the Netherlands (8%, Vreugdenhil *et al.* 2004), Korea (33% and 52% of incarcerated boys and girls, respectively; Chae, Jung and Noh 2001) and Germany (45% of incarcerated young males; Rösler *et al.* 2004). High prevalence rates of ADHD have also been found in adult prison populations (e.g., Eyestone and Howell 1994), with at least 25 per cent of inmates in Eme (2009) and Hurley and Eme (2008) reported as having ADHD. In one of the more comprehensive (N=3962) studies, 10.5 per cent of incarcerated individuals were found to have ADHD.

Although such prevalence data are difficult to interpret due to non-random sample selection, comorbidities and hierarchical rules that prevent a dual diagnosis, these estimate are higher than those for the general population (Cahill *et al.* 2012; Polanczyk *et al.* 2007).

There is also evidence that childhood ADHD predicts a trajectory of later delinquency and crime, although not every study has converged on this conclusion (e.g., Mordre *et al.* 2011). For children diagnosed at ages 5–12 years, Sibley *et al.* (2011) reported an increased risk of delinquency, a finding duplicated for children with both ADHD and oppositional defiant disorder. For children with ADHD and comorbid conduct disorder, the risk, especially for more severe delinquency, was much greater. In one of the few large-scale studies (N=3319) in which contextual variables (i.e., parental wealth, education, comorbid disorders and skipping grades) were controlled, Lundström *et al.* (2014) demonstrated that children with ADHD had an elevated risk for later violent crime (e.g., homicide, assault, arson, robbery, sexual crimes). Recall from our previous discussion of Lundström *et al.*'s study in Chapter 2, however, that, whereas ADHD emerged as a substantial risk factor for violent criminal behaviour, there was no evidence that a diagnosis of ASD elevated risk for violent offending.

As is the case with the other comorbidities discussed thus far, the mechanisms of ADHD effects on criminal involvement are poorly understood. An array of possible explanatory constructs, such as inattention, impulsivity or prosocial adjustment problems that increase susceptibility to antisocial and problematic behaviour (e.g., Colledge and Blair 2001; Young and Gudjonsson 2006), have been mooted but not resolved. This lack of clarity about the contributory mechanisms makes it difficult to pinpoint possible ADHD contributions to crimes involving people with ASD.

Oppositional Defiant Disorder, Conduct Disorder and Personality Disorder

Leaving aside the questionable reliability of the various comorbidity prevalence estimates shown in Table 4.1, it is clear that disorders such as oppositional defiant disorder, conduct disorder and personality disorders such as antisocial personality disorder represent potentially very significant ASD comorbidities. In the previous section we saw that the combination of ADHD and conduct disorder was a high risk factor for delinquency. The *ICD-10* identifies aggression to people or animals, destruction of property, deceitfulness or theft and serious violations of rules as diagnostic indicators of conduct disorder. Moreover, in a significant proportion of cases, conduct disorder develops into antisocial personality disorder, reflected in long-term patterns of manipulating, exploiting or violating the rights of others, often in criminal ways. This may lead to substance abuse and other mental health problems. Further, in adolescence and adulthood, persons with these disorders may be more vulnerable to arrest (Odgers *et al.* 2008), with antisocial personality disorder a strong risk factor for homicidal violence (Eronen *et al.* 1996).

There are two reasons why the presence of a comorbid oppositional defiant disorder also merits attention here. First, Wareham and Boots (2012) showed that the presence of oppositional defiant disorder was a significant predictor of both the prevalence of adolescent violence (though admittedly only a weak predictor) and the frequency of future violence, after controlling for various individual and environmental risk factors. While the effect may have been relatively small at the group level, Wareham and Boots' data highlight a potentially important influence on criminal behaviour at the individual level that may well co-exist with ASD. Similarly suggestive patterns of findings have been documented in other large-scale studies (Fergusson, Boden and Horwood 2010; Vogel and Messner 2011). Second, evidence from a large community sample shows that oppositional defiant disorder often, though by no means always, progresses to conduct disorder (e.g., Rowe *et al.* 2010). And, it has been suggested that it may sometimes progress to antisocial personality disorder in late adolescence or adulthood (Rey *et al.* 1995). As noted above, the presence of both disorders is clearly related to criminal behaviour. Thus, this particular comorbidity may be crucial for explaining the involvement of individuals with ASD in certain types of crime.

Summary

Examinations of psychiatric disorders that may be comorbid with ASD, and the possible links between those disorders and involvement in crime, are beset with interpretative problems but, nevertheless, suggest several broad conclusions. First, disorders such as the affective disorders, schizophrenia, ADHD, oppositional defiant disorder and, most likely, conduct disorder and other personality disorders probably are not infrequently comorbid with ASD. Second, there are reasonable grounds for concluding that these disorders either heighten the risk for criminal involvement or perhaps may do so by virtue of some kind of interaction with substance abuse problems. Third, it should come as no surprise that it is extremely difficult to assess the overall extent of the contributions of these comorbidities. These disorders often do not occur in isolation, and the clear and orderly separation of symptoms between disorders suggested by our classification systems is seldom the reality. Rather, attempts to tease out the relations between crime and psychiatric disorders will be thwarted because many of the potentially important variables are inextricably linked. Given the complex array of potentially influential interacting variables, it is no simple matter to identify either proximal or distal causal influences on, or risk factors for, criminal behaviour, not least because doing *clean* research into such issues is extraordinarily complex. Fourth, even at the level of the individual and their particular crime, it will often be difficult to isolate any contribution of these comorbidities, in part again because of the complex network of interacting variables but also in part because – as has been indicated in the preceding sections of this chapter – not a great deal is understood about the precise mechanisms via which these disorders affect individual behaviour.

Nevertheless, despite the numerous – and what perhaps may seem nearly insurmountable – complexities associated with researching causal links in this area and interpreting any empirical evidence that is produced, we believe that the identification of some comorbid conditions diagnosed in an individual with ASD should be considered much more plausible candidates for explaining some criminal behaviour than the presence of ASD. For example, we saw in earlier sections of this chapter that conditions such as oppositional defiant disorder, conduct disorder, antisocial personality disorder and ADHD not only often co-exist with ASD but also may be linked (alone or in combination) to certain types of crimes that are often too readily linked to the presence of ASD (e.g., arson, physical and sadistic abuse of others). In addition, whether as a precursor to or a product of the condition, adverse socio-environmental conditions that are known to increase one's likelihood of engaging in crime are clearly a contributing factor to this link. In many studies, controlling for these variables removes, or at least minimises, the reported link.

Socio-Environmental Factors and their Relationship with Criminality

There are numerous socio-environmental risk factors for criminal behaviour that have received attention in the criminological, sociological and psychological literatures. These include criminological factors as diverse as age of first conviction, number of convictions, familial involvement in crime and associating with criminals, as well as socio-economic factors such as parental unemployment, literacy, health problems, bullying and social rejection, and substance abuse. Coverage of this array of influences is outside the scope of this book. In this section we examine socio-environmental risk factors that may be associated with crime commission *and*, importantly, appear to constitute particular risk factors for persons with ASD. Similar to the picture we painted when discussing comorbid disorders, however, the causal role of these socio-environmental variables, either individually or in combination, is extremely difficult to disentangle. Many studies combine the socio-environmental predictor variables or collapse data across crime types, thereby making it extremely difficult to link specific crimes and risk factors. At best, generally all we are able to do is point to some plausible socio-environmental components within what is clearly a complex causal network.

Basic Demographic Factors

Some basic demographic factors probably heighten the risk of criminal engagement for persons with ASD. Being male, being single, having limited education, being unemployed and having been in foster care, all of which are criminological risk factors, are also reported as more common among adults with ASD (e.g., Howlin *et al.* 2004). For example, Salvatore and Taniguchi (2012) found that people who are married and have children have a decreased risk of (self-reported) offending, even after controlling for a range of variables such as age, gender, education, hours worked, religious observance and parental attachment. Given that persons with ASD are more likely to be single, this factor alone may increase the likelihood of criminal engagement. Having been in alternative care arrangements has also been linked to offending (Stephens and Day 2013) and, given the higher prevalence of children with ASD who have been in care (Hill 2012), this factor too could affect vulnerability. Adults with ASD may also lack some of the protective socio-environmental factors that might reduce the risk of criminal activity. For example, factors such as social support and personal resources are often lacking in persons with ASD. At the same time, they may also experience conditions that can serve as protective factors, the obvious one being the likelihood of more limited engagement with peers that necessarily reduces opportunities for potentially negative peer pressure. Although factors such as these are likely risk factors, they are not especially informative with respect to understanding how and why an individual with ASD came to commit a criminal offence. Two other social-behavioural influences do, however, warrant closer attention.

Bullying and Social Rejection

Given the difficulties that individuals with ASD experience in understanding and engaging in social relationships, it is not surprising that risk factors such as being exposed to bullying and rejection are frequently mentioned when trying to understand the social outcomes for individuals with ASD. Cappadocia, Weiss and Pepler (2012) found bullying to be a longstanding problem for 50 per cent of the 192 children in their sample of non-offending children with ASD. In a large sample study (N=1221) reported by Zablotsky *et al.* (2012), 37 per cent of parents reported that their children with AS aged 6–15 years had been bullied in the last month. Apparently reinforcing the bullying–criminal behaviour connection are Allen *et al.*'s (2008) findings that around 69 per cent of adult offenders with ASD were exposed to social rejection prior to their offending behaviour, while a further 50 per cent experienced sexual rejection. In addition, for 50 per cent of adult offenders with ASD, experiences of bullying preceded offending. At face value, such reports are persuasive. But, given the likelihood that most persons with ASD experience these social conditions, and perhaps quite regularly, it is likely that, at any given time, similar percentages of persons who haven't offended and have also experienced these social difficulties could be identified.

Evidence for a clear link between being bullied and later offending in individuals without ASD is mixed, even when the studies have captured large samples, as in the two studies reported next. For example, although Sourander et al. (2006) found the risk of later offending was predicted by having been a bully, they did not find that those who had been bullied were more at risk of offending (with the exception of drink-driving). In contrast, Wolke et al. (2013) reported that, when factors such as familial hardship and childhood psychiatric problems were controlled for, being a victim of bullying did increase the risk of self- or parent-reported offending.

It is clear, however, that being bullied does not, by itself, translate into criminal offending by individuals with ASD because, otherwise, prevalence estimates would be much higher. Nevertheless, for a couple of reasons at least, the possible relevance of bullying and rejection amongst a broader network of variables for some individuals should not be dismissed. First, the literature discussed above has largely been concerned with the aftermath of being bullied in childhood and has not focused on the consequences of sustained bullying of adults with ASD. Whether this would make any difference to the pattern of findings is unknown, but it could be important. Second, there is now a substantial literature demonstrating the powerful consequences of social rejection, or ostracism, for the behaviour of adults. Extended ostracism or social rejection is likely to lead eventually to a feeling of worthlessness and associated psychological problems, and in extreme cases it may lead to anger and aggression towards others (Williams 2009; Williams and Nida 2011). Indeed, Leary et al.'s (2003) analysis of school shootings in the US reported that 13 of the 15 shooters examined had experienced ostracism. Moreover, ostracised individuals may seek to repair the resultant diminished sense of belonging by joining and complying with the wishes or orders (even if unusual) of new individuals or groups that offer them some form of inclusion (Williams 2009). In other words, it seems likely that extended exclusion or social rejection may in some cases lead to behaviours that have the potential to culminate in criminal activity. Thus, just as some psychiatric conditions that sometimes co-exist with ASD – but are not specific to ASD – may eventually contribute to criminal behaviour, it is quite possible that extended bullying or rejection of the individual with ASD (assuming, of course, they are aware of it) may also have a similar impact.

Alcohol and Drug Abuse

Another socio-environmental influence that is clearly related to criminal activity is the abuse of alcohol and drugs (e.g., Boden, Fergusson and Horword 2012), although it is difficult to determine the extent of the problem in ASD samples. Based on records both of urine analysis and self-report data which had been collected by the Australian Institute of Criminology (from more than 40,000 persons who had been detained by police Payne and Gaffney, 2012), around two-thirds recorded positive tests for at least one drug other than alcohol (Gaffney et al. 2010). Moreover, 47 per cent of those arrested had also recorded another offence in the preceding 12-month period. These rates are higher than those reported in the general community (see comparative data at the Australian Institute of Health and Welfare 2008). Earlier in this chapter (see Table 4.1) we saw that the estimates for comorbidity of substance abuse and ASD span a wide range. Some studies suggest that these problems are less of an issue for individuals with ASD than they are for individuals with other psychological disorders (Mandell et al. 2012; Santosh and Mijovic 2006), although the use of alcohol and drugs among the ASD population did increase if someone had ADHD in addition to ASD (Sizoo et al. 2010). Indeed, Santosh and Mijovic (2006) reported that every participant in their study with ASD using drugs or abusing alcohol would have met ADHD criteria had ASD and ADHD been allowed to be concurrently diagnosed. Again, we are left with a very unclear picture about the extent of involvement of a variable that is clearly crucial in the non-ASD population.

Summary

A wide variety of socio-environmental variables have been linked to offending behaviour in the general population. Although many of these variables also appear to be represented in samples of offenders with ASD, they are also present in non-offenders. The data suggest similar conclusions to those we advanced with respect to the role of comorbid psychiatric conditions. That is, it is likely that such factors sometimes make some kind of causal contribution to criminal behaviour, although almost certainly as part of a multivariate causal network. But, given the obvious complexity of crime causation, it will always be difficult to pin down any such causal factor – and how big a role it played – with certainty. Again, there is a paucity of research investigating the role such factors may play in increasing the risk that an individual with ASD will engage in criminal behaviour. Nevertheless, we believe a couple of observations are particularly pertinent. First, when one of these socio-environmental risk factors appears to be strongly implicated, it may well be more important from a causal perspective than the presence of ASD. Second, the role of social rejection and bullying clearly warrants closer consideration and research attention, since it is a risk factor that is perhaps much more likely to come into play due to the particular deficits of individuals with ASD. However, given the frequency with which these circumstances occur among persons with ASD, we would perhaps expect greater criminal involvement, raising the obvious question as to why many adults with ASD share this proposed risk factor but do not offend.

Conclusion

The possible presence of comorbid psychiatric conditions and socio-environmental conditions that may heighten the risk of criminal behaviour makes it extremely difficult to pinpoint the key factors contributing to crimes involving people with ASD. Nevertheless, one thing is clear: when evaluating possible causal factors in such crimes, there may be numerous plausible candidates other than the fact that the person who committed the crime had an ASD. In order to assist in discriminating between such candidates, Chapter 5 concentrates on ASD-related mechanisms, specifically the cognitive, social and behavioural characteristics of individuals with ASD that may, given appropriate environmental conditions, play a role.

CRIMINAL VULNERABILITY
ASD-specific Influences

Chapter 3 highlighted the range of behavioural characteristics that we can expect to see – to varying degrees – in individuals with ASD. Chapter 4 reviewed comorbid psychopathologies and socio-environmental variables that may explain why some people with ASD become involved in criminal behaviour. In this chapter we focus on what are generally considered to be some core characteristics of ASD that are arguably associated with heightened criminal vulnerability. These characteristics are Theory of Mind (ToM) and restricted or circumscribed interests or obsessions. Given the low prevalence rates of criminality in ASD samples, we will not be arguing that any deficit in ToM or restricted interest can, in isolation, drive criminal behaviour. Rather, we will argue for a complex causal network that involves (a) an extremely broad (or pervasive) and severe ToM deficit, or (b) a quite specific and significant ToM deficit or limitation, or (c) the presence of a very strong and restricted interest or obsession, plus a pervasive or specific ToM deficit. Moreover, these deficits must occur in combination with a particular set or combination of environmental conditions to increase criminal vulnerability.

We are certainly not the first to implicate ToM deficits or dominating restricted interests as potential influences on criminal behaviour in individuals with ASD. Howlin (2004), for example, highlighted the possible contributory role of these and other characteristics of individuals with ASD and provided a number of case study illustrations. Indeed one or other, or sometimes both, of these factors have often been mentioned as possible causal mechanisms, especially in case study reports of crimes involving an individual with ASD. Rather, our contribution is a more detailed formulation of prior accounts of the mechanisms by which these factors – individually or in interaction – are likely to contribute to engagement in criminal activity. Then, in Chapter 7, we extend our account to encompass consideration of how these factors may influence the nature and outcomes of the interactions that individuals with ASD have with the criminal justice system.

As we have just indicated, it is common in case study reports of criminal activity involving individuals with ASD for a ToM deficit to be invoked as an explanatory mechanism. The offender with ASD may, for example, be described as not being able to:

> › anticipate or interpret the intentions or actions of another person
>
> › foresee the deleterious impact their own behaviour might have on other people or property
>
> › empathise with or relate to a person who is about to be, or has been, wronged or harmed or
>
> › negotiate their way out of a potential criminal involvement despite being aware of the wrongfulness of their prospective actions.

Although such descriptions are clearly strongly suggestive of ToM deficits, if this were all that were required, we might expect criminality to be rampant among individuals with ASD. So why might these ToM characteristics only be important for some individuals, some of the time?

In the following sections we try to answer this question by providing a much finer grained analysis of ToM deficits in association with ASD. We provide an overview of major empirical findings, focusing not only on consistent patterns therein but also on some inconsistencies that we believe are particularly informative about ToM in people with ASD. At first glance, some of the initial discussion especially may appear to be some distance removed from this book's focus on criminality. It is hoped, however, that the outcome will be a clearer understanding of ToM deficits in adults with ASD and, in turn, the complex role of ToM deficits in the emergence of criminal behaviour.

Theory of Mind

When Premack and Woodruff (1978) posed the question *Does the chimpanzee have a theory of mind?* they were interested in whether chimpanzees are like human adults in terms of being able to attribute mental states both to themselves and others, thereby allowing them to understand and predict the likely behaviour of others. These mental states are wide ranging, encompassing 'desires, emotions, beliefs, intentions, and other inner experiences that result in and are manifested in human action' (Wellman, Cross and Watson, 2001, p.655). Since Premack and Woodruff's explorations, the investigation of ToM has been a focus for basic researchers in cognitive and developmental psychology, with much of the research examining ToM in children. But, while Premack and Woodruff had assumed ToM was universal in adults, researchers have shown increased interest in ToM deficits as potential explanations for some of the cognitive and social characteristics, and deficits, observed in both children and adults with conditions such as ASD. In the following section we provide a brief overview of some of the key findings from empirical studies of ToM and ASD.

Empirical Findings on ToM Deficits and ASD

Although the focus of this book is on criminal activity, which is obviously most likely to be committed by adults and adolescents, brief consideration of research with children is useful from the perspectives of understanding the evolution of ToM research in relation to ASD and conceptualising the nature of ToM deficits. Much of the early ToM research focused on what are known as false belief tasks, which assess whether young children have the capacity to understand that another person may hold a belief that is at odds with reality (i.e., a false belief) and, moreover, that their behaviour can be predicted from this belief, rather than from the actual reality (see, for example, Bowler 1992; Wimmer and Perner 1983). In other words, the individual can recognise that, because a person's belief about a particular situation can be at odds with the reality of the situation, their behaviour can be shaped by, and hence predicted from, that belief. This research has used false belief tasks that vary in complexity to study ToM. The performance on such tasks by children at different developmental levels is considered to provide an indication of the child's understanding of the mental states of others, thereby indexing their ToM.

Although there has been considerable debate among researchers about precisely when these capacities are realised, and to what extent particular ToM tasks, or procedural parameters of such tasks, shape such conclusions, some broad generalisations emerge from the literature. First, the typically developing child's understanding of beliefs, and of other persons' minds, advances significantly in the early or preschool years (Wellman *et al.* 2001) – although this needs to be qualified by the observation that such tasks appear to be tapping only limited dimensions of a child's cognitive and social awareness. Second, the relatively poor performance of children with ASD on the same tests (despite being of equivalent or higher mental age when compared with the comparison control groups) led researchers to conclude that children with an ASD are characterised by a specific deficit in ToM (e.g., Baron-Cohen, Leslie and Frith 1985) that is independent of any associated intellectual deficit. Third, this ToM deficit has been described as a core deficit that constrains the child's capacity to understand and interact effectively within their social environment and is a key factor underlying the severe social impairment that characterises the condition (Baron-Cohen 1995, 2001).

As research progressed in this area, it became apparent that higher-functioning individuals with ASD could pass such tests by the time they reached adolescence (Baron-Cohen 2001; Happé 1994). Believing that (a) the ability to pass simple or basic ToM tests is insufficient evidence of intact ToM in older individuals with ASD (Baron-Cohen *et al.* 1997) and (b) the obvious social impairments observed in adults with ASD must reflect ToM deficits, researchers then focused on the development of more advanced or complex ToM tests that would provide more sensitive indices of subtle difficulties in social cognition in individuals with ASD who passed more basic (i.e., false belief) ToM tasks. One example of such tasks is Happé's (1994) *Strange Stories* test in which participants are presented with pencil-and-paper vignettes, or stories, about everyday situations where people say things they don't literally mean. Participants are required to answer questions concerning the accuracy of the story and to explain why a character said something. Items tap the ability to recognise instances of, for example, sarcasm, white lies, metaphors and double bluff. Participants with ASD who pass second-order false belief tests, including adults with HFA and AD, have been found to perform similarly to younger controls and those with much lower intellectual ability on the *Strange Stories* test (Happé 1994), and significantly worse than controls matched on age and IQ (Happé 1994; Jolliffe and Baron-Cohen 1999). Also, individuals with ASD generally have difficulty giving contextually appropriate mental-state explanations for characters' non-literal statements.

A second example of a more complex test designed to measure more advanced ToM is Baron-Cohen and colleagues' (Baron-Cohen *et al.* 1997; Baron-Cohen *et al.* 2001a) *The Reading the Mind in the Eyes Test*, which requires participants to select the correct mental state term (e.g., accusing, offended, serious) for a picture of a pair of eyes. Again, persons with HFA have, on average, performed worse than age- and IQ-matched controls, with test performance negatively correlated with scores on the *Autism Spectrum Quotient.*

Faux pas tests (e.g., Gregory *et al.* 2002; Stone, Baron-Cohen and Knight 1998) provide a third example that has produced similar differentiation between adults with ASD and those without (e.g., Spek, Scholte and van Berckelaer-Onnes 2010; Zalla *et al.* 2009). These tasks require a person to detect when someone unintentionally says something inappropriate that potentially produces emotional angst for another. Such research has suggested that individuals with ASD can be differentiated from those without ASD in terms of the ability to understand the emotional impact of socially inappropriate behaviour and the ability to correctly identify malicious intent. Zalla *et al.* (2009), for example, found that adults diagnosed with AS failed to understand that persons who committed a social faux pas did not do so intentionally (i.e., they tended to attribute instances of faux pas to maliciousness or a deliberate desire to offend on the part of the perpetrator of the faux pas). Further, they had difficulty describing the emotional state of the victim. Thus, while detection of socially inappropriate behaviour may be relatively well developed, participants with AS were impaired in their ability to interpret intent appropriately and their comprehension of other subtleties of complex social interaction.

The tests described above are perhaps three of the more widely known instruments that have been used for evaluating ToM in adolescents and adults. But a plethora of other tests and experimental tasks have been used to probe the ability of individuals with ASD to *read* the mental states or emotions of others. Taken together, the outcomes from these diverse approaches to the exploration of ToM have reinforced the widely held view that adults with ASD are characterised by deficits in more subtle aspects of social-cognitive reasoning. Not only has the prevailing view been that ToM deficits characterise individuals with ASD but this deficit has also been considered to be a core deficit that almost certainly underpins the problematic social-communicative deficits seen in association with ASD. Although the extent of this deficit is unknown, it is clear that the severity of the impairment is not universal and varies greatly between and within individuals and also across situations.

A couple of important qualifications or caveats warrant mention here because they emphasise the murkiness that surrounds the ToM construct and, in turn, the implications of ToM deficits for behaviour, including criminal behaviour. First, while most studies of measurement instruments developed to assess ToM contrast the performance of individuals with ASD with that of non-ASD controls, seldom do they employ discriminant validation approaches that see test performance validated against some independent criterion of social-cognitive functioning. Consequently, while the tests have frequently detected group differences between ASD and non-ASD samples, the functional significance of these differences is then inferred rather than demonstrated empirically. Consequently, we have little empirically supported idea of the range, severity or precise nature of ToM deficits in adults with ASD and how this translates into observable behaviour. We also have little idea of the nexus between specific areas or levels of severity of deficit and the individual's day-to-day functioning.

Second, the murkiness surrounding the ToM construct – and the precise nature and extent of ToM deficits in individuals with ASD – is further highlighted by consideration of the capacity for empathy in such individuals. A lack of empathy is not a characteristic listed in either the *DSM-IV* or *DSM-5* criteria for ASD. Both sets of diagnostic criteria do, however, refer to 'a lack of social or emotional reciprocity'.

Moreover, *DSM-5* highlights deficits in developing and maintaining relationships, exemplified by problems in areas such as adjusting behaviour to the particular social context and an absence of interest in people. We suspect that some might interpret these descriptors as signalling likely deficits in displaying appropriate empathy towards others in some form of difficulty or distress. Indeed, it is not uncommon for clinicians to describe individuals with ASD in these terms. Moreover, ToM researchers have explicitly stated that ToM – considered to be a core deficit of ASD – overlaps with empathy (e.g., Baron-Cohen 2008). It may, therefore, come as a surprise that the evidence on whether individuals with ASD have a diminished capacity for empathy appears to be both scarce and inconclusive.

As noted above when we described the faux pas task, Zalla *et al*.'s (2009) study showed that, while high-functioning adults detected the faux pas, they did not appreciate the emotional consequences that resulted, suggesting a lack of empathy. In a similar vein, Yirmiya *et al*. (1992) found, at the group level at least, that non-retarded 9–16-year-olds were inferior to matched controls in labelling the emotions of others, taking the perspective of others and responding empathetically. Yet, there were marked individual differences, resulting in considerable overlap between participants with and without ASD. Other studies, however, have reported differences in cognitive empathy (i.e., understanding another's perspective) but no significant differences in affective empathy, or empathic concern, between control participants and 9–16-year-olds (Jones *et al*. 2010) or adults (Rogers *et al*. 2007) with ASD, although in the latter study the effect size index was certainly consistent with a moderate difference in their empathic concern measure. Moreover, some researchers have questioned the commonly accepted view that individuals with ASD don't have the capacity for empathy, arguing that apparent empathy deficits may be explained as motivational phenomena (Chevallier *et al*. 2012). Zaki (2014), for example, provides a detailed motivational account of what might lead individuals to approach or avoid any engagement with the emotions of others and illustrates how it could be extended to explain empathy deficits observed in individuals with ASD.

Definitive conclusions regarding the presence or absence of differences in empathy between ASD and non-ASD samples are not just constrained by the lack of theoretical clarity about whether any differences are capacity-related or motivational in nature or about whether they reside in the cognitive or affective domains. They are also limited by a variety of methodological issues associated with the studies in this area (e.g., inadequate sample sizes, a reliance on self-report measures and the absence of assessments of reactions to live interactions). Consequently, while it may be tempting – and perhaps even fashionable – to explain some aspects of criminal behaviour, especially aggressive behaviour, observed in individuals with ASD in terms of deficits in affective empathy, such a conclusion is not at present sustained by firm empirical evidence.

Moreover, such conclusions are further challenged by evidence on the relationship between empathy and aggression. A recent meta-analysis confirms that this relationship is extremely weak (Vachon, Lynam and Johnson 2014). Although the weakness of this relationship may owe something to weaknesses of the commonly used measurement instruments, Vachon *et al.* (2014) also emphasised the importance of the distinction between low empathy where a person's feelings simply don't resonate with those of others and low empathy that also encompasses maladaptive sadistic and scornful responses such as enjoyment at seeing others in pain. Although the former may characterise individuals with ASD, the latter would appear to be more closely aligned with some of the disorders discussed in Chapter 4 (e.g., antisocial personality disorder, oppositional defiant disorder, conduct disorder) that appear to be often both comorbid with ASD and associated with aggressive and criminal behaviour.

Third, despite general agreement in the literature that ToM deficits characterise people with ASD, not only is there a lack of clarity about exactly what ToM encompasses, and the nature and extent of the deficits, but there are also fundamental differences in the way ToM has been conceptualised theoretically. On the one hand, we have the position that ToM is underpinned by a discrete cognitive system, likely supported by a dedicated neural system (cf. Baron-Cohen 1995; Fodor 1983; Scholl and Leslie 1999) – the core deficit position regarding ToM and ASD seems to be suggesting just that, although it does not require it to be the case.

On the other hand, some have argued strongly against this position (cf. Stone and Gerrans 2006), conceptualising ToM deficits as the result of the interaction between deficits in low-level mechanisms for processing social information (e.g., joint attention, recognition of emotional expression) and more general cognitive systems (e.g., executive function, natural language, attention), which notably do not include ToM. More recently, others have raised the interesting theoretical possibility that all of the deficits highlighted above may reflect a fundamental deficit in the flexibility with which people with ASD process and respond to violations of their expectations about people and situations (van de Cruys *et al.* 2014). While we believe it is important to be aware of these different perspectives, and the difference between these various positions may appear substantial, it is our view that the arguments we will present in this chapter regarding the characteristics of ToM deficits in adults are not undermined by adherence to any of these particular positions.

While the literature suggests a general acceptance of ToM deficits in association with ASD, it is not uncommon to find qualifying statements, and even some degree of uncertainty, associated with descriptions of the ToM–ASD relationship. In the next section we devote some attention to a few of the main qualifications that are noted in the literature. We do so because, taken together, we believe they offer critical insights for understanding how ToM deficits may play out in adulthood and contribute to the individual's often problematic interactions with the social environment.

ToM Deficits and ASD: Some Qualifications

It is clear that not all individuals with ASD display deficits on all measures of ToM (e.g., Ponnet *et al.* 2004; Roeyers *et al.* 2001). Indeed, it was these idiosyncratic patterns of performance between individuals that, at least in part, motivated the search for appropriate ToM tests for older – as compared with younger – samples. Doubtless it also motivated the development of many of the different instruments designed to probe ToM deficits in adults, as researchers searched for measures that might be sensitive to more subtle social-cognitive deficits than those tapped by instruments on which individuals with ASD might reach ceiling levels of performance.

Nevertheless, one of the qualifications encountered in the literature is that some individuals with ASD appear to have intact ToM. At face value this would appear to pose problems for the notion of ToM being a core deficit in ASD. Another qualification is that higher-functioning individuals, especially, may have the cognitive capacity to work out – or *hack out* as it is sometimes described – solutions to ToM problems if given the time to do so. For example, Frith (2004) argued that apparently intact ToM as indexed by some tasks may be called into question when an individual is confronted with tasks requiring more intuitive mentalising abilities. Examples of such tasks are, of course, abundant in everyday social contexts where people are often confronted with the need to make a rapid decision based on ambiguous or subtle social cues and information and don't have the luxury to sit down and analyse the situation in detail. Yet another – but clearly related – issue or qualification is that deficits associated with ASD may appear only when the task more closely parallels real life or naturalistic mindreading. For example, Ponnet *et al.* (2008) found that, when participants were required to infer thoughts and feelings of actors engaged in conversations, the deficits in inferring emotional tones in actors' thoughts and feelings associated with ASD were more striking when the conversations were more chaotic or unstructured (i.e., naturalistic) than they were when the conversations were highly structured. Yet another qualification is exemplified by perspectives such as Bowler's (1992) assertion that, while ToM deficits may exist, the key problem for individuals with ASD may lie in the application and generalisation of extant skills to social situations.

The preceding discussion highlights a number of different positions that have emerged from the literature about ToM deficits in association with ASD. One is that, maybe, ToM deficits do not characterise all individuals with an ASD and, therefore, ToM is not a core deficit. Another is that the deficit only becomes apparent when the task requires the individual to *read* social situations that mirror the more chaotic or less structured situations and interactions that are characteristic of many of our day-to-day experiences. That is, they are not given the opportunity to *hack out* a solution. A third is that individuals with ASD may not apply or generalise their ToM abilities effectively in social contexts. In the next section we consider how these sometimes conflicting perspectives can be reconciled, or integrated, as we develop an analogy between ToM development and intellectual development to illustrate our argument. The perspective we advance in the next section then provides a framework for showing how and when ToM deficits may become implicated in the complex causal network underpinning criminal activity.

An Analogy Between the Development of ToM and Intelligence

It is quite possible that other researchers in this area have drawn a similar analogy to the one we outline below, although we are not aware of it. We believe the analogy is helpful in two ways. First, it helps us to understand and integrate a complex literature on ToM that spans cohorts varying considerably in developmental level. Second, we believe it allows us to understand why ToM deficits may contribute to criminal vulnerability for some individuals with ASD in some contexts, yet apparently not have any negative consequences for others.

Theories of intelligence acknowledge a developmental progression in cognitive functioning, with intelligence progressively increasing from the infant years to adulthood. In addition, crystallised intelligence – encompassing those aspects of intelligence that draw on knowledge and experience – likely keeps developing throughout adulthood. Tests of intelligence reflect these developmental phenomena. They are comprised of items that get progressively more difficult and the expectation is that, with increasing age and the associated developmental advances, more of these items will be passed. Often, the test items are timed, with success dependent on the individual's speed of processing. The test items may be homogeneous in nature (e.g., the nonverbal problem-solving puzzles of the Progressive Matrices) or they may be sampled from a variety of different domains. For example, they may tap vocabulary, knowledge, working memory, processing speed, the deduction of verbal and spatial relationships and so on – but, importantly, the items become progressively more demanding, which allows the tests to differentiate high-functioning individuals from those at lower levels of intellectual development. Moreover, apart from the disjunction between early infant (nonverbal) tests and tests that are suitable for individuals with a verbal capacity, there is generally not an obvious disjunction between items expected to be passed by individuals at different levels of intellectual development. Rather, the items just get harder as one progresses through the test.

Many intelligence theorists consider that underpinning performance on such tasks is a general ability – usually referred to as g – which explains why performance on different test domains, or sub-tests, tend to be correlated quite strongly. But even if we accept that intellectual functioning is guided by the pervasive influence of a general ability or g, this does not mean that an individual performs at a similar level on all sub-tests of intelligence. Whereas scores for most individuals are reasonably consistent across the broad range of sub-tests, for others the profile is more idiosyncratic. Thus, some individuals may perform on one sub-test at or above their age level and on another at or below their age level. In other words, theorists generally acknowledge a broad profile of specific abilities over which individuals, even those of similar overall intellectual ability, typically show some variation. For example, some individuals may have particular strengths or deficiencies in holding items in memory, others in working out spatial relationships and so on. Failing to achieve the normative level of performance for one's age level on some sub-test, or on a test overall, does not, however, lead to the conclusion that the individual does not have intelligence while other individuals do. Rather, we say that these individuals are at different levels of intellectual development, with some more advanced than others.

Strengths or deficits in intelligence can contribute significantly to how individuals adapt to or cope with various environmental conditions or demands. Significant general intellectual deficits, of course, can by themselves cause major adaptation problems for the individual. Deficits in some specific area of intellectual functioning can also have negative consequences for the individual's adaptation given particular environmental conditions. And, intelligence may interact with other psychological characteristics to cause problems for the individual. For example, an individual who is unable to deduce (or estimate) how long it will take when braking to stop a car travelling at a certain speed – and has a particularly sensation seeking disposition – may endanger themselves and others, particularly under certain traffic conditions.

ToM is concerned not with intelligence per se – although some have argued there is likely a close relationship between the two or at least between ToM and verbal ability (Frith and Happé 1999) – but with social-cognitive reasoning and awareness. Just like intellectual functioning, ToM is clearly developmental in nature and some aspects of it may continue to develop into the later years, as evidenced by the variations in performance seen on instruments designed to tap ToM in adults (e.g., the recognition of faux pas). Whereas even the earliest attempts to measure intelligence explicitly acknowledged the developmental advances in cognitive functioning by incorporating items of progressively increasing difficulty, this has not been the case with theorising or test development in relation to ToM. The early research efforts focused on young children and the associated measurement instruments reflected that focus. As the empirical evidence unfurled, showing that older individuals with ASD master some tests of ToM, new tests were designed that were considered appropriate for older individuals. And this process has continued up through the age range. Thus, while the available tests of ToM reflect its developmental nature, that they do so is almost more by accident than design. Rather than researchers operating within a fully developed framework based on age-related expectations of performance, or norms, they have developed a variety of different measures for different sections of the age range. Tests designed for adults are more difficult, are designed to tap more subtle aspects of social-cognitive understanding or reasoning and may introduce time pressure or the processing of more complex unstructured interactions. And, like tests of intelligence, they may sample various domains of social-cognitive processing (e.g., recognising subtle interpersonal or social cues such as facial expressions or tone of voice, interpreting verbal expressions involving jokes, sarcasm, bluff or white lies, decoding the intentions of others, recognising the impact of one's behaviour on others and empathising with the outcomes experienced by others).

Yet, unlike tests of intellectual functioning, there are obvious disjunctions between tests of ToM designed for different age ranges. There are tests designed for certain broad developmental ranges and, contrary to what we see with intelligence tests, a test specifically designed for a higher developmental level generally does not represent a progression, in terms of complexity, of a lower-level test. So, when the observation is made that a person with ASD of a particular age has (or does not have)

ToM, or even has achieved a specific level of ToM, it ignores the developmental reality of the phenomenon and the fact that the test was only designed for individuals within a certain developmental range. Had the test tapped a greater range of social-cognitive understanding, the conclusion regarding the individual's ToM abilities may well have been different. And, as is typically observed with intelligence test performance, performance is likely to vary across tests of different aspects of ToM. For example, an individual may recognise a white lie but not sarcasm. Or an individual may have a particular deficit when it comes to decoding facial expressions that provide pointers to the nature of a social interaction. Thus, at the broadest level ToM may be likened to g in that there is likely something underpinning performance in different domains of ToM and on different sub-tests of ToM, and, hence, performance of an individual with ASD across different domains is likely to be reasonably correlated. But compared with the study of intelligence, what is missing from theorising about ToM, and the associated test development, is a detailed theoretical understanding of the development of ToM from childhood to adulthood and corresponding, developmentally sensitive test items.

We believe this intelligence-ToM analogy is informative because it suggests that, even if we accept that ToM is guided by the pervasive influence of some general social-cognitive ability akin to g, this does not mean that an individual with ASD will perform at a similar level on all sub-tests of ToM. As with intellectual functioning, some individuals may perform at or above their age level in one area of ToM (e.g., recognising the significance of particular vocal intonations or interpreting sarcasm) and below their age level in another (e.g., not recognising body or verbal language indicating that a person is upset or threatening). In other words, we are arguing for parallels between the various specific abilities that are incorporated in theorising about intelligence and the different sub-domains of ToM. Thus, just as it is probably not very surprising that adults with ASD may, because of differences in aetiology, display idiosyncratic profiles on sub-tests of intelligence, so too might we expect ToM profiles to vary across individuals.

A neat illustration of our perspective is provided by the literature on emotion-processing impairments observed in individuals with ASD. Impairments in this area are commonly associated with ASD and linked to the deficits in empathy that are also often attributed to individuals with ASD and considered to be indicative of ToM deficits. Yet, the literature indicates, for example, that atypical emotion-processing appears not to be ubiquitous in individuals with ASD and that its detection may be related to task demands and processing complexity, to the type of emotion (cf. Nuske, Vivanti and Dissanayake 2013) or perhaps even to the presence of alexithymia (cf. Cook *et al.* 2013; van de Cruys *et al.* 2014). Thus, in the typically complex scenarios presented by our day-to-day interactions, not all individuals with ASD will necessarily show the impairments that might generally be expected, or they might only do so under particularly taxing socio-environmental conditions (Nuske *et al.* 2013).

In sum, what we are arguing is that failing to achieve one's developmental level on some sub-test, or overall, does not lead to the conclusion that the individual does not have ToM while other individuals do. Rather, it suggests that these individuals are at different levels of ToM development and/or have different profiles – or strengths and weaknesses – with respect to ToM. This, we believe, is extremely important for understanding how individuals with ASD may differ markedly in terms of how they cope with day-to-day environmental demands and why only some individuals may encounter some difficulties under particular environmental circumstances, which may then lead to devastating consequences.

The Behavioural Implications of ToM Deficits for Adults with an ASD

We noted above that severe intellectual deficits obviously impose broad constraints on an individual's ability to respond adaptively to a wide variety of environmental demands. Similarly, it is likely that a broad and severe ToM deficit will undermine an individual's capacity to make effective social-cognitive judgements, such as accurately interpreting the intentions of others and recognising the potential impact of one's actions on others. It is likely that such pervasive and severe deficits will by themselves compromise the individual's capacity to respond appropriately in many situations requiring social-cognitive nous. Unfortunately, there is not much empirical evidence to inform us about the extent of these broad

ToM deficits in adults, nor about the specific level or type of deficit that would contribute to wide-ranging social difficulties – both being issues that we revisit when discussing assessment issues in Chapter 8.

Moreover, and again paralleling what we know about intellectual performance, very specific strengths or deficits in areas of ToM can contribute significantly to how individuals adapt to or cope with various environmental conditions or demands. Very specific areas of deficit in social-cognitive functioning may have potentially disastrous consequences – including engaging in criminal behaviour – given particular environmental or situational conditions. For example, imagine the problematic reaction of an individual with terrible burns to one side of his face who sees a young man staring at him in a pub. He says, 'Why don't you take a photo, it lasts longer?' The young man responds by taking a photo and the man with the burns hits him. Or, a young man gets into trouble because he steals garden gnomes from a garden after someone suggests to him, 'Why don't you take some of those garden gnomes, they have way too many?' And, two different individuals with ASD who show a similar deficit on a particular test tapping a specific sub-domain of ToM may differ substantially in terms of their vulnerability to criminal involvement because some specific area of ToM deficit will only prejudice successful adaptation given particular situational or environmental conditions. For example, a request made in jest (but not recognised as such) to a young male to point a toy gun at his father and demand $50 will have very different consequences to pointing the toy gun at and making an identical request of a bank teller.

We have tried to capture what ToM is and what the consequences of ToM deficits may be – often without any direct reference to the causal determinants of criminal behaviour. So let us just reiterate what we believe this all means. Some individuals with ASD are likely to have severe deficits that could compromise effective engagement, and potentially put them at risk, in a wide array of social interactions. Nevertheless, the appropriate environmental conditions would have to be present for their deficiencies to be translated into criminal behaviour. Other individuals may have one or more from a wide array of very specific ToM deficits, deficits that will often have minimal consequences in terms of likely involvement in criminal activity. But again, when aligned with specific environmental conditions, the likelihood of negative consequences may increase. In sum, what this means of course accords with the reality that many individuals with ASD may have significant ToM deficits and may in theory be at risk for criminal involvement – yet that risk will never be realised because there is never an alignment with the necessary environmental conditions.

Thus far, we have confined our discussions to deficits in ToM that may contribute to whether or not a person becomes involved in criminal activity. Of course, the world is more complex than this, with individuals regularly encountering tricky situations that involve somewhat more subtle decisions than choosing whether or not to commit some criminal act. It is important to emphasise, therefore, that the types of social-cognitive deficits we have been discussing may also constrain the ability of adults with ASD to *manage* interactions with other people in ways that will reduce the likelihood of the development of significant problems that may culminate in interactions with the criminal justice system. For example, it is easy to imagine how such deficits may lead to an individual being unable to recognise the tell-tale signs from the behaviour of others that an interaction is *turning sour* and, in turn, take the appropriate steps to prevent any exacerbation of the situation. Similarly, as we will illustrate in some of the case studies described in Chapter 6, an individual may become ensnared in criminal activity because they don't have the social-cognitive resources to recognise where an interaction is heading, or they may end up being a victim or exploited by others for exactly the same reason. In the current era of extensive internet communication, the risks for the individual with significant ToM deficits are perhaps even greater, as the warning cues or signs are generally much more subtle than those available in face-to-face interactions.

As we outlined at the start of this chapter, however, other characteristics of ASD are also likely to be crucial in determining the likelihood of involvement in criminal activity. One such characteristic is the presence of a strong and restricted interest or obsession. Here we will argue that the interaction between a very strong restricted interest and either a broad or very specific – but severe – ToM deficit may also explain why some individuals with ASD can become involved in criminal activity.

Restricted Interests

Chapter 3 provided a detailed discussion of the diagnostic criteria for ASD. Prominent among those is the presence of restricted and repetitive behaviours and interests, which encompass stereotyped movements and speech, excessive adherence to routines, abnormally strong and restricted interests and unusual reactivity to sensory stimuli within the environment. Our focus here is on the abnormally strong and restricted interests (akin to obsessions) that are particularly prominent among higher-functioning and older individuals with ASD.

The Characteristics of Restricted Interests

The restricted interests or obsessions documented among persons with ASD are many and amazingly varied (cf. Baron-Cohen and Wheelwright 1999). They include intense preoccupations with machines, vehicles, spinning objects, physical systems, computers, astronomy, buildings, people, plants, animals, illness, reproduction, biology, geography, nature and so on. Take the example of a young man with ASD who could be located any time of the day at his nearby train-line watching the trains go by, knowing the timetable explicitly and becoming very distressed if a train was only minutes late. Or that of a young girl obsessed with *anime* who became fluent in Japanese after watching thousands of hours of these Japanese cartoons. Or a young girl obsessed with digital watches feeling the need to grab the wrist of any passer-by sporting a digital watch so she could have a closer inspection. These restricted interests or obsessions can be totally consuming, with some persons spending many hours a day in pursuit of their special interest or obsession. The preoccupations may not, however, be confined to one domain. Such interests or preoccupations are unusual in that they may dominate the individual's time and activities, potentially interfering with friendships, work and other regular daily activities – as was the case with one young girl who, once engaged in a drawing, was unable to stop until it was complete, with some of her drawings spanning 24 hours. The individual may not, due to ToM limitations, recognise the impact their restricted interest or obsession has on their own daily functioning or their interactions with others. In this sense there is a suggestion of a parallel with OCD in that the biased processing by people with that disorder is considered to come at a cost with respect to processing other stimuli (e.g., Radomsky and Rachman 1999; Tata *et al.* 1996).

Yet, although these behaviours are thought to differ from the obsessions ('recurrent and persistent thoughts, urges, or images that are experienced as intrusive and unwanted'; APA 2013, p.235) and compulsions ('repetitive behaviors or mental acts that an individual feels driven to perform in response to an obsession or according to rules that must be applied rigidly'; APA 2013, p.235) that characterise OCD, there is a great deal that we do not know about these behaviours. For example, we know relatively little about the neurobiological, neuropsychological or developmental origins or causes of these behaviours (Leekam, Prior and Uljarevic 2011). We also know little about efficacious treatment or intervention approaches (Leekam *et al.* 2011).

We do know, however, from the *DSM-5* diagnostic criteria – and, of course, from numerous clinical case studies and anecdotal reports – that we should expect the severity of these restricted (and repetitive) behaviours to vary markedly across individuals. But hard data on issues such as the relative frequencies (or prevalence) of various special interests or obsessions, the severity levels, whether some special interests tend to be more consuming than others, the nature and extent of any disruption produced and so on are in short supply. One factor contributing to the paucity of data on such issues has been the absence of a uniform measurement protocol. Measurement approaches have, for example, included verbal reports (e.g., self, parents), questionnaires and interviews, and observational procedures. Sometimes, the protocols used have been part of the diagnostic assessment process; on other occasions they represent separate measures (see Leekam *et al.* 2011 for a comprehensive overview). And, regardless of the measurement approach, seldom is the focus a detailed evaluation of exactly how the restricted interest shapes the individual's day-to-day functioning and decision making.

The paucity of informative data is even more striking when considering the characteristics of restricted interests in adults. Nevertheless, data for one reasonably sized sample have been reported by Esbensen *et al.* (2009) and, unlike other studies that used information from the ASD diagnostic instrument to chart target behaviours, Esbensen *et al.* were able to compare 251 adults aged 22–62 years with similar-sized younger cohorts on an independent measure, namely, the *Repetitive Behavior Scale-Revised* (*RBS-R*, Bodfish *et al.* 2000). Three aspects of their findings deserve mention but, as we will see shortly, their interpretation is not straightforward. First, on the Restricted Interest sub-scale, scores ranged across the entire scale, from 0 ('behaviour does not occur') to 3 ('behaviour occurs and is a severe problem'). Second, on this 0–3 scale the mean item sub-scale scores were at the low end, ranging from .95 (*SD*=.87) for adults in their 20s down to .64 (*SD*=.65) for adults in their 30s. Third, the problematic nature of restricted interests declined from childhood through adulthood. But what are we to make of these data patterns? First, the study was cross-sectional in nature rather than longitudinal, so it is difficult to conclude that there was a reliable developmental trend and, in turn, that such interests or obsessions are not a problem in adults. And as Esbensen *et al.* pointed out, the data were based on parental reports and likely to have been shaped by the parents' familiarity with and adaptation to the particular behavioural issue, perhaps explaining why mean scores were at the low end of the scale. Second, although the descriptive statistics indicate that a range of severity levels should be expected across individuals, it is completely unclear as to how respondents were operationalising severity. For example, does 'a severe problem' mean the behaviour is clearly out of the ordinary and attention grabbing, presents problems for other people with whom the individual interacts, dominates the individual's life and, hence, interferes with other aspects of their daily functioning, or perhaps that severe problems arise when the individual's pursuit of the behaviour is interrupted? In sum, comprehensive and decisive objective data that reveal the nature and extent of such restricted interests and clearly delineate the behavioural consequences appear to be non-existent.

Basically then, what we are left with, apart from parent report data such as those described above, are:

> the *DSM-5* criteria, which suggest that, at least for some individuals with ASD, there is a potential for these restrictive repetitive behaviours to interfere markedly with day-to-day functioning and, if interrupted, cause considerable distress to the individual,

> various case study reports of the apparent behavioural consequences of interrupting the pursuit of an obsession or powerful restricted interest (Barry-Walsh and Mullen 2004)

> some single-case behavioural intervention studies that report the behavioural consequences of interrupting very complex stereotypies in very low-functioning adults or children (e.g., Murphy *et al.* 2000).

One consequence of this lack of understanding of the precise nature and consequences of restricted and repetitive interests in adults with ASD is that it is even more difficult than it might otherwise be to impute links between such behaviours and involvement in criminal activity. However, guided by case study evidence, we suggest that these behaviours may be implicated as part of a complex causal network via the mechanisms outlined in the next section.

The Contribution of Restricted and Repetitive Interests to Criminality in Adults with ASD

Although case study research has highlighted the apparent contribution of very strong restricted interests to the involvement of some individuals with ASD in criminal acts, restricted interests do not feature among the prominent predictors of crime (Copeland *et al.* 2007; Samuels *et al.* 2004). And, given that they represent diagnostic features of ASD, we should not expect a direct restricted interest–criminality link given that criminality is not widespread amongst people with ASD. Clearly, for a strong interest or obsession to lead to inappropriate social behaviour and, ultimately, criminal activity, other factors must be involved.

Again we suggest that, first, there must be an unfortunate alignment with a set of environmental conditions that provide an opportunity for a criminal act to occur. Additionally, however, there must be a ToM deficit that undermines the capacity of the individual to respond adaptively. Imagine, for example, that – as in the example below – an individual is pursuing an intense special interest, is interrupted and the interruption provokes intense anger and an act of aggression towards the person responsible for the interruption.

A young male with ASD who is obsessed with the *Wheel of Fortune* television show is watching the show at his apartment when his room-mate returns home from work. The room-mate asks him to change channels so he can watch the football, but the young male says he cannot because he has to watch his favourite show. When an advertisement starts, the room-mate tells the young man there is a parcel for him in the kitchen, which he can fetch during the advertisement. As soon as the young man goes to the kitchen, the room-mate changes the television channel to watch the football. The young man returns and pleads repeatedly for the channel to be switched back to allow him to watch *Wheel of Fortune*. The room-mate refuses his requests, simply saying that it's his television and he can watch what he wants. The young man becomes increasingly agitated until, eventually, he picks up a lampshade and strikes the unsuspecting room-mate viciously on the back of the head, injuring him badly. Then he simply sits back down, changes the channel back on *Wheel of Fortune,* and continues to watch it, oblivious to the injury to his room-mate.

The inability on the part of the individual with ASD to foresee the negative consequences of his socially inappropriate, aggressive response to the interruption is what would be required for the restricted interest to be implicated as a contributing factor in a criminal act of aggression.

Alternatively, an individual with ASD may have a very strong restricted interest that becomes inextricably linked with a sequence of behavioural events that culminates in a criminal act – but, as the events unfold, his ToM deficit prevents him appreciating the adverse social and legal ramifications of his behaviour. The following scenario provides an illustration of such a case.

A teenage male with ASD, who has an obsessional interest in iPhones, bumps into a female acquaintance on the street. After he shows her, and she admires, his new iPhone, she opens the box she is carrying, revealing around 20 iPhones. When she notices two police officers on foot patrol drawing near, the female becomes flustered and asks her male friend if he could look after the box of phones for a while at his house, perhaps storing them under his bed. She also asks him not to tell others about the phones. The young male, clearly oblivious to the warning signals provided by his friend's behaviour and the unusual nature of her request, enthusiastically takes the box of (stolen) phones, promising to look after them.

What we have identified in this chapter are specific characteristics of ASD – namely, severe deficits in ToM and intense restricted interests – that, under an appropriate set of environmental conditions, may interact to increase the likelihood that the individual commits a criminal act.

This amalgam of conditions may not occur often but, when it does, the consequences may be dire. Yet, the criminal act is clearly not one that is planned, nor is it characterised by what we might normally think of as criminal intent. In Chapter 6 we provide an array of case studies that illustrate such mechanisms at work.

Other Characteristics of ASD Associated With Criminal Behaviour

Before progressing to those case studies, however, we should point out that there may well be other characteristics associated with ASD that may also contribute to the shaping of some criminal behaviour. Some researchers have speculated, for example, that factors such as poor impulse control (Allen *et al.* 2008) or problems associated with moral reasoning (Barry-Walsh and Mullen 2004) may be contributory. Given that (a) such characteristics are, of course, not confined to individuals with ASD and (b) there is no firm empirical evidence demonstrating their contributions to criminality in individuals with ASD, we have not extended this speculation here. But we do briefly consider one other characteristic of ASD that has not attracted much attention in considerations of factors shaping criminality, yet may explain some very unusual though probably relatively infrequent behaviours that may culminate in a criminal act.

The coverage of the *DMS-5* for ASD in Chapter 3 indicated that one category of restricted or repetitive behaviours and interests was hyper- or hyposensitivity to, or unusual interest in, sensory stimuli. Although this category did not emerge in the formal diagnostic criteria until the *DSM-5*, sensory-perceptual abnormalities such as hyper-and hyposensitivity to stimuli have been frequently documented in the ASD literature, and have for some time been an integral part of many of the diagnostic tools, (e.g., *Childhood Autism Rating Scale* (CARS), *Autism Diagnostic Interview-Revised* (ADI-R), *Autism Diagnostic Observation Schedule* (*ADOS*)). Kanner's (1943) original description of autism noted such sensitivities and referred to these environmental stimuli as a 'dreaded intrusion' (p.244). Further, he described children reacting with 'horror' to loud noises and moving objects and even experiencing major panic when feeling the wind. Hans Asperger (Wing 1981) also noted the sensitivity (and the insensitivity) of persons with AS.

Such sensory processing difficulties may be life-long and may be so consuming that they cause significant disruptions to a person's life, affecting the food they eat, the clothes they wear, the places they can visit and the relationships they form (Schaaf *et al.* 2011). For example, consider the plight of a young lady who is refused work in a bakery because she cannot wear enclosed shoes, a young man evicted from a library for loudly sucking a chewing ring, a young girl who freezes all winter because she cannot wear her prickly school jumper, or a young man whose aversion to certain foods has led to anxiety and food refusal. The consequences of these sensory issues are immediate and obvious. Moreover, sensory processing problems are also thought to be linked to other ASD characteristics such as stereotypical and rigid behaviours (Rogers, Hepburn and Wehner 2003; Schaaf *et al.* 2011).

Importantly, from the perspective of crime causation, clinical observations suggest that this unusual reactivity to sensory stimuli within the environment, when coupled with significant ToM deficits, may also render the individual with ASD vulnerable to committing a criminal act under particular environmental circumstances. An individual for whom tactile contact from others is extremely aversive might conceivably react adversely – and inappropriately from a legal perspective – in some situations. Imagine this individual, for example, in a discussion with a police officer or a social welfare worker over some matter and the latter person puts a comforting arm on their shoulder. An inability to recognise the intentions of the other person, combined with the adverse reaction to the physical contact, may produce a sudden aggressive avoidant behavioural response that could see the individual with ASD confronting an assault charge. In a similar vein, a person with ASD who is preoccupied with touching certain surfaces or textures could find themselves in significant legal difficulties if this behaviour involved unwelcome and perhaps repeated physical contact with part of another person's body, and the unwelcome nature of the physical contact was not immediately appreciated by the offender. In both of these examples, the critical variables are the individual's atypical sensory reactions coupled with obvious deficits in recognising social-communicative signals from other individuals.

The literature contains reports of case studies illustrating connections between such sensory sensitivities and criminal acts. For example, Schwartz-Watts (2005) described a case in which an eight-year-old boy was shot and killed by a man with autism after the boy ran over the man's foot; the man was apparently hypersensitive to sensory input and over-reacted to being touched. Cooper, Mohamed and Collacott (1993) detailed the sensory-seeking behaviour (hyposensitivity) of a transvestite with AS who enjoyed touching stockings being worn by other women. In Chapter 6 we also provide further case study illustrations of the difficulties that may be produced by the operation of such mechanisms.

A Final Comment

In Chapter 4 we discussed the often confusing evidence about the possible contributions of comorbid conditions and socio-environmental variables to criminality in individuals with ASD. In this chapter we have focused on some special characteristics of individuals with ASD that we believe may heighten criminal vulnerability. But we have again been at pains to emphasise that simple and direct causal paths are not easily identified and likely do not exist. Rather, we argue for a complex network of interacting variables. First, there has to be a certain set of situational or environmental conditions in place. Without those necessary – or enabling – environmental conditions, a criminal act may never be triggered or *get off the ground*. In other words, we are suggesting that there is definitely an element of bad luck involved. Then, the individual needs to have a ToM deficit, both the nature and severity of which are likely important. It might be severe and pervasive so that it leads to a failure to recognise the intentions and expressions and remarks of others or to detect the annoyance or distress or anger of others. Or it might be a specific deficit in some area of ToM that means they are not responsive to quite specific types of social-cognitive cues that are important for appropriate behavioural adaptation under particular conditions. And it may be that in some highly structured situations these deficits are not prejudicial to effective and appropriate social interaction. Yet, in the hurly-burly chaotic world of many ongoing social interactions, such deficits may be crucial in allowing certain unplanned maladaptive behavioural outcomes to eventuate. Finally, we have suggested that while the alignment of a significant ToM deficit with apposite environmental conditions may shape a criminal act, often much more will be required. This may include an unwanted interruption to an individual's intense pursuit of a particular preoccupation or restricted interest, an interruption that provokes an angry, aggressive and socially inappropriate response. Or it may involve the continued pursuit of some special interest – or perhaps sensory preoccupation – while seemingly completely oblivious to the fact that it may be taking the individual down a path that will culminate in a criminal offence.

It is under these types of conditions that we believe we may see the emergence of criminal behaviour that may be specifically linked to ASD. The combination of conditions will not occur often and, hence, prevalence of such criminal behaviour will not be high. The criminal behaviour may range from relatively minor to extremely severe, spanning a variety of types of offence – but the behaviour is different from much criminal behaviour in terms of the offender's (lack of) intent and appreciation of what they were doing. In Chapter 6 we provide an array of case studies that, we believe, illustrate such mechanisms at work.

Chapter 6

>>>>>>>>>>>>>>>>>>>>>>>

ASD-SPECIFIC INFLUENCES
Case Studies

Chapter 5 was concerned with some of the unique characteristics observed in individuals with ASD that may contribute to an increased likelihood of involvement in criminal activity. We argued that the existence of a ToM deficit, either general or specific, and obsessive special interests or behaviours could combine with an enabling set of situational or environmental conditions to produce criminal behaviour. In this chapter we present a number of case studies that highlight the apparent meshing of ToM deficits, obsessive behaviours and enabling socio-environmental conditions in ways that have contributed to the occurrence of criminal behaviour. Clearly these case studies do not establish causation. But we believe they are strongly suggestive of the key factors that may lead a person with ASD to become involved in criminal activity, though not through intent or malice. One of the striking features of these cases is that, although they are very different in numerous respects (e.g., the crime, the characteristics of the individual, the context), some common themes consistently emerge in relation to the apparent contribution of several of the characteristic features of ASD.

Six of the cases we present in this chapter involve individuals within the normal range of intellectual ability (Cases A1–A6). As discussed in Chapter 4, the presence of an intellectual disability is commonly found in association with ASD. Given the likelihood that many of the ToM deficits we have described may also be observed in individuals with a significant intellectual disability, we obviously cannot be sure whether behaviours apparently contributing to criminality in individuals with ASD and a comorbid intellectual disability are influenced by ToM, intellectual deficits or both. Likewise, we believe it may be difficult to distinguish between repetitive or stereotypical behaviours that characterise ASD and similar behaviours that are sometimes seen in individuals with an intellectual disability (Deb and Prasad 1994; Hartley and Sikora 2010; Wing 1981). Consequently, we focus first on case studies involving high-functioning individuals only. For these individuals, the deficits that we are suggesting may be pivotal in crime causation cannot be explained away by reference to the individual's low level of intellectual functioning. However, individuals with ASD and a comorbid intellectual disability may also sometimes find themselves involved in criminal activity that looks very similar, in terms of lack of intent and malice, to the sorts of crimes that we suggest may be particularly ASD-related. For that reason we also present four additional case studies (Cases B1–B4) involving culprits who met criteria for both ASD and intellectual disability and for whom the mix of ToM deficits and a particular restricted interest or obsession also appeared to be crucial. In none of these cases was there evidence of other environmental or socio-economic risk factors that are so often associated with criminality in individuals with an intellectual disability. We clearly cannot be certain that it was not a low level of intellectual functioning that was the key factor in these latter four cases (or in other similar ones we have encountered). Nevertheless, we have chosen to include them because they are likely representative of a broader array of cases in which, as noted above, the culprit acted without intent or malice.

Each case involves an individual with ASD who had been referred for a psychological assessment either to determine suitability to stand trial or to provide advice to the court about matters that might assist the judge when sentencing. All the assessment details form part of the public record as they were prepared for lawyers and presented before the courts. To preserve confidentiality, able clients (where possible) signed informed consent to allow their information to be included and were provided with drafts prior to publication. In the event that this was not possible, three approaches were used to preserve anonymity: disguise, obfuscation and/or the creation of composite identities. Real names have been replaced with pseudonyms. The information provided is based on formal assessments, interviews with the individual and, sometimes, a significant other, and legal and medical records. The amount of available background information available varies considerably across cases. In most cases, police apprehension reports and witness statements were also available.

Case A1: Ashley
The Crime
Ashley (aged 29 years) informed a court-appointed psychologist that his 'friend' Chris had told him the 'phone lines were down' at a local service station, and this meant he could use his debit card to buy things. Chris informed Ashley that when the lines are 'down' the computers cannot communicate with the bank and you can withdraw more funds than you have available. Ashley accompanied Chris to the service station and they collectively made purchases using Ashley's card. The value of the purchases was more than $600, well in excess of the few dollars Ashley had available in his account. Ashley bought groceries as well as vouchers to enable him to purchase apps and music for his iPhone.

When they returned from the store, Ashley returned his debit card to a safe location in his room. He then went outside to have a cigarette while Chris remained in the house. It was not until Ashley checked his bank balance some time later that he realised there were other purchases on the card. He checked the glove box in his car where he kept his card and it was missing. He did not think to report his card as stolen. Several days later the police arrested him for theft and damage of property. The card had been used at a number of stores. The phone lines in all cases, including the first store, were deliberately cut. Ashley denies any involvement in the cutting of the lines. Although facing up to ten years jail, Ashley's primary concern was that he would not be allowed to have his phone in jail.

Background and Assessment Information
> Ashley was diagnosed with ADHD at two years of age. Although he believes a few psychologists have, over the years, suggested a diagnosis of AS, he was never formally diagnosed with this condition until he became involved with the criminal judicial system in connection with this particular crime.

> He was raised by his mother and father in a rural working-class environment until his father left home when he was about eight years of age.

> He was exposed to abuse from a series of 'stepfathers'.

> He believes his mother and two older siblings are still alive but he is unsure of their ages or whereabouts. He has no contact with any relatives.

> At interview with the court-appointed psychologist he said school was boring and he attended infrequently. He left school at the end of Year 8 because he did not pass any of his subjects and then spent time at home, before his mother sent him back to school.

> At age 15 he left school and home. He was initially homeless and lived on the streets before moving between numerous shelters and places of residence over a three-year period. He spent some time living on a city street but found this annoying as he had to travel to the local mall to locate a power outlet where he could charge his phone.

> Although he has hundreds of friends on Facebook he does not know any of them personally. He only has a few friends but he has been informed that most people tend to 'use him'. He was unable to explain what is meant by this or provide any examples.

> Intelligence testing placed him above average on both verbal and perceptual sub-tests. He met DSM-IV-TR criteria for AS and DSM-5 criteria for ASD.

Behavioural Indicators of ToM Deficits and Restricted Interests

From speaking with Ashley it is clear that he is socially naive, lacks reciprocity in social interaction and is obsessed with his phone. Conversations are one-sided and he constantly goes off on tangents, typically producing lengthy monologues about transformers and nuclear power. He admits to being socially inappropriate at times – or at least he reported that he is frequently told that he is. He does not engage in eye contact; instead he will flick through his phone while talking.

He can identify if someone is angry or happy but admits that he has problems recognising any other emotions. During his interview with the psychologist to assess his fitness to stand trial, countless examples of this were provided. He showed the psychologist numerous photos of his phone chargers and he did not detect her deliberate display of boredom when she crossed her arms and looked at the ceiling during one monologue. Ashley also engaged in a lengthy monologue about how he was planning to build a nuclear-powered bike and how he had bought uranium on eBay to help him achieve this goal. He then proceeded to show the psychologist photos of the tin of uranium he had purchased. When questioned about the validity of the purchase, he showed a Geiger counter reading on the side of the tin as proof, and noted, 'See I told you it's real and it cost me $40.' In sum, he is very gullible.

He has a collection of phones, phone chargers and transformers. These collections are now littered throughout his house but, when he was homeless, he used to carry them wherever he went. He has a very strong attachment to his iPhone 4S. He chose street locations on which to sleep that allowed him access to power to charge his phone.

He displays some repetitive motor movements such as flicking his phone and shaking his leg. He also uses idiosyncratic phrases such as 'You lost the game' repeatedly and out of context. He likes to line up his phone chargers carefully and says he would feel distressed if they were moved (and would feel the need to realign them). He is resistant to change and becomes distressed if unable to engage in his routines.

He is hypersensitive to light. He reacts badly to babies crying and traffic, as these sounds irritate him. He does not like certain textures and fabrics. Despite his limited education, he is articulate and, consistent with his intelligence test results, does not present as a person one might consider to have an intellectual disability.

Contributing Factors

Ashley is gullible and would like to have friends. He was coerced by a 'friend' into using his own debit card at the service station and did not contemplate the legality of what he was doing. He was motivated by his desire to impress this person as well as the opportunity to engage his current obsession (i.e., collecting apps for his phone). He is unsure whether he thought about the card being traced to him at the time, but believes he knew it would be. He did not, however, foresee or consider the consequences of his behaviour at the time. Further, he did not suspect that his friend had deliberately damaged the lines, nor did he question the friend as to how he knew the lines were down. He also did not consider that his friend might steal his card for future dishonest behaviour. These behaviours show a marked inability to read the behaviour of others in interpersonal interactions and to recognise possible motives of people. He also did not appreciate the seriousness of the offence as he thought the purchases were coming out of his debit card and, thus, he believed he would have to pay for it at some time. He claims it was an impulsive decision to use his card but he had to 'think on the fly'.

Case A2: Alicia
The Crime
Alicia is a 15-year-old girl who was watching television with her one-year-old nephew while the adults present in the house at the time were in another room. Alicia spontaneously removed her nephew's nappy to have a look at his penis, and possibly pulled at the foreskin. It was only when the young boy started to cry that, by her own admission, Alicia realised she should not be doing this and ran to another room. The adults, investigating the crying, returned to the room where the two had been watching television and noticed the removed nappy of the nephew. They questioned Alicia who initially denied any involvement. She later confessed to her mother, after continuous questioning, that she had removed the clothing to have a look at the child's penis. Her mother took her straight to the police. Alicia's recount of the events reported to the psychologist was consistent with those recorded in the police apprehension report.

Background and Assessment Information

> Alicia was diagnosed with AS at the age of 15 – some months after the alleged crime – although she had been on the waiting list for an assessment with the local Autism Association well before the incident.

> Her speech was delayed at 18 months. She produced odd babble and subsequently had speech therapy.

> She is very articulate but her speech is pedantic and at times perseverative.

> In the absence of friendships, Alicia's mother encouraged her to follow her passion of reading and to go to the library if she was being hassled or lonely.

> She has indicated that ultimately she would like to become a nurse.

> Her verbal reasoning abilities are in the very superior range (exceeding those of 99.9% of her peers) and her nonverbal reasoning ability is average.

> Her score on the CARS (Schopler et al. 1980) placed her above the scale cut-off for clinical significance in terms of autism.

Behavioural Indicators of ToM Deficits and Restricted Interests
Alicia has never been able to read the emotions or facial expressions of people and make friends because, as she stated, she doesn't know how to engage properly. Unless she sees tears or some very obvious signs of distress, she cannot interpret the nonverbal communication of others. At times she may not express the expected emotion for the situation.

For example, while her mother cried throughout the police interview about the incident described above, she was unperturbed by her mother's behaviour and continued to make a full confession and talk openly, showing no embarrassment for her actions. Her presentation in the police interviews could best be described as clinical. Oblivious to social norms regarding appropriate approaches to interaction or maintenance of personal space, Alicia might rub people's backs or touch their hair in a bid to get people to like her.

She has always played by lining things up and she also likes to look at things from unusual angles. She makes up a new word every week and says it repetitively. For example, she may say 'dewar' meaning pineapple and insist everyone else refer to pineapples as dewars. She follows a number of routines and does not like it if she is told something will happen and it doesn't. She obsesses about walking her dog and will repeatedly ask when this will occur, even when the timing is inappropriate. For example, when she went to visit her gravely ill father in hospital she greeted him by saying, 'You need to walk the dog.'

She has had many obsessions, which have changed throughout her short life. At present she has two major obsessions or special interests. One is train timetables and routes. She will spend the whole time she is on a train with her mother talking about the way they will go home. She will often give her mother train travel options but her mother has learned to question these, as Alicia will often suggest routes that have them travelling several hours in a non-direct route. The other special interest is the male reproductive system. To satisfy this interest her mother directed her towards books on the subject.

She also has many sensory sensitivities, avoiding some sensory input while pursuing other sensory interests. Before she puts anything in her mouth she will smell it. When she was younger, Alicia did not like to wear long sleeves as she did not like the feel of these on her skin, and she would also continually remove her shoes.

Contributing Factors

Alicia is an 15-year-old girl with ASD who had an intense interest in the reproductive system. Out of curiosity she decided to look at a young baby's penis and explore it. Alicia's actions do not appear to have been premeditated. She did not intend to commit a sexual assault, the crime for which she was charged. She claims she meant no harm, and it was not until the child cried that she appreciated the wrongfulness of her behaviour. It appears that she did not understand the impact that her behaviour would have on her nephew. She had an intense interest in, or obsession with, body parts, specifically, the male reproductive system, an interest fuelled by a book series *How Your Body Works* given to her prior to the assault. Given the other pointers to her ToM deficits, it seems unlikely the impact of her behaviour on the infant would have been considered. This apparent indifference was evident during her questioning. For example, as she became aware of the seriousness of the offence (during the two-year legal process that followed), she would respond to questions by asking, 'Will this prevent me from being a nurse?', thus showing an inability to appreciate the reactions of others to her behaviour.

Case A3: Ricci
The Crime
Ricci is an elderly man who was charged with possessing child pornography (knowing of its pornographic nature) and using a carriage service to access child pornography. He pleaded guilty to all charges. At the time of his arrest he had collected more than 27,000 photos on his computer. Most of these, however, remained in unopened zip folders until they were examined by police.

Background and Assessment Information

> Ricci is an elderly man with ASD who has lived alone since his parents died.

> He has never had any friends outside of the family.

> He describes himself as 'the child who was always picked last to be in a group activity' and, although he remembers trying to make friends, he believes he isn't worth knowing.

> He was sexually abused by a much older stepbrother from the age of 7 to 14 years, but did not realise it was abuse at the time. His lack of knowledge about the previous abuse was not because he had a poor memory of events, but because he did not appreciate that allowing someone to play with your penis was not a prerequisite for social interaction.

> He only learned that these events in his childhood constituted child sexual abuse when he commenced rehabilitation for his possession of child pornography.

> His disability only became apparent to professionals when he was required to undertake sexual counselling after pleading guilty to accessing child pornography. He had never seen an allied health professional such as a psychologist and no previous diagnoses had been ventured.

> He was referred to two specialists in the field who supported an ASD diagnosis.

> His IQ profile was idiosyncratic, with verbal comprehension in the low average range but perceptual reasoning in the average range of intelligence.

> Formal testing for depression, anxiety and stress using the *Depression Anxiety Stress Scale – 21 (DASS-21) – a self-report questionnaire used to assess symptoms common to depression, anxiety and stress* – showed elevated anxiety.

Behavioural Indicators of ToM Deficits and Restricted Interests

Ricci reported ongoing difficulties with eye contact, preferring to look at the floor or over people's shoulders than looking at people in the eye. He also reported that his facial expressions can be quite flat although at times he can become quite emotional and experience a 'flood' of reactions. He noted that if he is sad or hurt he prefers to keep this to himself. If someone else becomes upset or hurt, he may notice and will want to provide comfort, but will often burst into tears in accompaniment and simply sit and watch. Ricci has always experienced extreme difficulty making and maintaining friendships, stating in his police interview that he 'struggled' in all social situations. He reported difficulties initiating and maintaining conversations, stating that he does not know 'what to say or what to do' and that he has 'no idea' if people are interested in what he is talking about. Thus, he assumes that no one is interested in him and has disengaged from the community due to his constant feelings of awkwardness and rejection.

Ricci has a history of strong special interests. When younger he was interested in the Kennedy assassination, even writing a letter to the President's office; he also collected stamps and was fascinated by sand. He is currently obsessed with his computer and surfing the internet, focusing on family history and pornography. He reported that he would spend six to seven hours per day working on the history of the US presidents and does not like to be interrupted. He admits that his preoccupations have stopped him from participating socially as he can become so focused on his interests that everything else is forgotten.

He also has difficulty adjusting to changes in his routine. He prefers to have a plan or sequence to his day. He always puts on his left sock before his right sock, and does likewise with his underpants and shirt. He will only turn right when walking, thus turning 270 degrees to the right to make a left turn. He reported that everything in his room has a place and cannot be moved. He noted that his father would always arrive home from work at 6:05 and he would panic if he wasn't home on time. Changes to his routine used to make him angry but he has learned to control this.

He has repetitive and unusual motor mannerisms. Several times a day, he will rub his hands together and engage in hand wringing. He will also wiggle his fingers, but only on the right-hand side. He often finds himself rocking and covers his ears in response to the sharp pain he experiences when he hears noise. He is not well coordinated and describes himself as clumsy.

Contributing Factors

Ricci is an elderly man with ASD who has had obsessions all of his life. His particular history of abuse shows a general naiveté in sexually related matters, as well as in terms of understanding the intentions of others. His sexual curiosity led him to explore the internet, as he did when pursuing other areas of interest. He collected the photographs that were sent to him, just as he had collected stamps when younger. He chose not to open the files sent to him, partly due to a lack of interest as well as the fact that many of the files were zipped and he was scared of computer viruses. However, he continued to accept the files because he was thrilled people were inviting him to join their chat groups. But he denies any interest in child pornography and never considered what he was doing was illegal. His poor ToM prevented him from appreciating the motives of the persons making the requests or the impact his behaviour had on the children involved. While he enjoys collecting pornography, his enjoyment comes mostly from collecting and the involvement with people, rather than the pornographic content. He did not consider the pictures as real-life pictures; rather, they were just two-dimensional objects to collect. He never considered these photographs were depicting children being exploited. However, he did not know how to stop it or whether he may offend his new 'friends' in opting out of these requests. It is only through his rehabilitation that he realises these pictures depicted children being exploited and appreciates the severity of his crime. He now knows these are children who are too young to make decisions and he appreciates how his conduct contributes to the ongoing exploitation of these children. He is now ashamed of himself.

Case A4: Jason

The Crime

Jason is a 26-year-old male charged with unlawful sexual intercourse. He had sexual intercourse with his then girlfriend who was aged 15.

He alleges that she placed his penis in her vagina, and he had complied despite suggesting he had been unable to gain an erection.

Background and Assessment Information

> Jason has a high-pitched voice, is lean and has the physical appearance of a teenager.

> He attended mainstream school where he recalls having friends, although he could not recall much about them or what he did with them, other than perhaps playing computer games. He thinks he was bullied at school but could not recall why, other than perhaps because he was small. He completed school and went to university to study science.

> When asked to tell the psychologist about himself, he started by saying he was born on a Wednesday, then added he was born overseas and came to Australia when he was five. He required prompting to talk about his family, but described a reasonably happy, working-class upbringing. However, he noted that his mother would hit him with a long stick when he was naughty, though he was rarely naughty.

> He believes he had delayed speech and recalls requiring speech therapy. He was unable to explain why speech therapy was deemed necessary, despite presenting with a debilitating stutter.

> Although two psychologists had previously suggested he had AS, it appears this was never formally diagnosed. He had, however, previously been diagnosed with depression; no other diagnosis has been provided to his knowledge.

> He was sexually abused from the age of 11 to 15 years by a perpetrator who was two years older than him. He believes there may have been around 20 sexual encounters over the years. He does not recall why it stopped but thinks it was because the perpetrator became attracted to women and realised he wasn't gay. Jason thought the abuser must have been 'just practising for a cute girlfriend'.

> He is a member of a fundamentalist religious group. When asked what it meant to be a member of this church, he simply provided a list of things you cannot do, continuing until he was interrupted. Like many persons on the spectrum, religion appears to cause confusion for Jason due to the abstract nature of the content.

> He has had two relationships with girls, one of whom was the victim of the crime he is alleged to have committed. He had been in a relationship with this girl for some months and, although her father was

aware that Jason was his daughter's boyfriend, he had, until the night of the incident, thought Jason was the same age as his daughter.

› During the police interview he stated that his girlfriend had lied to her father about his age. He indicated that he was not supportive of this lie and could not understand his girlfriend's motives for perpetuating it. He saw no difference between two 15-year-olds engaging in sex and his situation.

› He seeks contact with others through the internet and information he has posted on the net indicates he seeks out people with whom he can have intimate and possibly sexual encounters. When asked about some of the slang he used, he simply stated he had copied it but was not sure of what it meant.

› His online interactions were mostly with young girls. When asked why he gravitated towards younger females, he said that he sent out many requests online and would correspond with whoever responded. It appears younger girls were likely to accept his requests and he acknowledged this, though he does not believe he is a paedophile. He described his ideal woman as anyone up to the age of 50. He further volunteered that he preferred a C cup and hair on the vagina, and had no reservations about stating these desires at interview.

› He revealed that he was unsure of the age of consent. When told it was 17, he asked if he could have sex with a 16-year-old. When he was told this was illegal he was confused, as he knew that some 15-year-olds were having sex. When asked if there were any differences between a relationship between a 22-year-old and a 15-year-old and one between two 15-year-olds, he said there were not.

› He was surprised that the girl's father had politely asked him to leave when he found them in bed together, but later had called the police. He could not appreciate that the girl's father would be unhappy with the situation.

› When asked what penalty he thought might be imposed, he suggested it would likely result in family mediation. After becoming aware that it is typically a custodial offence, he appeared more concerned about the wrongfulness of his actions in the eyes of the church than the courts.

› He met sufficient criterion in the DSM-5 classification system for a diagnosis of ASD. Intellectual assessment indicated that verbal comprehension, perceptual reasoning and the ability to process simple or routine visual material without making errors were in the superior range, and the ability to sustain attention, concentrate and exert mental control was in the average range.

> He was studying at university at the time of the offence, but has since been jailed due to a breach of his bail conditions, involving making contact with the victim.

Behavioural Indicators of ToM Deficits and Restricted Interests

Jason is socially very awkward, though very polite and respectful. His voice is shaky with a pronounced stutter, and he has a restless leg. He was very frank in his discussions relating to the charges and other sexual matters, some of which most people would consider embarrassing. Even when interviewed by a young female student, he showed no signs of embarrassment talking about his sexual interests and activities. When interviewed, he would present to the interviewer things he had brought along that were of interest to him. For example, he showed photos of his previous girlfriend or floor plans of his victim's bedroom. There was no sense that he thought any of what he presented was inappropriate.

He admits to learning social and sexual expressions from the internet. Conversation with him is difficult, though this varies with the subject matter. His ability to read the emotions and actions of others appears very limited. Although he maintains good eye contact, he has a constant smile on his face, which could be perceived as odd. His social interactions are scripted and seem unnatural. He says he has friends, apparently mainly developed and maintained through the church (but some through sport), with them reflecting a shared interest in electronics. However, based on his accounts the interactions could be best described as parallel rather than cooperative.

He observes a number of routines: he lines up his belongings; he eats in his room; he eats the same food every day and he does not eat vegetables; he can't leave the house without a shower and, if he returned to the house and left again, he would require another shower. He has never liked tags on his clothes, and likes to stare at the sun, as he feels this makes him more alert. He is obsessed with gaming, becoming agitated if asked to cease. He also appears to have an obsessive interest in sexual matters and the female body – particularly their navels. He said he likes to ask girls to show him their navels because, as this is not a sexual organ, it won't get him into trouble.

Contributing Factors

Jason is a 26-year-old man who looks like a teenager, presents as socially awkward, remains sexually naive, but has an obsession with females.

He had always struggled with developing and maintaining friendships, gravitating towards younger peers and seeing nothing unusual about this. Throughout his questioning he continued to state his victim gave consent even though he had been informed she was a minor at the time of the offence and could not do so. He saw no issue with the difference in their ages and did not realise what he had done was illegal, although he knew it was inappropriate in the eyes of the church. He saw other 15-year-olds experimenting sexually with peers, and considered it appropriate for him to be thus involved. In pursuit of his obsessive sexual interests, and with an apparent lack of consideration for the victim or the family, he committed a criminal act. He was surprised by the reaction of the victim's father. All of these responses are consistent with deficits in knowledge about sexual relationships in relation to the law, as well as ToM deficits.

Case A5: Kallen
The Crime
Kallen lives in a self-contained unit at a residential care facility with 14 other residents. At this location Kallen allegedly sprayed deodorant in his carer's eyes. The incident occurred when the carer entered his unit to investigate why his lights were going on and off. Kallen was doing this as part of his nightly ritual – a ritual with which the new worker was unfamiliar. The carer then began to scream and he 'freaked out' and grabbed her by the throat. A scuffle in the darkened room ensued. The carer alleged he grabbed her breast and crotch. Kallen denied this allegation. Kallen was subsequently charged with assault. The police were called and he was also charged with assaulting a police officer and resisting arrest.

Background and Assessment Information

> Kallen is a 17-year-old male who was diagnosed with ASD when he was four years of age. With the exception of speech his early milestones displayed typical development. He required speech pathology services due to language delay as well as pronunciation difficulties.

> His parents separated when he was five years of age. He later moved to a country town with two of his four siblings. He did not see his father again until he was 16 years of age.

> He maintains a good relationship with his mother and she is the only family member with whom he has contact. When asked about his grandparents he suggested they were 'pretty much dead'.

> He has few friends and sees no need in pursing relationships with anyone. He did have a girlfriend for about five months but he felt she was too needy. He is not interested in contacting his siblings.

> He attended mainstream school until Year 11. He reported that he did not find the schoolwork difficult, just *boring*.

> Formal testing using the *Social Communication Questionnaire (SCQ)* (Rutter *et al.* 2003) was indicative of an ASD, as was *The Childhood Asperger Test*.

> Overall his IQ was in the average range, with above average scores on the nonverbal tasks.

> He scored in the significant range for depression and anxiety using standardised testing.

> He is incredibly literal. He was unable to interpret expressions such as, 'One frost doesn't make a winter' or 'If you can't bite, don't show your teeth'. He did not recognise these were metaphors.

> He has a lot of sensory issues, including sensitivity to noise; he reported he would freeze if people shouted when he was younger.

> When asked at the police interview if he had ASD, he replied, 'Yes, just barely. I look like everyone else.'

> He claims that his behaviour has improved, as he hasn't bitten anyone since primary school.

Behavioural Indicators of ToM Deficits and Restricted Interests

Kallen will tend to take any conversation back to what interests him and, in doing so, can enter into lengthy monologues. He will tell people about things but the interaction is never reciprocal. He struggles to understand the emotions and intent of others. He has a lack of affect and a monotone that, together, make him difficult to read. He often thinks people are angry when they are not. He would need to see tears to recognise sadness. His mother states that he cannot tell a friend from a foe. His poor ToM was evident when he was asked whether he understood the victim was hurt by the spray to her eyes. He replied, 'But you don't walk into a room when someone is spraying.' There was no remorse, as he was sure he had done nothing wrong. He assumed the carer would know he was spraying deodorant. He did not appreciate the fear or pain she may have been experiencing, but instead was consumed by his own pain.

He likes to have things done in a particular way, and has to follow certain routines. He engages in a ritual of flicking his room lights on and off, behaviour that can last up to 15 minutes and typically occurs when he is agitated. He does not like people to touch his belongings. He used to collect coins, models, rocks and fishing rods. He does not like to be touched.

Contributing Factors

Kallen is extremely sensitive to noise. On the night of the assault he had been awake smoking, as he was unable to sleep due to music coming from his neighbour's bedroom. He then began his ritual of switching his lights on and off. The lights caught the attention of his carer, who was unaware of this routine and came to investigate. Kallen maintains that the carer walked in as he was spraying deodorant to hide the smell of his cigarettes in his room. He states that he did not spray the carer because he was angry or anxious about having his routine interrupted; rather, he was simply spraying the deodorant to disguise the smell. The carer unfortunately inadvertently entered the darkened room and walked straight into the deodorant being sprayed. His poor ToM caused him to believe the carer should have anticipated that he would be spraying deodorant, despite the carer having no way of knowing this. Instead, the carer was sprayed directly in the eyes, causing her to scream in pain. Kallen was not concerned by the victim's pain, but rather by his own pain from the noise. When asked why the victim's screaming had caused him to panic, he said he had never heard screaming that loud and it had hurt his ears. When asked why he had grabbed the victim, Kallen explained it was to stop her screaming. When asked whether he had held the victim, Kallen explained that he had tried to sit her on the couch and she had fallen, dragging him with her. Kallen remains adamant that the carer should have anticipated he was going to spray deodorant and, hence, he feels no remorse.

He denied that he had grabbed the victim by the throat and strangled her at the door. When the police came to his bedroom to arrest him, he became highly agitated. He is sensitive to touch and did not respond well to being touched by the officers, pushing them away when they tried to arrest him. He said the officers hurt him with their handcuffs. Kallen's account indicates a complete lack of appreciation of the impact of his behaviour on others and of why they may have behaved as they did.

Case A6: Garrison
The Crime

Garrison is a 22-year-old male with no criminal record, who has been charged with the offence of stealing. Armed with bolt-cutters he, together with his co-accused, stole copper piping from 35 new hot-water service installations on housing estates over a period of several months. Garrison knew he was 'not supposed to take them' and that his behaviour was unlawful. At the time of the thefts he recognised that it was a crime that would involve the police should he be caught.

Background and Assessment Information

> His development was described as typical until he was about two years of age, when his behaviour became 'difficult'. He pulled objects apart and was described by his mother as determined, mischievous and destructive.

> Garrison 'body-rocked' from a young age. He has also been known to pace and would sleep on his stomach while head-butting his pillow.

> When Garrison was younger he licked and smelled objects. He continues to have some sensory-seeking behaviours, including touching objects around him. He will not wear jeans due to tactile sensitivities.

> Initial diagnoses included oppositional defiant disorder and ADHD, as well as antisocial behaviour (e.g., exposing himself).

> Garrison was diagnosed with AS and conduct disorder when he was 13 years of age.

> IQ assessments place Garrison in the average range of intellect with notable weakness in his speed of processing.

Behavioural Indicators of ToM Deficits and Restricted Interests

Garrison cannot engage in reciprocal conversation; rather, he simply states his own point of view. He only responds to people if they initiate conversation and he shows little interest in what they have to say. He demonstrates his lack of interest by walking away, yet will randomly approach unfamiliar people. His mother described him as gullible.

Although he may notice if his mother is sad, he does not know how to show comfort or affection in this or any other situation. He cannot easily read the nonverbal cues of others. His eye contact is poor and his facial expressions are often inconsistent with his mood. At one time during his interview with the psychologist his mother left the room. When asked why she had left he stated he was unsure, but upon reflection he suggested 'she is probably upset'. He seemed oblivious to the fact she had been teary for some time prior to her departure. He has a flat affect and has difficulty expressing his own emotions.

He has not been able to develop or maintain relationships with others, and moves from one acquaintance to the next without forming any solid friendships. Over the years he has developed many fixated interests, including computers and other electronics, trains, matchbox cars, stamp collecting, dragons, watches and fishing. During his early adolescence he developed an interest in matches and lighting fires. He has also developed strong attachments to objects, exemplified by his carrying a bum-bag containing his wallet and headphones and always having a hat with him.

Contributing Factors

Intrinsic to his diagnosis, Garrison was socially isolated with no friends and a limited social network. He was having problems at home when a person he met at a factory where he was gaining work experience offered him a place to live. These new living arrangements further exacerbated this isolation, resulting in reduced contact with his family and no money or ability to contact people. As payment for board, Garrison was asked by this man (now his co-accused) to give him his entire government allowance. Garrison was also required to run errands (e.g., he would be sent on errands such as getting coffee, cigarettes and basic food supplies). He did not have access to his own money, the internet or phone credit. His mother commented that the co-accused had him 'on a leash'. During his time living with the co-accused he often wore dirty clothes and had access to only limited food. He lost 13kg during his time living with the co-accused.

Garrison stated that the first time he went for a drive with the co-accused he did think it was a 'bit weird' that the co-accused was carrying a bag with bolt-cutters. Someone with a well-developed ToM would likely consider this to be more than a bit weird. He did not think to ask questions when he witnessed the co-accused removing copper piping from a property being completed at a new housing estate. He accompanied the co-accused on one more outing of this nature before being given addresses and asked to conduct the thefts on his own. In order to stop the repetitive requesting of the co-accused and to ensure he had food and lodgings, he complied with the requests. He was not involved in the on-selling of the copper piping, nor did he receive any financial gain. He was manipulated into the criminal activity and, while he was aware of its criminal nature, he did not have the social maturity or social scripts to extricate himself from this situation.

Case B1: Kosta
The Crime

Kosta (a 19-year-old male) allegedly walked into a fast food chain brandishing an imitation firearm and demanded cash from the till. In the police report it is alleged that Kosta approached the cashier and said,

'Give me the money or I'll shoot you.' The cashier was unable to open the till and he left empty handed. Kosta was charged with attempted aggravated robbery.

Background and Assessment Information

> Kosta is a 19-year-old man with ASD and in the borderline range of intellectual functioning.

> His teacher noted he was experiencing difficulties at age six years and requested assessments from school guidance officers.

> Social immaturity and difficulty in maintaining friendships were noted in subsequent assessments.

> He was teased at school until he responded like 'fireworks'.

> He has had no friends aside from a family friend called Renee; he has never been invited to birthday parties.

> When younger he wanted to wear red shoes, even though he was teased about it at school.

> His score on the SCQ was suggestive of ASD. Scores on the ADI-R were all clinically significant for ASD, and his CARS score placed him in the mild range for AD.

> His verbal reasoning abilities were in the low average range and much better developed than his nonverbal reasoning abilities, which were in the extremely low range. His ability to sustain attention, concentrate and exert mental control was also in the extremely low range.

> A parental report using a standardised assessment tool placed him in the extremely low range across all adaptive behaviour domains (e.g., self-care, getting along with others).

> He was presented informally with some ToM tasks from Happé's (1994) *Strange Stories* test. While he failed most items, he was occasionally able to take the perspective of others, and he also understood why it might be appropriate at times to tell a lie instead of hurting someone's feelings.

Behavioural Indicators of ToM Deficits and Restricted Interests

Examination of Kosta's files indicated he had little insight into the thoughts or behaviours of others. Most of his social behaviours needed explicit teaching and they remain scripted. As his diagnosis suggests, he clearly lacked social and emotional reciprocity and would not offer comfort if someone was hurt. His facial expressions are hard to read and he has difficulty interpreting the emotions of others. He also appears to have no appreciation of the personal space of others.

His language has caused problems throughout his life, commencing with early speech delays. While his speech has become more fluent with age, there remain issues relating to reciprocity in his speech and repetition of phrases. For example, he will wake up every morning and say the same phrase. He cannot engage in small talk. He still has problems with pronouns, often confusing *he* and *she* or referring to himself in the third person. He sometimes says socially inappropriate things such as, 'She has big gazongas.' His nonverbal gestures were delayed and he did not point. He is quite literal in his interpretation of speech and, if told something was going to happen in a minute, he would become upset if it didn't happen in exactly 60 seconds.

He has not displayed obsessions to the degree often found in persons with an ASD, but periodically he has had some intense interests, which have included motor bikes and the colour red. He does, however, have a number of repetitive behaviours such as lining up his shoes and flicking switches, and he likes a strict routine. Kosta has displayed a number of sensory issues such as tactile sensitivity and may pace and stare blankly into space.

Contributing Factors

Kosta was a young naive man with ASD who wanted to be part of a group. He had developed a network of people whom he perceived as 'mates'. The reality was that these mates were simply a group of young men Kosta had regularly seen at the fast food establishment near his home. He was unable to name any of the young men or provide any personal information about them. Further, he was unable to provide any evidence of interacting with them prior to the evening upon which the crime occurred – despite the fact he considered himself part of the group.

On the evening of the robbery, Kosta had been given a water pistol. For reasons that remain unclear, he decided to take the water pistol to the restaurant. While sitting alone at a booth playing with his pistol, two of the men approached him. Possibly sensing his naiveté and vulnerability, they suggested he use the water pistol to demand money from the cashier. Kosta remains unclear why he complied with the request, although it appears it was an attempt to impress his 'mates'. He reported that he did not think he was intending to rob the store and, at the time, he did not think it was a robbery. He did not think the cashier would believe the gun to be real and he could not understand why the cashier was so distressed. He also found it curious that she remained distressed after being told by police it was not a real gun. He demonstrated poor ToM in his ability to appreciate the intent of the men or the reaction of the cashier. This lack of ToM is also apparent from his inability to understand the fuss and why people continued to refer to it as robbery when he didn't steal anything. Unlike many of the crimes discussed in this chapter, his crime did not appear to be related to any intense interest. He was, however, interested in making friends but showed obvious deficits in reading their behaviour and anticipating the possible consequences of his own behaviour.

Case B2: Aaron
The Crime

Aaron is 24 years of age. He is very close to his father and together they would habitually frequent a local shopping mall to collect stamps for his book. They often rode their bikes there. On many occasions they had seen a man (John) en route to the mall. On the day of the alleged assault, Aaron and his father saw John inside the store and John spoke to them. Aaron interpreted John's approach as harassment and said John was teasing him – a claim John denied. Aaron became highly agitated due to John's presence and decided to leave the store. His father left with Aaron and unlocked his own bike, but Aaron was unable to unlock his bike due to his highly agitated state. Aaron placed his helmet by his side as he fidgeted with his bike lock. At this point John approached Aaron, picked up his helmet and offered it to him by tapping his shoulder with it. Aaron reacted by spitting on him. John argued that he was merely being friendly and, when he realised that his approach had upset Aaron, had followed him to apologise and explain he meant no harm. John argued that he was just trying to help. Aaron was charged with aggravated assault as a result of the spit landing on John.

Background and Assessment Information

> Aaron was diagnosed with AD and a mild intellectual disability when he was 12 years of age.

> His disability is readily apparent, prompting his arresting officers to terminate their interview with him on the basis of a potential medical condition.

> He reports having few long-term friends aside from cousins, some friends made through Scouts and old classmates with disabilities.

> He was often bullied at school and suspended for retaliation. He left school at 14 years of age due to the constant bullying. He has weaknesses in all areas of adaptive functioning (e.g., poor self-help skills and hygiene) and has never been employed.

> He reports being bullied or teased wherever he goes and, thus, chooses not to interact with people outside of his family.

> He lives at home with his mother and father and had no prior criminal history.

> His scores on the SCQ and the ADI-R place him above the scale cut-off for clinical significance in terms of AD, and he met DSM-IV criteria for AD.

> His overall cognitive ability could not be easily summarised because his verbal reasoning abilities are not as developed as his nonverbal reasoning abilities. His verbal and nonverbal ability scores were in the mild and borderline range of intellectual disability, respectively. His ability to sustain attention, concentrate and exert mental control was in the mild range and the processing of simple or routine visual material was in the borderline range.

Behavioural Indicators of ToM Deficits and Restricted Interests

The psychologists' reports suggest Aaron has little insight into the thoughts of others or their behavioural intentions. Most of his social behaviour has been taught and it remains scripted. As indicated by his diagnosis, he clearly lacks social and emotional reciprocity. Language impairments have been evident throughout his life; his speech is echolalic and full of jargon, and he engages in lengthy incoherent monologues (including during his interviews). He has difficulty interpreting nonverbal cues (e.g., facial expressions to indicate not understanding the message, boredom, etc.) and interprets the speech of others literally. He appears not to appreciate social norms and thus makes social mistakes. Aaron's mother reported that he has little awareness of his difficulties and how his behaviour affects others.

Aaron has always had obsessions and special interests. He has always collected things and lined them up and, currently, he spends every day collecting stamps and placing them into a book. He routinely visits the local mall to collect stamps for his book. His mother reports that he becomes agitated if this activity is interrupted. He also has hypersensitivity to both touch (e.g., he cuts the tags out of his clothes) and noise, and he becomes anxious if his senses are overloaded.

Contributing Factors

Aaron is a young man with a mild intellectual disability who meets diagnostic criteria for ASD. No other comorbid conditions were identified in extensive court-ordered assessments from three professionals (two psychologists and one psychiatrist). He was engaging in his daily ritual of going to the shops with his father and engaging his obsession of collecting stamps for his books. His ToM deficit appears to be pervasive and his special interest consuming; interrupting his special interest produces considerable angst. He is also hypersensitive to touch. John interrupted Aaron's routine and, believing John was teasing him, Aaron became agitated and responded by spitting at John. Aaron claims to have found John's approach to be anxiety-provoking and was adamant that his actions were a response to the approaches of the victim who had been harassing him – but he was unable to provide any examples of harassment from either John's verbal or nonverbal behaviour. John strongly denied any harassment, arguing he was simply being friendly to people he had seen on numerous occasions at the store. It appears that Aaron misread John's approach and did not recognise how his behaviour would affect John and was surprised when he was arrested.

Case B3: Bradley
The Crime
On the day of the alleged offence, Bradley had been agitated by his bus schedule changing and, in a distressed state, he caught the wrong bus home. Realising his mistake, he got off the bus near a primary school. He entered the school and asked for directions to enable him to get home. While walking back to the bus stop, Bradley approached two young girls who were playing on the footpath and tried to show them some of his rock collection, which he always carried with him. The girls screamed and Bradley reached out – without any intention to harm – with the intent to quieten them, causing the girls even more distress. He too became distressed and left but was subsequently charged with attempted kidnapping.

Background and Assessment Information

> From early childhood, Bradley's mother thought he was different from her other children. Despite attempts to teach him things, he just did not appear to learn – characteristics that became more apparent when he started school.

> A diagnosis of AD was made by the local Autism Association when he was six years of age.

> He is employed at a sheltered workshop for people with disabilities. The bullying and teasing he experienced at school persists in the sheltered workshop.

> Nevertheless, he tries to initiate friendships but has had no success and remains socially isolated. His mother's reports indicate his keenness to

engage with people but a lack of requisite social skills. He is always keen to please but is socially naive and vulnerable.

› He is well known in the street where he lives and many people, mostly children, visit the family home to say hello to him and his mother. When Bradley meets people, he always offers to show them some of his rock collection from his backpack, which he takes with him wherever he goes. This behaviour is well received in his neighbourhood and encouraged by his mother.

› Bradley's intellectual assessment shows similar verbal and performance IQ profiles and is consistent with a mild intellectual disability.

Behavioural Indicators of ToM Deficits and Restricted Interests

Bradley's mother indicated that Bradley has problems with social skills and comprehension that undermine his social interactions. His behaviour can at times be inappropriate and obsessive, and his slow and deliberate speech causes some people to lose interest and disengage.

He is obsessed with his rock collection. His collection cannot be disturbed and his mother must negotiate what she is allowed to move or discard. He carries his most recently collected rocks with him wherever he goes. He also has a number of motor stereotypies, which include twitching, pacing and shaking, and he is hypersensitive to noise.

Contributing Factors

Bradley has AD and a mild intellectual disability. Wing and Gould's (1979) description of a subgroup of persons with AD as 'active-but-odd' – that is, people who actively seek interaction with others but do so in an odd, awkward and often overly persistent manner – aptly describes Bradley. He is interested in social interaction, but does not know how to approach people. As a result, he engages in inappropriate attempts to communicate, often involving interactions with children in his neighbourhood. He has a rigid daily routine of travelling to and from work by bus, then walking home from his bus stop and showing his rock collection junk mail to passers-by who have become accustomed to this practice. On the day of the crime, this routine was broken when Bradley became agitated by the change in his bus schedule and, subsequently, got on the wrong bus. While trying to get home he approached two young girls and engaged in his obsession of showing his rock collection. His ToM deficits meant that he did not anticipate the girls' reactions to his attempt to interact with them, nor their reactions to his attempts to subdue their screams, which would have been particularly aversive given his hypersensitivity to noise. The outcome was the very serious charge of attempted kidnapping.

Case B4: Frederick
The Crime
Frederick (aged 22 years) received a rare invitation to attend a party by his sister and her new boyfriend, whom (at their request) he drove to the party. While there, a friend of the new boyfriend, whom Frederick had never met before, approached Frederick, who was sitting alone, and asked him if he would be able to look after a bag for him. Frederick agreed to do this and the man later returned with a large bag and escorted Frederick to his car where he placed the bag in the boot of his car.

Frederick returned home later that night and took the bag from his car, carrying it to his room. Out of curiosity he looked in the bag, only to find a collection of knives, knuckle-dusters and other weapons inside. He re-zipped the bag and placed it under his bed. It was at this point that he realised that something was wrong but, by his own admission, he did not know what to do. He described feeling 'panicky' when he saw the contents of the bag.

Several weeks later the bag was found by a cleaner, who called the police. Frederick was subsequently charged with illegal possession and storage of prohibited weapons, as well as drug-related offences. The drug offences related to illegal steroids he had purchased on the internet and a marijuana plant he was growing in his room. During the police interview Frederick stated that he did not anticipate any wrongdoing when he agreed to look after the bag. When he looked in the bag and realised there were weapons inside, he did not know what to do. He panicked and threw the bag under his bed.

Background and Assessment Information

> Like many persons with ASD, Frederick had previously been labelled with many disorders, including ADHD, OCD, central auditory processing disorder and oppositional defiant disorder.

> None of these labels appeared to be based on formal diagnoses, but reference to them appears periodically in medical reports.

> Suspicion that Frederick may have ASD arose during questioning by a lawyer, who asked the court to order an assessment. (Four years prior to the offence a prominent local paediatrician in the area of ASD had apparently suggested Frederick had ASD but the diagnosis was never pursued.)

> The court-ordered assessment highlighted a history of speech difficulties, inappropriate behaviour in social settings, a tendency to engagement in lengthy monologues, resistance to change, obsessive behaviours

and a low tolerance for noise. All domains of the *ADI-R* and the *SCQ* (completed by his parents) yielded scores considered to be clinically significant for ASD.

> Intellectual ability assessments placed Frederick in the range of borderline to mild intellectual disability (at the most recent assessment). His IQ score has progressively declined with each assessment, perhaps due to drug use, limited schooling and/or motivation. His ability to provide oral solutions to everyday problems and to explain the reasons for certain social conventions was also noted to be significantly impaired during formal assessment.

Behavioural Indicators of ToM Deficits and Restricted Interests

The court-ordered psychological report stated that Frederick does not seem aware of and is not responsive to the feelings of others. His language is repetitive and at times he speaks about issues that are out of context. His eye contact is poor. His parents stated that he has never really had friends and his peers used to tell him to go away. Although he rarely directs his anger at people, he does find other avenues to express his frustration. His parents reported an example of this where he put petrol in the fishpond when he had been bullied at school. He is known not to display affect, and people, including his parents, find him difficult to 'read'. He states he is unable to 'read' the emotions of others.

At times he has been obsessive about particular persons, attaching himself to a favourite person and then annoying them. He has become obsessive about his body image, believing that if he was more muscular, people would like him more. This has led to an obsession with exercise and supplement use.

Contributing Factors

Frederick is a naive young man obsessed with finding friendships, but lacking the requisite social skills. To gain a friendship, he accepted the request of a person (previously unknown to him) to look after a bag for him, never considering the possibility of contraband being in the bag. He was unsure when his suspicions were aroused, but believes it wasn't until he saw the content of the bag. It is evident from his behavioural presentation, the associated case reports and the events outlined above that Frederick had significant ToM deficits. Given the situation in which he found himself, most people with well-developed ToM would recognise something was not quite right as there were a number of cues that should have made him suspicious. For example, his sister's boyfriend asked him to drive them to a party, yet he had never conversed with him prior to this. Further, most people would consider it highly unusual to be asked at a party to look after the bag of a person whom they'd never previously met. Thus, it appears that his obsessive desire to have friends, coupled with his ToM deficits, conspired to undermine his capacity to recognise that he was being led into criminal activity. Moreover, once he realised that he had the weapons in his possession, he lacked the insight to respond appropriately. He did not appreciate that, had he gone to the police, they may have accepted his involvement as naive. Instead, he took no action, thus incriminating himself further. He also was at a loss to understand that the steroids he had purchased on the internet were illegal. He simply could not understand that if you bought something on the internet it could be illegal. He did know his marijuana possession was illegal, but claimed it was for medicinal purposes to minimise his high level of anxiety and to help with his sleep.

The Message from These Case Studies

On many occasions throughout this book we have cautioned that case studies such as those presented in this chapter are, at best, suggestive of mechanisms that may underpin the involvement of persons with an ASD in criminal activity. And we repeat that message here. Nevertheless, we believe that there are several prominent themes that emerge from these case studies that should be highlighted because they have important implications for the operation of the criminal justice system.

First, none of the crimes identified in the case studies we have outlined appear to have been premeditated by the accused or committed with malice or intent to harm. In all but one of these cases the likely outcome of the behaviour appears to have received no consideration at the time of the offence. In the case of Kallen (Case A5), he was coerced and motivated by self-preservation rather than any deliberate attempt at wrongdoing. In all cases the perpetrator needed to be educated about the seriousness of the offence and the impact their behaviour had on the victim. Second, in all cases the perpetrator of the crime showed what in everyday terms would likely be called very poor judgement. In other words, the perpetrator appeared not to recognise or understand the intent of another person or seemed oblivious to the potential impact of their behaviour on other people. As we have seen in earlier chapters, these deficiencies are commonly observed in some form and with some degree of severity in many people with ASD. And, as we argued in Chapter 5, they may – given certain enabling environmental conditions – explain how a person with an ASD may sometimes behave completely inappropriately and unlawfully – indeed naively or unwittingly – without any intent to violate the law. Third, in many of the cases the individual's behaviour was related in some way to their pursuit of an extremely strong restricted interest or obsession and, occasionally, to hypersensitivity to sensory stimuli. In other words, it is as if the special interest or obsession (or hypersensitivity) increased the likelihood that they were blinded to the intent of others or the consequences of their own actions – or exacerbated the potential impact of their ToM deficit(s) in particular situations.

There are two other noteworthy characteristics of some of these cases. One is that the offender appeared to become involved because they acceded to the wishes of someone they hoped to befriend or, perhaps, impress. It is as if there was a meshing of their social-communicative limitations and ToM deficits, deficits that are of course not independent of each other. A feature of the disorder is that affected individuals lack the requisite skills to form friendships, and they behave in ways that constrain their capacity to make friends. This, in turn, may increase the individual's vulnerability to comply with requests from people who appear to provide them with an opportunity to secure a friendship and yet are inviting them to engage in criminal behaviour. In so doing they may sometimes have severe reservations about the appropriateness of their (criminal) behaviour, or even know it to be wrong, yet it is as if they cannot recognise that they are being exploited. This is clearly quite a sophisticated or advanced aspect of understanding the thoughts and intentions of others (i.e., ToM). In such cases it also appears as if something is missing in terms of the individual's ability to balance or weigh up the apparent positive consequences of securing a much-needed 'friend' versus the likely negative consequences of their behaviour for themselves and others. Whether this cognitive-moral balancing problem could also be considered to be, at least in part, a reflection of poorly developed ToM – or simply indicative of poorly developed moral reasoning (or some other deficit) – is arguable. Regardless, it does seem to be a particular issue that is obviously not unrelated to the social-communicative deficits that define the disorder.

A second noteworthy feature is that the inability of the accused to explain or justify their behaviour when interacting with the police or judicial system often appears to have exacerbated the situation and led to legal outcomes that were far more serious than might be expected based on the behaviour described. For example, it is surprising that a person showing another person a rock collection or spitting on someone could end up on charges of attempted kidnapping and aggravated assault, respectively. It seems likely that the unusual and probably misunderstood characteristics of the accused shaped the reactions of the victims and the police towards the accused, with much more serious charges being laid than might otherwise have been the case.

Although we find the messages we have distilled from these case studies persuasive, it is appropriate to add some qualifying statements. First, we reiterate that the last four cases (Cases B1–B4) were distinguished from the others by the fact that they involved individuals with a diagnosed intellectual disability, which – rather than any ToM deficit – may have been crucial in explaining their behaviour. Second, although in most of these cases formal assessments of intellectual functioning and ASD, and checks for other comorbid disorders, have at some stage been conducted, this is certainly not the case for ToM. Neither the police nor the courts had the advantage of the wisdom that might be provided by the availability of assessments using standardised measures of ToM. In other words, there was no objective information on the nature and extent of ToM deficits; rather, all the *evidence* is actually clinical observation and inference. A similar observation needs to be made about the documentation of special interests or obsessions. The obsessions documented here most likely stand out for those who are not so familiar with the disorder as unusual or bizarre. Nevertheless, our conclusions are again reliant on clinical observation, without supporting hard data on the strength of the obsession, the extent to which it takes control of the individual and the degree of impact on the individual's functioning when it is interrupted. These are very important issues, not only from the perspective of understanding crime causation but also from that of the criminal justice's system's approach to evaluating culpability. In Chapter 8, the focus of which is on assessment and intervention, we address these issues in more detail.

Third, the potential causal factors discussed above are unlikely to be the only influences that may have been relevant to the emergence of the criminal behaviour. In many cases there was clear evidence of social-environmental variables (e.g., troubled home environment, bullying, abuse) that may well have shaped the individual's behaviour in ways that increased the likelihood that the ASD-related deficits would play out in the way that they apparently did. And, there may well have been undetected comorbid psychiatric conditions that shaped the eventual outcomes. Nevertheless, we believe the case evidence is at least consistent with the hypotheses advanced in Chapter 5 about the vulnerability of individuals with an ASD who have severe deficits in ToM and extremely strong preoccupations or obsessions.

In the next chapter we shall see that the story does not end here, as we argue how the characteristics of people with ASD may sometimes prejudice the outcomes of their interactions with the criminal justice system. It is notable, for example, that none of the offenders described in these case studies had reserved their right to remain silent or requested legal assistance. In all cases a lawyer was appointed by the court. Moreover, the case histories suggest that their behaviour subsequent to the crime had served to further incriminate them. In Chapter 7 we examine how the behavioural characteristics of people with ASD may define the direction that their interactions with police, lawyers, judges and jurors may take and indeed compromise the outcomes of those interactions.

Chapter 7

>>>>>>>>>>>>>>>>>>>>>>>

INTERACTIONS WITH THE CRIMINAL JUSTICE SYSTEM

Thus far our focus has been on how ToM deficits, in conjunction with dominating circumscribed interests or sensory sensitivity, may – given certain enabling environmental conditions – contribute to an individual with ASD becoming involved in criminal activity. In this chapter we argue that there are particular behavioural characteristics of ASD that may not only render an individual vulnerable to involvement in criminal activity but also adversely affect the progress and outcomes of their interactions with the criminal justice system.

Here we consider what might happen should an individual with ASD come into contact with the criminal justice system as an offender, suspect or victim. We examine how the behavioural characteristics of individuals with ASD may (a) shape the course of their interactions with police who may be investigating a crime, and with prosecution and defence lawyers and (b) influence the evaluations of the judiciary and jurors should a case culminate in a trial. It is important to recognise that there is very little empirical research that directly address these issues. How police, lawyers, judges and jurors interpret and react to the behaviour of individuals with ASD has not been the subject of systematic and controlled scientific research. Consequently, much of what we have to say in this chapter relies upon establishing links between what we know about (a) the behavioural characteristics of individuals with ASD and (b) how people perceive and respond to such behavioural characteristics, independent of any connection with ASD. Whether our generalisations in this chapter about such perceptions and reactions are appropriate must await the outcomes of future research. Nevertheless, we believe it is useful – even if only from the perspective of stimulating research – to highlight an array of variables and issues that potentially have a major bearing on the outcomes of criminal justice system interactions for offenders, suspects, victims or even witnesses with ASD.

In line with the position advanced in the previous two chapters, we again argue that those core deficits considered to heighten criminal vulnerability – ToM, restricted interests or obsessions and sensory sensitivity – may, under certain conditions, also place individuals with ASD at a severe disadvantage in any interactions they may have with the criminal justice system. First, we consider how ToM deficits that influence social-cognitive processing may shape the course of interactions between a person with ASD and individuals from the various sectors of the criminal justice system (i.e., police, lawyers, judiciary and jurors).

Behavioural Manifestations of ToM Deficits

We suggest that many of the behavioural manifestations of ToM deficits observed in association with ASD may have a significant impact on the perceptions and evaluations of a person with ASD by various individuals within the criminal justice system with whom they interact. Moreover, this impact is perhaps likely to be even more significant if those individuals working within the criminal justice system do not have an appreciation of the disorder and its behavioural characteristics or, conversely, have misperceptions about the disorder. We consider some of the ways in which ToM deficits are likely to manifest behaviourally when an individual with ASD is being interviewed by police in relation to crime commission or criminal victimisation, interrogated by lawyers as a suspect or victim, testifying before a judge and jurors after being committed to stand trial, or simply providing evidence as a victim or perhaps as a witness. We focus on the impact of both nonverbal and verbal behavioural characteristics of individuals with ASD, and we also consider how individuals with ASD are likely to interpret the nonverbal and verbal characteristics of those with whom they are interacting.

Nonverbal Behaviours

Effective social communication is critically dependent on the ability to display socially appropriate nonverbal behaviour during interactions with others. The diagnostic criteria for ASD highlight abnormalities in eye contact and body language, including deficits in the use of nonverbal facial and gestural communication. This includes the inability to express emotions and read the emotions of others. The presence of such deficits in individuals who do not appreciate how such behaviours shape the perceptions and reactions of others – that is, in individuals characterised by ToM deficits – is not particularly surprising. But what is likely to be surprising to professionals within the criminal justice system is that there are good grounds for thinking that such behavioural characteristics will affect the direction and outcomes of their interactions with an individual with ASD, even though these characteristics offer little in the way of probative information.

Consider the impact of behaviours such as lack of eye contact (referred to in the deception–detection literature as gaze aversion) or apparently nervous fidgeting, shuffling or personal grooming on the part of a suspect or victim with ASD during an interview with the police or under questioning in a courtroom.

For example:

> A young man was walking to the shops to buy his midnight Subway sandwich and became extremely agitated when his routine was suddenly interrupted by a police officer stopping him and asking him questions. The young man began to pace backwards and forwards while gazing at the ground and, despite being told several times to stand still, he could not oblige the officer's request. His consistent failure to comply made the officer suspicious and he then arrested the young man.

It is well documented in the deception–detection literature that people tasked with assessing the likely veracity of a person's statements – whether they be laypeople, police or customs officers – consider nonverbal cues such as gaze aversion (e.g., looking down or away while communicating) and nervous fidgeting to be indicators of lying, despite the fact these behaviours prove not to be diagnostic of veracity (cf. Granhag and Vrij 2005). We might, therefore, expect police to interpret such behavioural indicators from a suspect as confirmation that their suspect is indeed the culprit. Or, should the behaviour be displayed by a suspect during testimony, we might expect it to diminish the credibility of their testimony in the eyes of the judge or jury. Consequently, police may neglect to consider alternative hypotheses about the identity of the criminal and focus only on a search for evidence that adds further weight to their suspicions. Or, they may take a victim's testimony far less seriously than they should, purely because they have relied upon non-veridical indices of veracity. Lawyers, jurors and judges may well do likewise. In other words, despite the fact that such nonverbal behaviours do not reliably diagnose attempts to deceive, their prevalence in individuals with ASD may well prejudice the assessments that others make of them when they come into contact with the criminal justice system.

To our knowledge there has been no systematic empirical work that directly targets these issues in the context of a suspect, defendant or victim with ASD. Nevertheless, apart from the body of work demonstrating the pervasiveness of the belief that these behaviours signal lying or attempts to deceive, there is also a limited body of work using mock-juror experimental paradigms that assesses how manipulations of witnesses' nonverbal behaviour or demeanour affect perceptions of probability of guilt and verdicts. For example, several studies have reported that when a defendant displayed nonverbal behaviours typically associated with deception (e.g., poor eye contact, fidgeting), the likelihood of guilty verdicts from mock-jurors was higher than in the absence of such behaviours (e.g., Feldman and Chesley 1984; Pryor and Buchanan 1984).

Other studies have focused on the impact of (nonverbal) emotional displays of victims, an area in which individuals with ASD are (on average) likely to differ from those without ASD. These studies suggest that assessments of a victim's credibility are shaped by the extent to which the emotional presentation or demeanour of the victim accords with social norms or expectations regarding such behaviour. Thus, for example, exactly the same verbal testimony of a female rape victim has been judged as more credible when the victim presents as emotional or despairing rather than in either a neutral or positive manner (Bollingmo et al. 2009; Kaufmann et al. 2003; Wessel et al. 2006). Interestingly, precisely the same pattern of results has been found when experienced police investigators made credibility judgements of the testimony of rape victims (Bollingmo et al. 2008). A similar pattern of findings has been reported in other experiments where victims of (non-rape) crimes may be judged more or less favourably depending on whether their emotional response appears to be calibrated with the seriousness of the crime (Rose, Nadler and Clark 2006). Together, such research certainly points to the possibility that some of the characteristic nonverbal behaviours of individuals with ASD that are unrelated to veracity – specifically, gaze aversion, fidgeting and shuffling, an absence of appropriate affective displays – may undermine their credibility when interacting (as a suspect or victim) with police, lawyers and the courts.

Verbal Behaviours

Also commonly observed in individuals with ASD are distinctive verbal communication characteristics that have the potential to prejudice interactions with the criminal justice system. Perhaps most salient among these is a reduced sharing of affect or emotion in normal social interactions. For an individual with ASD being interviewed in relation to the commission of a crime, it is quite likely that verbal displays of affect or emotion that appear to reflect a sensitivity to the nature and impact of the crime on a victim will be missing. Likewise, perceptible expressions of remorse for victims may be notable for their absence.

For example:

Simon was accused of having sex with a 12-year-old girl. He told the police she had said yes to having sex. The police told Simon that was irrelevant because she was a minor and therefore not legally able to consent. Simon responded, 'Well I wish she hadn't consented because she was a dud root.' When asked during the interview if he had said anything to her about her sexual performance, he said, 'No but I told the others as I walked out of the room.' When asked if she may have heard that remark he responded, 'I don't know what she heard but I did offer to drive her home.'

Or:

YB, after being arrested for rape and placed in the back of a police vehicle at 3:00am, asked the officers if he could enquire about his stolen mobile phone while at the police station. The police officer replied, 'Yes I am sure there would be plenty of people at the station well-equipped to deal with this matter at this time of day,' to which YB replied, 'Great.' He then continued to chat about his previous encounters with the law, showing disregard for how this might prejudice the officer's opinion of him. Further, when asked if he had fondled the girl's vagina while she slept, he said, 'Yes,' but then added, 'I said I was sorry and bought her some lollies.'

What is the likely impact of a failure to display what might be considered to be normative levels of affect or emotion? Intuitively, we might imagine that observers of such behaviour in a suspect or defendant would almost certainly perceive the individual as callous and indifferent to the consequences of their purported criminal activity. Police may, therefore, see such behavioural displays as confirming their hypothesis about the person's guilt and perhaps neglect to consider alternative hypotheses about what might have transpired in the event under consideration. Maybe lawyers would do likewise. Perhaps jurors would interpret such behaviour as consistent with that of a guilty person or, at a minimum, callous. And, maybe judges would interpret a lack of appropriate expressed affect towards the victim as indicative of an absence of remorse that justified a more severe sentence than might otherwise have been the case.

To our knowledge there has been no systematic empirical work that directly targets these issues. There has, however, been a limited amount of research (unrelated to ASD) using mock-juror experimental paradigms to assess how manipulations of witnesses' verbal presentation or demeanour affect perceptions of probability of guilt and verdicts. For example, Salekin et al. (1995) manipulated the emotional expression of a defendant giving testimony when charged with second-degree murder of their two children. A female defendant who showed flat affect throughout her testimony was judged more likely to be guilty than when she displayed moderate or high affect (e.g., crying and other emotional responses) that is likely to be considered normative for such a situation. These patterns were not replicated with male defendants. In a similar vein, Jehle, Miller and Kemmelmeier (2009) assessed mock-juror reactions after watching a mock-trial of a person charged with shooting his neighbour after a property dispute. Compared with an absence of remorse (i.e., monotone voice and continual eye contact), displays of remorse (i.e., trembling voice) increased the likelihood of a guilty assessment from jurors but moderated the severity of punishment recommended. But, there is certainly not a strong and consistent pattern of findings to guide predictions regarding likely outcomes. Moreover, the available findings are derived from relatively small samples, based on a restricted set of relatively low fidelity simulations and, importantly, do not involve assessments of witnesses, victims or defendants with ASD. Rather, evidence such as that just outlined comes from studies where the defendant or victim merely displays behavioural characteristics that diagnostic criteria suggest are, on average, more likely to be prominent in people with ASD than in those without.

It is difficult, therefore, to draw firm inferences about likely reactions on the part of police, lawyers, jurors or judges to such patterns of behaviour. Although these behaviours may potentially prejudice outcomes for individuals with ASD, perhaps one of the legacies of the many and varied experiences of seasoned criminal justice professionals may be that they don't rely on such heuristics when evaluating the individuals they encounter but rather are much more discerning evaluators of the people and information that comes before them. We suspect this is unlikely – especially given the previously described results of the Bollingmo *et al.* (2008) study with police investigators – but there is very little in the way of hard evidence to support our suspicion.

Occasionally, other verbal characteristics of people with ASD are noted in anecdotal clinician reports as potential moderators of legal outcomes. For example, clinicians have noted that the person with ASD may, under questioning, engage in a lengthy monologue when responding, apparently oblivious to the reactions of the questioner. In the forensic context such behaviour may increase the likelihood that the interviewee discloses potentially incriminating detail or, at least, detail that is perceived as incriminating.

For example:

Seth was asked to describe the house where the minor with whom he had sex lived. He asked if he could draw it. He then spent 40 minutes detailing and describing a comprehensive floor plan of every room in the house, including the bedrooms where younger children slept, their wardrobes, what they kept on the dressers and so forth. While this might be consistent with the eidetic memory seen in some persons with ASD, to the majority of persons the behaviour may be seen as odd – even creepy – and lead to further investigation about his involvement with the other minors.

Or:

> One young man, pulled over after running a red light, was asked whether he knew he had run the red light. He responded that he had not realised the light was red because he was talking on his mobile at the time. The police officer said rhetorically, 'Of course you were talking on hands-free,' to which he responded, 'No,' and then engaged in a lengthy monologue about how he was trying to make a call but was frustrated because he was unable to put credit on the phone he had bought from a mate.

To our knowledge, however, there is no empirical evidence documenting the likely prevalence of such behaviour or demonstrating its impact on criminal justice professionals. In a similar vein, clinicians occasionally note that individuals with ASD may swear excessively in contexts where such behaviour is likely to be regarded as socially inappropriate.

For example:

> Persons with ASD often fail to modify their behaviour to suit the social context and thus may continue to swear inside the courtroom or in other formal settings. One young man repeatedly told the psychologist interviewing him to 'fuck off' when he was asked questions, before going on to answer the questions to the best of his ability. When his father was asked to join the interview he told his son to refrain from such language. He then explained to his father that the psychologist was 'cool with it' and continued telling her to fuck off before answering each question posed. It was clear he enjoyed his conversation with the psychologist and was responsive to the questions, despite the response to 'fuck off' before he continued with each answer.

Or:

> When one young man was asked in court why he had assaulted his carer, he described his victim as, 'a fat-arsed dumb slut', precipitating audible gasps from the jury.

Inappropriate communications may, of course, take a variety of other forms, with timing sometimes being all important. For example:

> When Steven was asked to accompany the officers to the police station, he asked if he could put a shirt on. He returned wearing a shirt with the inscription, 'It's not illegal until you're caught'.

Again, though we have no evidence documenting the prevalence or impact of such behaviour, it is not difficult to imagine that it might prejudice the assessments made by people within the criminal justice system.

Interpretation of Nonverbal Behaviours

Effective social communication is a two-sided process. Our knowledge of the social-communicative deficits of individuals with ASD indicates that not only are socially expected or appropriate nonverbal and verbal behaviours unlikely to be forthcoming but it is also likely that individuals with ASD will be less adept at reading or interpreting the nonverbal and verbal characteristics of those with whom they are interacting – with potentially important ramifications.

In Chapter 5 we noted that performance on *The Reading the Mind in the Eyes Test* was negatively correlated with autistic symptomatology. In other words, we should expect individuals with ASD to be less perceptive of, and responsive to, nonverbal expressions emanating from the eye region. Similarly, we should expect reduced sensitivity to facial expressions of emotion (e.g., Celani, Battacchi and Arcidiacono 1999; Gross 2004; Pelphrey *et al.* 2002; Tantam *et al.* 1989). Although there is no work that we are aware of in the forensic context, these findings suggest that adults with ASD may not be particularly perceptive of what others are thinking and perhaps planning. Moreover, they are also unlikely to be sensitive to the facial expressions and gestures of those with whom they are interacting, cues that – if accurately decoded – would provide valuable information about the impact they are having on other people and lead them to modify their behaviour. Thus, they may be relatively insensitive to subtle cues that indicate how a police interviewer, lawyer or juror is receiving or interpreting their testimony. They may be less likely to recognise that a police interrogator or lawyer is angry, accusing, confused or even leading them. In turn, they may be less aware of when they should stop talking or when they should elaborate or clarify. Alternatively, they may misperceive the officer's questions as hostile. In sum, they are perhaps less likely to behave in accord with normative expectations and may be evaluated harshly as a result. Of course, deficits in reading nonverbal signs that point to the likely behaviour of others may also sometimes place individuals with ASD at greater risk of becoming a victim of a criminal act. For example, a failure to recognise facial expressions or gestures that signal that a person with whom they are interacting harbours some malicious intent towards them could well result in their becoming an assault victim.

Interpretation of Verbal Behaviours

The nuances of verbal behaviour provide an extremely rich source of cues about how an interpersonal interaction is progressing and how one might adjust their communication to manage the impressions they are making on others. Again, our knowledge of the communicative deficits associated with ASD provides a strong pointer that such individuals may be at a disadvantage in their interactions with the criminal justice system. The scientific literature suggests a variety of ways in which individuals with ASD may be unable to capitalise on conversational cues, all of which could prejudice their interactions with the criminal justice system.

Verbal Intonation

One source of information about the intentions of others is provided by the characteristics of their verbal intonations when communicating, with different verbal intonations allowing people to identify the emotions of the person with whom they are interacting (e.g., Bachorowski and Owren 1995; Banse and Scherer 1996). There is some evidence, admittedly again quite limited, to suggest adults with ASD may be less effective at exploiting such cues to ascertain the emotional reactions of those with whom they are interacting. Hobson (1986a, 1986b) asked participants to listen to vocal expressions of different emotions and match the vocalisations to pictures of faces or gestures. Individuals with ASD performed more poorly on this matching task than IQ-matched control participants, although they no longer detected such differences when samples were matched for verbal mental age and participants had to match verbal expressions (rather than vocalisations) to facial expressions (Hobson, Ouston and Lee 1988). Exploring this theme further, Kleinman, Marciano and Ault (2001) examined whether the performance of high-functioning adults with ASD differed from that of controls when they listened to recordings of a sentence expressed with different intonations reflecting various emotional expressions and then indicated which of an array of emotional expressions matched the expression conveyed by each intonation. While the non-ASD controls performed at close to ceiling levels, the adults with ASD were much more variable and, on average, were less effective at attributing emotional expressions to expressions varying in voice intonation. Similar findings of difficulties in recognising mental states based on intonation or vocal stimuli have since been reported by Paul *et al.* (2005) and Golan *et al.* (2007).

We are not aware of any empirical evidence showing the failure of a suspect with ASD to respond as expected to fluctuations in verbal intonation that might signal that a police investigator, lawyer or judge is, for example, becoming bored or perhaps even angry or disgusted by their testimony. Nevertheless, it is not difficult to imagine that such a lack of responsiveness might lead to increasingly negative evaluations of the individual.

Literal and Metaphorical Language
It is widely accepted that individuals with ASD have great difficulty understanding nonliteral utterances or metaphorical expressions. That is, they interpret verbal communications from others literally (e.g., Frith 1989; Martin and McDonald 2004). It has been suggested that this is due to the fact that they are unable to exploit important contextual information that helps make sense of the communication. For example, critical communicative cues such as facial expressions, intonation and background information relating to the event are not integrated with the content of the verbal message and, consequently, the resulting interpretation is a purely literal one.

There is debate about the exact nature of this deficit, with some researchers arguing that there may be no qualitative difference between individuals with AS (though not other individuals with ASD who have language or intellectual impairments) and those with a normal history of language development or non-ASD controls. That is, individuals with AS can benefit from contextual information but, for reasons related to their much narrower experiences in social interaction and communication, they are simply likely to be less familiar with metaphorical expressions. As Giora *et al.* (2012) showed, individuals with AS are similar to non-ASD controls in that they can integrate contextual information when processing verbal communications and they can understand metaphors (especially if they are familiar), but they perform worse when processing novel metaphors (and likewise when processing novel literal expressions). But, from the applied perspective of the forensic context we are addressing, the findings of Giora *et al.* (2012) suggest that, on average, when contrasted with non-ASD individuals, the processing of (unfamiliar) metaphorical expressions by those with AS will be slower and more prone to error – and, to the extent that literal statements are familiar, processing of the latter will be more efficient. Thus, it seems likely that a literal interpretation will often trump a metaphoric or an ironic interpretation.

For example:

> After providing a response judged by the police officer as fictitious, the officer responded, 'Do you think I was born yesterday?' The accused then responded, 'Of course not, I would assume you were born more than 30 years ago.'

Or:

> When another young man was asked why he chose to talk after he was told he had the right to remain silent, he responded, 'What about my right? I have the right to talk too.'

Or:

> Another man who was asked how he was able to get home from the hotel where he was drinking, responded, 'In a dual-cab Toyota Hilux.'

Or:

> Another man, when asked why he did not ask for a solicitor, responded that he had been told he could have a relative, friend or solicitor present. Given his mother was present, he assumed he could not request a solicitor. Ironically, he later asked, 'What's a solicitor?'

Or:

> YB who was charged with rape after the police officer asked seven times if he had placed his finger in the vagina and anus of a young girl. On each of the six initial requests he replied, 'No.' By the seventh request, perhaps sensing he was providing the wrong answer, YB responded, 'Not the anus.' The police took this as an admission that he had placed his finger in the vagina of a young girl. YB was charged with rape, read his rights and placed handcuffed into the back of a police vehicle. Ironically, it was subsequently revealed he did not know what an anus was.

A specific example of nonliteral expression that has been closely examined in samples with ASD is the detection and interpretation of irony or sarcasm. It is not uncommon in normal social interaction for people to say something that suggests a meaning that is exactly the opposite of what is intended. It is also generally accepted that the ability to detect irony or sarcasm is much more likely to be impaired in individuals with an ASD than in normal individuals. Indeed, this feature of behaviour in ASD individuals is central to the claim that ToM deficits characterise the disorder. Illustrative of this claim are the typical deficits shown on ToM tests by adults with ASD that include decoding of expressions of sarcasm or irony (e.g., Happé 1994; Jolliffe and Baron-Cohen 1999), as well as evidence from experimental studies showing that individuals who are socially inclined (based on the AQ social sub-scale score) discern the difference between ironic and literal expressions much more rapidly than those who are much less socially inclined (Spotorno and Noveck 2014).

Such interpretative deficits have the potential to affect significantly an individual's interaction with the criminal justice system.

For example:

> YB did not understood an offer of a threesome on Facebook was a joke, even though it was followed by 'LOL'. Given every comment YB posted ended with LOL, it is not clear he understood the appropriate use of this term. For example he would say, 'Shall we meet at 4 LOL?' and 'I'm going to the shops LOL.' YB failed to understand that joking on Facebook about threesomes did not constitute permission. A further example of his literalness can be found in the transcribed record of an interview. In that interview YB was asked if he smoked marijuana daily. He responded, 'Yeah, daily and night time.'

Bluff, Deception and White Lies

The performance of adults with ASD in ToM tests also illustrates that they may be vulnerable to misreading various other verbal behaviours or expressions in ways that may prejudice their interactions with the justice system. For example, it is not uncommon for people to use tactics involving bluff, deception or white lies in an effort to *manoeuvre* an interpersonal interaction in a particular direction. Again, the performance of samples with ASD in advanced ToM tests show that, on average, individuals with ASD are less likely to read the intention of such communications.

Moreover, as the following examples illustrate, the use of such tactics can easily become a part of the repertoire of police and lawyers attempting to steer an investigation in a particular direction.

For example:

> One young man was asked to show his downloads on a computer to a police officer. The police officer, looking at the computer, said, 'That one looks interesting, two 16-year-olds fuck a 14-year-old, what is that like?' The young man responded, 'I don't know, I haven't opened it yet, I can't get the passwords.'
>
> Later he was asked, 'What is in those files?' and he responded, 'Just photographs of children.' The police officer then asked, 'Do you have even younger children?' to which the young man replied, 'I think so', further incriminating himself by indicating his knowledge of the age of the children.

Or:

> When the police suggested to a suspect, 'If you just tell us you did it, we can all go home,' the suspect willingly acknowledged that he did it and was then surprised that he didn't get to go home.

Other Misinterpretations

Frequently, we see cases involving a person with ASD that start out in a relatively benign manner and would normally not have been expected to proceed to arrest or court action. However, the lack of ToM or social-communicative skills, which are so crucial if an individual is to negotiate a smooth passage through such situations, clearly contributed to an escalation of the situation, precipitating an arrest and perhaps other much more severe legal consequences than should have been otherwise expected. The following cases illustrate this progression.

> Despite being articulate, Daniel has always struggled to remember his address. While investigating a fire in a nearby rubbish bin, Daniel's awkward gait and pacing attracted the attention of the police. They approached Daniel, who would not look at them despite repeated requests from the officers to do so. The officer's notebook states the accused 'was acting in a suspicious manner and appeared agitated when approached'. Further, when asked his name and address, he could not recall his address. The police interpreted this as evasive and oppositional behaviour, instead of part of his disorder. He was arrested for failing to provide police with his address. He responded badly to being touched,

and abused the officer in the process. Both officers grabbed him and he hit one of the officers.

Or:

Police were called to a public library after a young man, who was approached by staff for speaking too loudly, became hostile towards staff he perceived were harassing him. He eventually left, only to be confronted by the police arriving to investigate. The situation escalated when his phone rang and the officer told him to let it go. He became very distressed. The phone continued to ring, causing the young man to become increasingly distressed and, although told to place his hands in the air, he reached into his jacket pocket for his phone. He was subsequently tackled to the ground. At interview the young man could not appreciate that the officers were concerned he may have been reaching for a weapon. He responded repetitively by stating, 'But I didn't have a weapon.'

Or:

Randall was being interviewed for the purpose of determining his knowledge of the wrongfulness of the crime at the time of the offence. Randall was asked if he knew that having sex with a minor was an offence. He said, 'Yes.' He offered no further explanation or qualification. He was then asked how he knew this, to which he replied, 'I read it on a pamphlet.' He was then asked, 'Where did you find that pamphlet?' and he said, 'In the legal services commission.' He was then asked if this was after the arrest and he said, 'Yes.' A person with insight, who was aware of the intent and implications of this questioning, might immediately inform the person posing the questions that they had just learned this and didn't know it at the time of the alleged offence.

Restricted Interests and Their Possible Consequences

As earlier chapters clearly indicated, social-cognitive deficits that reflect ToM limitations are not the only characteristics that are commonly observed in individuals with ASD. The other key feature that has been emphasised involves the presence of restricted repetitive behaviours, including stereotyped movements and speech, excessive adherence to routines, abnormally strong and restricted interests, and unusual reactivity to sensory stimuli within the environment.

It is conceivable that, under particular conditions, such behavioural characteristics may also sometimes affect the course that interactions with the criminal justice system take. Again, however, we are hamstrung by an absence of hard empirical data that are informative with respect to the impact of such behaviour on police, lawyers, judges and jurors. Thus, we are totally reliant on speculation and anecdotal case reports. Nevertheless, we believe that some brief speculative observations are warranted to sensitise readers to possible issues and to suggest potentially valuable lines of research enquiry. Simply hearing about the very nature and strength of some individual's restricted interests is likely to strike many observers as unusual in the extreme and may, therefore, contribute to negative stereotyping of the individual. To the extent that pursuit of the special interest overlaps with the person's interactions with criminal justice system professionals, it may well have a similar effect. For example, police officers, lawyers or jurors who have no appreciation of the degree of frustration likely to be associated with any interference in the pursuit of a special interest may be very surprised to hear a person charged with a serious assault say, 'I struck him because he interfered with me playing with my electric train set,' – and, in turn, may judge the person very harshly. More generally, most observers who have no detailed knowledge of the disorder would find it extremely hard to comprehend that the obsessive pursuit of any particular special interest could provide an acceptable explanation, let alone justification, for any criminal act that directly or indirectly resulted. Unfortunately, however, there are so many potential moderators of people's reactions (e.g., knowledge of the disorder and its characteristics, attitudinal states, the context in which the behaviours are encountered) that it is difficult for us to say anything more definitive than this.

Anecdotal reports also point to the possibility that the hyper- or hyposensitivity to sensory stimuli (e.g., lighting, noise, crowding, touch) commonly observed in individuals with ASD may sometimes prove problematic in the context of the justice system. Thus, it has been argued that being interviewed by police or lawyers within a hectic visual or auditory environment may prove quite unsettling for an individual with ASD (Maras and Bowler 2014). It is, of course, easy to imagine how a person's sensory sensitivities lead them to touch or smell objects or people excessively or inappropriately. But being touched by another may also sometimes trigger an extreme and totally unexpected reaction in an individual with ASD. For example, a police officer who places a reassuring hand on the shoulder of a person with an ASD may find herself the recipient of an aggressive physical response that simply reflects the individual's hypersensitivity to touch.

For example:

A teenage boy was distressed by a replacement social worker who attended his house for his weekly appointment. The boy was quite anxious as a result of this change and his behaviour appeared agitated. In an attempt to calm him, the social worker touched him on the shoulder. Frustrated, the boy reached for a can of fly spray and sprayed the social worker in the face. This led to the police being called and they too had problems containing the boy, who resisted their attempts to calm him. They too tried to touch the boy to restrain and cuff him. The outcome was the boy was arrested and charged with aggravated assault.

Or:

A young man who seeks tactile stimulation was arrested for touching a woman's tights. Although he was not sexually aroused by the feel of the material, he enjoyed the sensory stimulation the fabric provided.

Broad Implications

In this chapter we have highlighted a number of characteristics commonly observed in people with an ASD that may influence their interactions with the criminal justice system, whether these are in the role of a suspect, victim or witness. We need to re-emphasise two things. First, the characteristics we have highlighted will not be present in all individuals; nor, when present, will they be represented to the same degree or have the same impact. Second, while the evidence regarding the characteristics of the disorder is robust, to our knowledge there is generally very little empirical evidence supporting our broader hypotheses about the possible prejudicial effects of these behavioural characteristics. So, it is possible that, in some areas, our speculation has been stretching the bounds of credibility. Judgement on that will have to await the gathering of data from what will clearly need to be a very substantial and wide-ranging research exercise. Meanwhile, as we foreshadowed earlier in the chapter, we believe our speculation is useful both from the perspective of guiding such research efforts as well as alerting criminal justice system professionals to potentially important issues that can affect the administration of justice.

Although the available evidence may be flimsy and we have often been drawing a relatively long bow based on clinical inferences, we suggest that a lack of understanding of the behavioural features of ASD may have wide ramifications. Obviously, negative perceptions of suspects or victims may develop among police investigators, lawyers, and judges and jurors. Moreover, such perceptions may, in turn, shape decisions by police to seek further evidence, to consider alternative hypotheses about the crime and the culprit's identity, and so on. They may also influence a prosecuting lawyer's decision as to whether to proceed with a case and a defence lawyer's recommendations to their client about how to plead and present their arguments. Finally, they could exert a significant influence on how jurors and judges weight the evidence and assess the culpability of the defendant. It is hoped that future research will provide answers to these questions.

Testimonial Limitations Associated with ASD

Thus far, our focus in this chapter has been on characteristics often observed in association with ASD that may compromise the interactions that people with ASD have with criminal justice system professionals. In this last section we shift tack a little to consider some of the possible characteristics of the actual testimony – rather than the nonverbal and behavioural characteristics of the person providing the testimony – that individuals with ASD may provide when interacting with police and the legal fraternity as a witness, victim or suspect.

There is a body of research on the memory performance of individuals (although often with child samples) with an ASD that suggests the potential for problematic testimony because individuals with an ASD have been shown to display impairments in episodic memory and in the reporting of personally experienced events and are more susceptible to source monitoring errors (e.g., Farrant, Blades and Boucher 1998; Lind and Bowler 2008; Maras and Bowler 2014). Such deficits suggest the possibility of impaired recall of a crime event in which they had been involved, suggestibility and misinformation effects whereby they might unwittingly incorporate into their testimony information obtained from other sources, and difficulties in discriminating repeated events and the temporal order of events.

Thus far, research that directly explores eyewitness memory for people and events provides ground for some optimism about the reliability of the testimony of individuals with ASD, although there are two very important qualifiers. First, most of the studies have been conducted with high-functioning individuals (i.e., average IQs in the range 105–110). Second, the body of empirical work is still quite small so there exists little in the way of replication of findings or examinations of the generalisation of findings across stimuli or forensically relevant conditions. Although there is not yet any convincing evidence to indicate greater suggestibility among high-functioning adults, a number of studies reported by Maras and colleagues (for a review, see Maras and Bowler 2014) suggest that under free-recall conditions, adults with ASD may make more errors in reporting than non-ASD control. They may not differ from controls in terms of reporting details about the physical environment but, perhaps not surprisingly given their relative insensitivity to social cues, they may report fewer person and person-action details. However, the interviewing technique, the Cognitive Interview, which has been widely recommended for forensic interviewing and has substantial evidential backing (Fisher and Geiselman 1992; Powell, Fisher and Wright 2005), may not afford the same advantages for people with ASD as it does for other samples. The Cognitive Interview typically incorporates a (sometimes variable) suite of techniques designed to enhance memory reporting quantity and accuracy, and emphasises features such as rapport building, context reinstatement, varying the order and perspective of recall, and imagery-guided probing. This literature provides some suggestion that varying the order and perspective of recall may produce difficulties for individuals with ASD, while the efficacy of the context reinstatement component may also be questionable if it relies purely on mental (rather than physical) context reinstatement processes (cf. Maras and Bowler 2014).

The research discussed above represents a promisingly systematic approach to understanding the possible limitations in the testimony provided by adults with ASD. As we have already noted, however, the extent to which these findings are likely to hold up as replications and extensions emerge in the literature, and as more diverse samples are examined, is unknown. Again, the message that reverberates from this chapter is that there is a substantial number of significant research questions to be addressed, the answers to which may well have important ramifications for how interactions between criminal justice system professionals and individuals with an ASD need to be managed.

Chapter 8

ASSESSMENT AND INTERVENTION

Previous chapters highlighted a number of characteristics of ASD that may either contribute to an individual with ASD becoming naively enmeshed in criminal activity or may prejudice the outcomes of their interactions with the criminal justice system. Chapter 4 drew attention to a wide array of psychiatric and socio-environmental conditions that are sometimes comorbid with ASD and may constitute risk factors for criminal involvement. Establishing a direct association between these diverse social and cognitive deficits, comorbidities and criminal activities is of course extremely difficult, if not impossible. But, in any particular criminal case, a comprehensive assessment that incorporates a careful consideration of these various potential influences is likely to be suggestive of causal mechanisms and assist the police and the courts in understanding whether there may exist some impairment that might have affected the culprit's conduct, their understanding of the wrongfulness of their conduct or their ability to control their conduct. Depending on the particular legal jurisdiction, the presence of any such impairments may affect whether the courts judge a culprit as being mentally competent to have committed the offence or perhaps even the extent to which they might be considered culpable for their actions and their consequences. In the first section of this chapter we discuss what we believe should be the key considerations in the assessment process.

In subsequent sections of the chapter we focus on some crucial targets for intervention efforts. We consider the nature and focus of intervention programmes that might enhance the adaptive skills of individuals with ASD, which may be crucial in their recognising and avoiding criminal behaviour or influential in ensuring efficacious interactions with the criminal justice system.

We also discuss intervention programmes that can prepare criminal justice system professionals for dealing with adult suspects, defendants or witnesses who have an ASD in ways that ensure those interactions are not prejudicial to the outcomes of any investigation or court proceeding involving such individuals.

Assessment Issues

Within an adversarial justice system, it will almost certainly be the defence lawyer or perhaps the judge – rather than the police or prosecuting lawyer – who draws attention to the possible causal role of a psychological disorder in a defendant's criminal behaviour. Here, however, we ignore such distinctions and simply examine assessment issues and requirements from the perspective of what is required to best inform all sectors of the justice system regarding crime causation and culpability.

In some cases it may become apparent early in a police investigation that their suspect has a formal diagnosis of ASD. Likewise, this information may be known to a lawyer or judge from the outset of their interaction, although being aware of such a diagnosis and understanding the possible ramifications of the disorder for the individual's behaviour and its management is not the same thing. Sometimes, however, police, lawyers and judges may find themselves dealing with a suspect or defendant who has an undiagnosed ASD or whose diagnosis is not made known to them. Given these possibilities, a number of obvious questions are suggested. For example, how can the disorder be recognised? What kind of assessment is required to confirm a diagnosis? Are there other comorbid disorders present or socio-environmental influences that may help understand the individual's criminal behaviour? Are there assessments over and above those that are required to provide a diagnosis that are likely to be crucial for an understanding of causality and mental competence?

Recognition of ASD Symptomatology

There are a number of cues that might sensitise police, lawyers and judges to the possibility that a suspect, defendant or witness has an ASD. These have already been foreshadowed in earlier chapters in which we examined diagnostic criteria, ToM deficits, restricted interests and hyper- and hyposensitivity to sensory stimuli. We summarise these below, but with the following caveats. First, individuals with ASD may differ in terms of which of these characteristics they display, the context in which they are displayed and the extent to which they are apparent. Second, some of these characteristics may manifest in people with other disorders, or in people without any known disorder. In other words, these behaviours are cues to – though not guarantees of – the presence of the disorder, although the presence of a wider range of these behaviours or more frequent and severe forms of the behaviour would obviously represent stronger evidence of the disorder's likely presence.

Table 8.1 summarises some of the tell-tale signs or cues (many of which overlap to some degree), loosely grouped under the *DSM-5* diagnostic criteria with which they are probably most closely aligned (although some could readily fit under multiple criteria).

The presence of such symtomatology in a witness, victim, suspect or offender should cue criminal justice system professionals to the possible presence of ASD. As will become clear later in this chapter when we outline appropriate intervention strategies, ideally this should also trigger adaptive reactions to managing interactions with such individuals. But, in some cases where understanding the disorder is likely to provide important contextual information about the crime and the culprit, confirmation of a diagnosis of ASD will be important, especially when the individual concerned is a suspect or known to be the culprit. In the next section we outline the assessment process required to confirm a diagnosis.

Table 8.1 Behavioural Indicators of ASD Categorised According to DSM-5 Criteria

---

A1 and A3. Deficits in social-emotional reciprocity and developing and maintaining relationships:

- low interest in social interaction
- difficulty understanding intentions, motives, expectations and behaviour of others (e.g., inability to recognise bluff, irony, metaphor, sarcasm or other ambiguities in language)
- difficulty in initiating, maintaining or reciprocating in conversations
- communication characterised by pedantic language, excessive detail, use of scripts
- difficulty interacting in groups
- verbal bluntness or lack of tact
- apparent lack of empathy
- lack of social awareness, social vulnerability or naiveté
- faux pas
- difficulty seeing perspective of others
- difficulty recognising subtle social hints
- social anxiety.

A2. Deficits in nonverbal communicative behaviours used for social interaction:
violation of personal space of others (touching, standing too close, talking too loud)

- lack of appropriate eye contact (gaze aversion, staring)
- poor understanding of nonverbal behaviour of others that signals intentions, motives, expectations and behaviour (e.g., facial expressions, vocal intonation).

B1, B2 and B3. Stereotyped behaviours, adherence to routines and strong restricted interests:

- stereotyped or repetitive speech (e.g., echolalia or idiosyncratic phrases, unusual noises)
- stereotyped or repetitive movements (e.g., rocking, walking, finger movements)
- repetitive use of objects
- ritualised patterns of verbal behaviour (e.g., repetitive or pedantic questioning)
- ritualised patterns of nonverbal behaviour (e.g., lining up of objects, walking patterns)
- excessive adherence to routines or resistance to change (e.g., wearing same clothes, eating same food, travelling same route)
- restricted and intense special interests that may dominate their life, be the subject of monologues
- extreme distress at small changes to routine (e.g., clothing, arrangement of furniture, daily routines) or interference with special interests.

B4. Hyper-or hyposensitivity to sensory stimuli:

- fascination with lights or spinning objects
- preoccupation with smelling, touching or licking objects or people
- adverse reaction to specific sounds, textures, types of clothing, touch
- insensitive to pain, heat, cold.

Assessments Required to Confirm Diagnosis

A request from an individual's lawyer or a judge (or perhaps even the police) for the conduct of an assessment to confirm a diagnosis of ASD, or perhaps to investigate the possibility of some psychiatric disorder, signals the beginning of quite a complex process. How and when such an assessment process is initiated, what the assessment is likely to involve (e.g., screening for ASD or other comorbid conditions) and who is expected to conduct it (e.g., psychologist, psychiatrist) is likely to vary across jurisdictions, depending on historical factors, local legislative requirements regarding competency and so on. While acknowledging these considerations, our focus is on detailing what we believe should be the key elements of such assessments.

First, the provision of a diagnosis of ASD demands that the assessment be conducted by a trained professional who is familiar with ASD. Second, even though the clinician's mandate may be to screen for ASD, there is a body of background information that would be of interest in any clinical interview in order to better understand possible contextual influences on the individual's development. Although these influences do not speak in any direct way to issues of causation or mental competence, they may be particularly informative in terms of resolving issues such as the most appropriate disposition of a case and sentencing. This potentially relevant background information would span variables such as:

> family history: parenting, home life and socio-economic status; exposure to domestic or other violence, criminality and drug use; experiences of bullying, physical or psychological trauma; extent of social support

> educational and employment history: achievement history as well as experiences of bullying and other psychological trauma

> personal characteristics: medication, alcohol and drug use; membership of a minority or disability group leading to bullying or ostracism; history of aggression towards people or animals.

Although the routine appraisal of these more general background factors is important, the provision of a diagnosis of ASD is far from routine and involves a number of essential requirements. A minimum of one adult diagnostic test should be administered. *The Autism Diagnostic Observation Schedule* (second edition, *ADOS-2; Lord et al.* 2012b) – a semi-structured assessment of communication, social interaction and play – is the preferred assessment instrument. It is appropriate for children and adults of differing developmental and language levels. There are several alternative (or complementary) instruments for assessing adults. One is the *Ritvo Autism Asperger Diagnostic Scale-Revised* (*RAADS-R*; Ritvo *et al.* 2011), a diagnostic instrument developed specifically for adults, which examines developmental pathology in language, sensory-motor and social relatedness. Useful complementary screening (but not diagnostic) devices are the *AQ* (Baron-Cohen *et al.* 2001b), developed specifically for adults and the *SCQ* (Rutter *et al.* 2003) for children and adults. The administration of this assessment occurs in the context of a clinical interview, ideally incorporating the *ADI-Revised* (Rutter, Le Couteur and Lord 2003). This comprehensive process needs to ensure that ASD diagnostic criteria (cf. *DSM-5* or *ICD-10*) are met, including establishing that the symptoms were present in childhood.

Of course, this diagnostic process will not necessarily provide a comprehensive picture of the individual who is the focus of the assessment, nor of the potential contributing factors to a crime. Some of the gaps may be filled by investigating comorbid psychiatric disorders and socio-environmental variables that may help understanding of the individual's criminal behaviour.

Assessments for Comorbid Disorders

In Chapter 4 we provided an overview of psychiatric disorders that may be comorbid with ASD and also examined evidence for their possible links to criminality. Three broad conclusions emerged from that examination. First, the range of comorbid disorders is wide, although it is difficult to establish their prevalence with ASD with any precision. Second, some of these disorders appear to be clear risk factors for criminal behaviour, although again it is difficult to be precise regarding the extent of their influence (either in terms of number of cases or within any particular case). Third, the risk may become more pronounced, and significant, when the comorbid disorders co-exist with other conditions or particular situational variables (e.g., mood disorders such as mania coupled with a serious drug problem).

Chapter 4 highlighted some psychiatric conditions that clearly (a) are sometimes likely to be comorbid with ASD and (b) provide an extremely plausible and alternative explanatory mechanism for some instances of criminal behaviour observed in individuals with ASD and inappropriately attributed to the ASD. Thus, it is crucial that any formal assessment process screens for and identifies such comorbid conditions if we are to isolate those cases where characteristics associated with ASD have been pivotal in terms of crime causation.

As for an assessment for ASD, the first requirement of this screening is that it should involve an experienced and trained professional (psychiatrist or psychologist) with an intimate knowledge of the *DSM* and a capacity to make the sometimes subtle discriminations between disorders with overlapping symptomatology (cf. Chapter 4). Making these discriminations can be extremely challenging and has sometimes stimulated the development of new assessment instruments: for example, the Autism Spectrum Disorders Comorbidity for Adults (*ASD-CA*) was developed by LoVullo and Matson (2009) in response to the difficulty associated with identifying comorbidity in individuals with both an ASD and intellectual disability. Professionals have a number of tools available to supplement their clinical judgement. For example, apart from commonly used self-report measures for conditions such as anxiety and depression (e.g., *DASS*), there are semi-structured interviews (e.g., *SCID-I*, First *et al.* 2002; *SCID-II*, First *et al. 1997*) for making the major diagnoses that we highlighted in Chapter 4 as potential risk factors for criminal behaviour. As we foreshadowed in Chapter 1 when reviewing various high-profile criminal cases in which the presence of ASD was implicated, we suspect that a systematic application of appropriate assessment techniques will, in some cases, highlight the presence of a comorbid condition that may provide a much better explanation for an individual's criminal behaviour than attributing the behaviour to the presence of ASD.

Finally – and this may seem so obvious as to not warrant further elaboration – the likelihood that an individual with ASD has a comorbid intellectual disability is high. Apart from any impact this may have had on the individual's involvement in crime, it clearly has implications for their ability to understand and respond appropriately to trial processes and, therefore, raises the issue of the individual's competence to stand trial. Thus, the importance of screening individuals with an ASD for a comorbid intellectual disability is crucial.

Additional Assessments for Understanding Causation and Culpability

It will be clear from the position we have taken in preceding chapters about crime causation that, for many crimes involving an individual with ASD, the types of assessments described thus far will not be sufficient to pinpoint the contributions of ASD to crime causation and criminal culpability. Here we argue there is a need for psychological assessments that go beyond those required to provide a diagnosis of ASD and that they are crucial for achieving an understanding of causality and mental competence.

In the concluding section of Chapter 6 we observed that:

> none of the crimes reported in the case studies appeared to be premeditated or committed with malice

> in most cases the culprit appeared neither to foresee nor appreciate the negative consequences of their actions

> the culprit appeared to have some kind of ToM deficit

> the culprit's behaviour was often associated with pursuit of a very strong interest or fixation or sometimes with a particular sensitivity to some sensory stimuli

> there was an unfortunate or unpropitious set of prevailing environmental conditions, in the absence of which (viz. with better luck) the crime would probably not have occurred.

In other words, understanding the precise nature and severity of any ToM deficit and the intensity or controlling influence of any special interest or obsession is, for some crimes, likely to be crucial for determining both causation and culpability. The following sections focus, respectively, on the assessment of ToM and restricted and repetitive interests.

Assessment of ToM

In Chapter 5 we argued that some individuals may have ToM deficits that are wide ranging, whereas others' deficits may be more specific, undermining their ability to read facial expressions or gestures or decode particular types of verbal expressions such as sarcasm, metaphor and so on. Moreover, the severity of these deficits, whether they are specific or general, is likely to vary considerably. This is perhaps particularly likely to be the case in adults, although we don't have detailed normative data to confirm this suggestion. As we saw in Chapter 5, there are tests that appear to tap various aspects of ToM (e.g., *Strange Stories*) and others probing more specific limitations such as interpreting facial expressions (e.g., *Reading the Mind in the Eyes Test*) or recognising faux pas. But major question marks surround the use of such instruments for the forensic purposes we are considering here.

Consider some of the key criteria that we would like such assessment instruments to meet. First, they obviously have to be designed to assess advanced or upper-level ToM in adults. In other words, there needs to be empirical evidence that, at a minimum, the instruments discriminate adults with ASD from non-ASD samples. This minimal criterion is met by a number of instruments (e.g., the *Strange Stories* test, Jolliffe and Baron-Cohen 1999; *The Awkward Moments Test*, Heavey *et al.* 2000; *The Movie for the Assessment of Social Cognition* (*MASC*), Dziobek *et al.* 2006; *The Reading the Mind in Films* (*RMF*) task, Golan *et al.* 2006).

Second, the tests need to ensure that they don't allow the test-taker to hack out a strategy and response to test items, something that may be possible using pencil-and-paper tests. In other words, the tests need to limit the time available to apply analytic reasoning skills, thereby simulating the real-life situation in which people are required to make fast decisions based on ambiguous social cues and subtle social information. Again, there are various instruments available that have taken this tack, requiring the test-taker to react to acted-out social interactions between individuals. *The Awkward Moments Test*, the *MASC* and the *RMF* task – mentioned above – and *The Awareness of Social Inference Test* (*TASIT-R*, McDonald, Flanagan and Rollins 2011) provide several examples of there. One challenge with these is to ensure that performance is not dictated by other higher-order cognitive skills (e.g., information retention, executive function and central coherence).

Third, reliable normative data are required if the test is to be used for clinical decision making, as distinct from research purposes. This means, of course, the recruitment of sizable standardisation samples which will provide data that not only speak to the meaning of the overall or global test scores but also permit the detailed breakdown of performance on the various items and ToM sub-domains tapped by such tests. As we have argued thus far, it is quite possible that the involvement of an individual with ASD in a crime may have been linked to a significant deficit in some particular area of ToM that is unlikely to be pinpointed reliably by a test that samples each of an array of behaviours with a very limited subset of items and normative database. Of course, the existence of reliable normative data also involves an expectation that scores on the instrument are not only internally consistent but also stable both within the individual test-taker and across observers, requirements that also involve a significant effort in data collection. All of these requirements are, not surprisingly, extremely difficult to meet given the difficulty of recruiting large samples of individuals from what is a quite exclusive population.

Fourth, if the instrument is to be used as a basis for any forensic (or other kind of) decision making, it is absolutely crucial that there exist comprehensive validity data. For most instruments, concurrent validity data, usually in the form of a modest correlation with one of the mainstream measures of ToM, can be found in the scientific literature, thereby suggesting that the measures are tapping something in common. There also exists some kind of evidence of discriminant validity for some instruments. For example, despite equivalent performance on the physical items among ASD and non-ASD matched participants, the *Strange Stories* test discriminates these groups using the social sub-scale (Happé 1994). Similarly, other scales have reported discrimination between ASD and non-ASD samples on items tapping ToM items but not on those tapping memory.

It is in this area, however, that existing tests fall short in terms of their suitability for the type of forensic assessment process under consideration here. First, evidence that the scales predict performance on relevant criterion-related indices of adults' social-cognitive functioning in everyday living contexts is missing. In other words, while the measures may have high face validity, we are generally lacking evidence that any ToM deficits that manifest on the tests are predictive of ineffective adaptations or responses to the social challenges that may confront the individual in their day-to-day life.

Second, the validity data for the various scales do not speak to the potential utility of the instrument as a predictor within the type of forensic contexts we have been discussing. For example, there is no independent evidence that performance on these measures – regardless of whether it is overall test performance or performance on specific items or sub-scales – is likely to indicate or predict (a) the possibility that an individual may naively or unwittingly become involved in criminal activity, (b) an apparent complete lack of understanding of the possible adverse physical and emotional consequences that criminal behaviour may have for the victim(s) of the crime, or (c) unusual and prejudicial responses to questioning from the police or in the courtroom. In sum, there simply are not the requisite data available to demonstrate that a general ToM deficit of a certain order of magnitude is sufficient to explain how an individual became involved in a particular crime. Nor are their adequate data to show whether some very specific significant ToM weakness is severe enough to explain the criminal behaviour of an individual in a particular situation or the problematic behaviour of the individual during police interrogation. Put simply, existing ToM tests have neither been designed nor evaluated for forensic applications. Moreover, we don't have any systematic body of evidence that is informative about the likelihood that an individual with ASD is able to recognise or foresee the possibility that particular courses of behaviour on the part of themselves or others may culminate in a criminal outcome, arouse the ire of police or attract negative evaluations from judges and jurors. Thus, when evaluating the possibility that an individual's criminal behaviour and presentation in the legal system might reflect some unique social-cognitive characteristic(s) of ASD, we really remain largely dependent on clinical judgement or inference.

And furthermore, intrinsic to poor ToM is one's inability to determine the nature of a relationship with another individual. For example, should another person be considered as friend or foe? Poor ToM and, hence, a limited ability to detect and interpret subtle verbal and nonverbal cues will make it difficult for a person with ASD to determine if the actions of another person are genuine or dodgy and, if the latter, to recognise that they are possibly being exploited. Further, the desire for friendship on the part of the individual with ASD may reduce their ability to perceive possible exploitation. There are, however, no tools to identify one's ability to detect dodgy behaviour. It may be that the construct is strongly correlated with ToM and adequate measures of ToM will encapsulate the perception of dodginess. Furthermore, it may be that ToM is a sufficient predictor of vulnerability to exploitation in crime. Alternatively, we may need purpose-built tools to probe more specific skills related to one's ability to detect dodgy behaviour or that problematic situations are arising.

Clearly, a major challenge for future research will be the development of ToM measurement instruments designed for use with adults, based on sufficiently large samples to provide robust normative data and evaluated systematically in terms of their capacity to discriminate test-takers' ability to discern likely criminal versus non-criminal outcomes of particular sequences of behaviour. We are hopeful that some of our current endeavours that are pursuing these broad objectives will be among those to yield fruit in the ensuing years.

Assessment of Restricted and Repetitive Interests
The assessment of restricted interests is also beset with problems, at least from the forensic perspective of interest here. Restricted interests are specified by the diagnostic criteria of the *DSM-5* and, from a purely clinical-descriptive perspective, are probably quite easy to classify. But formal assessment of their severity, impact on general adaptive functioning and possible causal role in the forensic context is not so straightforward.

Some of the major difficulties were summarised in Chapter 5. First, there is no uniform measurement protocol. Second, the trajectory of such behaviours into and during adulthood is poorly understood. Third, and most importantly given our focus here, our understanding of precisely how such behaviours affect day-to-day functioning is poor. We know that the *DSM-5* criteria categorise severity of these behaviours in terms of their interference with daily functioning, the distress caused when they are interrupted and the difficulty of directing behaviour away from these interests. But, as we noted in earlier chapters, these classifications are highly subjective and the inter-observer reliability of such categorisations remains unknown.

Although the possible assessment methods are diverse, potentially encompassing verbal reports (e.g., self-reports, parent reports), questionnaires such as the *RBS-R* developed by Bodfish *et al.* (2000) or the *Cambridge University Obsession Questionnaire* (Baron-Cohen and Wheelwright 1999), or behavioural observation, what is missing are the key reference points provided by a normative database. We lack objective guidelines for determining the intensity of the restricted interest and the extent to which it might *control* the individual's behaviour, the likelihood of being able to redirect the individual away from the activity or the strength of any resulting distress from disruption to the activity. In the forensic context these are pivotal considerations. In earlier chapters we presented case studies that highlighted the possible contribution of such factors to criminal involvement. But while the case study evidence appears persuasive, in the absence of any assessment procedure that allows the behaviour to be benchmarked against normative data, it is extremely difficult to make a watertight argument that a blinkered pursuit of the restricted interest or the angst caused by its disruption – that is, specific diagnostic characteristics of ASD – might have made important contributions to crime causation. In turn, we are denied valuable insights into the possibility that an individual offender's culpability was shaped by inherent features of their disorder.

In the preceding section we pointed to the extensive research effort required to deliver adult ToM measures and normative data that could be deployed in forensic assessments. A similar type and scale of research exercise is necessary in relation to measures of restricted and repetitive interests. First, for example, the requisite normative data must capture the frequency and extent of adults' involvement in the special interest(s), the difficulty of redirecting behaviour away from the interest, the degree of distress caused by interruptions to the interest and any behavioural consequences that flow from that. Second, in the absence of any existing tools that can clearly link these behaviours to criminal vulnerability, criterion-related validity data are required that permit inferences to be drawn about the likely parallels between behavioural characteristics identified by the test(s) and those evidenced in the lead-up to and during the crime.

Final Comment on Issues of Mental Competence
The issues in the preceding discussion related to the determination of possible roles of ToM deficits and restricted interests in crime causation are relevant, of course, to determinations of issues such as whether an offender is judged *mentally competent* to have committed an offence. For example, an individual with a severe deficit in ToM that rendered them unable to appreciate the wrongfulness of their criminal conduct, or one whose pursuit of a restricted interest appeared to be beyond conscious control, might arguably be considered as not competent to have committed a particular offence.

These are complex legal issues, which we (i.e., the authors) clearly do not have the expertise to address. Moreover, the law on such matters doubtless varies across jurisdictions, making it difficult to provide universally relevant comment. Nevertheless, we believe that several general – although perhaps obvious – comments are warranted. Purely to anchor these comments, we use as a guide the relevant law in our own legal jurisdiction. The South Australian Criminal Law Consolidation Act 1935 (Division 2, Section 269C) indicates:

> A person is mentally incompetent to commit an offence if, at the time of the conduct alleged to give rise to the offence, the person is suffering from a mental impairment and, in consequence of the mental impairment –
>
> › does not know the nature and quality of the conduct; or
>
> › does not know that the conduct is wrong; or
>
> › is unable to control the conduct.

Within this particular jurisdiction, therefore, it seems possible that an individual with ASD, shown to have a significant ToM deficit or an all-consuming restricted interest, such as those we have described in earlier chapters, might meet one or more of the above criteria for being judged mentally incompetent to commit the offence. But, with the assessment devices currently at our disposal, such a determination would rest entirely on clinical judgement and be unsupported by any objective evidence from a rigorous psychological assessment of these characteristics.

Intervention for Adults with ASD

The major focus of this section is the consideration of approaches to intervention, and the efficacy thereof, that:

> › target the development of social-cognitive skills that should increase the capacity of individuals with ASD to recognise and avoid criminal behaviour, as well as enhancing the likelihood that their interactions with criminal justice system professionals proceed in a manner that does not negatively influence the outcomes

> permit the management of restricted and repetitive interests so that they don't consume the individual in ways that may potentially blind them to potential criminal consequences of their actions

> reduce sensory hypersensitivities that may under particular stimulus conditions contribute to problematic reactive behaviour.

ToM Deficits

Previous chapters have emphasised how significant deficits in ToM – whether they be deficits of a pervasive nature or in some specific aspect of ToM – may increase an individual's vulnerability to becoming involved in criminal behaviour. From an intervention perspective, numerous important but as yet unresolved issues are raised by this observation. Knowing exactly what should be trained to produce sustained and flexible improvements in ToM would be invaluable. For example, is it possible to design training that produces a meaningful reduction in the degree of deficit and its impact? Knowing what form that training should take would also be invaluable, as would knowing whether training needs to target specific dimensions of ToM or could perhaps be designed to effect a generalised improvement in ToM. We also need answers to questions such as whether any improvement in specific areas of ToM will depend on producing a general ToM improvement, whether any gains produced by training will be maintained for any meaningful period following training and whether any beneficial effects seen in response to training can be detected in the broader social-communicative behaviour of the individual – that is, can any evidence of transfer or generalisation be produced? There are also fundamental considerations related to when training should occur. At present we do not know, for example, if training is effective regardless of whether it occurs in childhood, adolescence or adulthood. Nor do we know whether training in childhood or adolescence provides an important platform that facilitates subsequent adaptive development of ToM. Unfortunately, given our present state of knowledge, many, if not all, of these issues and questions are either unresolved or the answers come with significant qualifications attached.

We distinguish here between two very broad (and not completely independent) classes of studies. In one, the focus of the intervention is on the development of deficient social skills, which often includes some components that address specific ToM deficits. In the other, the focus of the interventions is explicitly on ToM deficits.

Social Skills Interventions

Given that deficits in social communication and interaction are the hallmark of ASD, and have wide-ranging implications for various aspects of day-to-day living, it is not at all surprising that intervention efforts have targeted social skill development. Indeed, the proliferation of intervention programmes within the community is likely to be widespread, although systematic evaluations of such programmes are much less prevalent.

Children are more likely to have been the targets of programmes reported in published evaluations, although programme outcomes with adolescents have been reported. Very few participants in any intervention studies were older than 20 years (Edwards *et al.* 2012). The skills targeted in such programmes vary and are likely to depend on the developmental status of the sample, but may span smiling and eye contact, basic conversational skills (e.g., asking and answering questions), interpreting non-literal language, locating and maintaining friends, appropriate verbal behaviour and use of electronic communication, recognising emotions, use of humour, dealing with teasing or conflict and so on. The intervention may be implemented daily over many weeks, may involve individualised or group instruction and typically will incorporate instructional elements such as didactic teaching and Socratic questioning (i.e., challenging the individual's current thinking), modelling of behaviours, structured practice and role play, feedback and homework accompanied by parent or caregiver instruction. Many and varied outcome measures are reported, ranging from measures of parent or client satisfaction with the programme, parent and teacher checklists or rating scales such as the *Social Skills Rating System* (Gresham and Elliott 1990) and observational data. Sometimes, performance on at least some of the outcome measures is re-examined for skill maintenance subsequent to programme completion. Study designs also vary, spanning single-case (e.g., multiple baseline) designs with very small sample sizes through to randomised control trials (but with the control condition often only comprising a wait-list control).

Given the enormous variability in the makeup of samples, the focus of the intervention programme, the study design and the duration and method of intervention – together with the usually quite small sample sizes, even in designs involving group contrasts – it is completely unsurprising that findings, and hence conclusions regarding the efficacy of these programmes, are mixed. Interpretation of programme efficacy is also hindered by factors such as the lack of any uniformly applied outcome measures (which is a major problem), non-blinded programme evaluators and long-term follow-up assessments (cf. Magiati, Tay and Howlin 2012; Rao, Beidel and Murray 2008; White, Keonig and Scahill 2007). In very broad terms, what we can say is that there is evidence of the efficacy of social skills training programmes with children (e.g., Lopata *et al.* 2010; Thomeer *et al.* 2012; White *et al.* 2007), adolescents (e.g., Laugeson *et al.* 2009) and young adults (e.g., Gantman *et al.* 2012). There is also limited evidence that treatment gains may persist for several months post-intervention (e.g., Thomeer *et al.* 2012), although measures taken at longer term follow-up are more likely to be parent satisfaction assessments than objective performance measures. Follow-up studies into adulthood have not been documented (e.g., Magiati *et al.* 2012) and it is extremely difficult to support a claim that durable and meaningful social skills transfer will be detected beyond the training environment (cf. White *et al.* 2007).

In sum, it is unfortunate that we cannot be certain about exactly which social behaviours or skills are likely to be most responsive to intervention, at what age(s) responsiveness is likely to be greatest, how long any training effects will last and how much generalisation of trained skills across different contexts is likely to occur. In other words, we are left with the conclusion that we are unable to answer many of the questions that we raised at the outset of this section. In particular, we are able to say very little about how to go about ensuring that adults are able to take into their day-to-day interactions a repertoire of social skills that will allow them to function adaptively.

ToM Interventions

Some of the social skill interventions documented in the research literature clearly focus on deficits that we associate with, or recognise as, ToM deficits. For example, amongst the repertoire of social skills targeted may be the recognition of facial emotional expressions, vocal intonations and so on. Nevertheless, while acknowledging the sometimes apparently arbitrary distinction between some social skills and some aspects or dimensions of ToM, this section focuses specifically on interventions designed to improve ToM. In other words, the concern is with interventions designed to improve the individual's capacity to recognise and anticipate the thoughts, intentions and emotions of others – and to appreciate the impact of their own behaviour on how others will react.

If we reflect for a moment about what this means, however, we will begin to appreciate the complexity of this task. As we illustrated in Chapter 5, the operationalisation of ToM from both the conceptual and measurement perspectives has varied, particularly when considered in the context of different developmental levels. There is neither a particularly well-formulated account of precisely what ToM is, especially in the adult context, nor (despite the plethora of measures) is there a generally accepted measure of ToM that spans developmental levels. In other words, there are no detailed reference points for the development of a comprehensive intervention programme, let alone precise outcome goals. Consequently, if we set out to try to improve ToM in an individual with an ASD, it soon becomes clear that there are again many unresolved issues with respect to the focus of the intervention. We do not know whether it might be better to try to achieve some broad or pervasive improvement that spans all aspects of what is generally considered to be encompassed by the term ToM or to effect improvement in some specific areas or dimensions of ToM that appear to be in deficit. In other words, at present it is unclear whether the intervention should target some overarching social-cognitive capacity or focus on sub-areas of functioning that might, for example, be reflected in performance on a false belief task, the *Strange Stories* test or perhaps *The Reading the Mind in the Eyes Test*. It is also unclear as to how either approach should differ depending on the developmental level of the individual. Finally, assuming that efficacious interventions may exist or can be developed, significant questions remain as to what exactly has to be targeted at early developmental levels – and when – to ensure the attainment of sophisticated social-cognitive skills when a person reaches adulthood.

We have a perspective on such questions but we emphasise that we offer it with the qualification that we have no supporting empirical evidence. Given the rather imprecise operationalisation of ToM, we find it difficult to believe that a comprehensive broad ToM intervention package could be developed that would produce improvement across the diverse array of areas of social-cognitive functioning that are considered to reflect intact (or deficient) ToM. We suspect that the most appropriate strategy might be to target specific aspects of ToM that appear lagging relative to developmental level. This, of course, would require a systematic analysis of normative ToM capabilities across developmental levels and the development of associated intervention programmes that span the sorts of expressive and receptive nonverbal and verbal aspects of ToM functioning discussed in earlier chapters. Moreover, consideration has to be given to three significant issues associated with programme implementation. First, we need to establish what constitutes sufficient intervention or training. It is often not clear from reports of intervention studies whether the duration and intensity of the programme has been determined by the individual participants' attainment of performance criteria or by practical exigencies associated with the programme's delivery. Second, we must determine what is required to ensure maintenance of any programme benefits. Clearly, this involves some guesswork and trial and error but it also requires careful planning for examinations of maintenance over extended timeframes. And third, we must identify how transfer of training can best be ensured. In other words, what has to be done to ensure performance gains extend to new and different contexts? Consideration of how training should be enacted to realise these objectives is beyond the scope of this book, but guidance would be provided by the extensive scientific literatures on instruction and training. Suffice it to say that these represent mammoth challenges for future researchers.

Let us examine what has happened in the field thus far with respect to ToM interventions. Some of the published studies have focused on putative precursors of ToM, some of which were of course encompassed in social skills programmes that we discussed in the previous section. These precursors include, for example, recognition of nonverbal, vocal and verbal emotion expressions, joint attention and imitation. As was noted in the previous section on social skills, studies vary considerably in methodology, the adequacy of control conditions and outcome measures. Nevertheless, several broad generalisations regarding programme efficacy can be offered. Perhaps the most attention has been devoted to training the recognition of emotions, typically relying on recognition of different affect in facial expressions or voice intonation. Although positive effects have been demonstrated at the group level (e.g., Golan and Baron-Cohen 2006; Young and Posselt 2012), convincing evidence for transfer beyond the training context to different faces or voices or to holistic judgements of emotion based on the behaviour of people in a life-like context is not available (e.g., Fletcher-Watson *et al.* 2014; Golan and Baron-Cohen 2006). Whether transfer would be more likely to occur with extended or more intensive training, or perhaps in response to training embedded in more realistic or life-like contexts, has not been resolved by research reported to date.

A small number of studies have developed interventions specifically designed to train ToM and have evaluated outcomes with ToM measures (e.g., Begeer *et al.* 2011; Fisher and Happé 2005; Hadwin *et al.* 1997; Paynter and Peterson 2013). The samples were relatively small and comprised entirely children or adolescents. The training programmes' tasks varied, including thought-bubble (or thought-picture) training to depict beliefs, perspective taking regarding the thoughts and feelings others, understanding humour and so on. The findings across studies converge, with meaningful gains detected on ToM outcome measures that were essentially those behaviours targeted in the programme, gains that were sometimes maintained for at least several weeks or months post-intervention. However, none of these studies reported positive effects of the interventions on broader ToM understanding, which would have positive implications for day-to-day-functioning, or on independent evaluations of social performance in daily life. Nor have any of these studies examined the impact of interventions with adult samples, established long-term positive effects or, importantly, provided evidence that the intervention facilitated subsequent developmental progress in ToM acquisition (cf. Fletcher-Watson *et al.* 2014).

We should note that there are various other published reports of intervention studies targeting the social-cognitive deficits that characterise individuals with an ASD. Although the effects reported in some of these appear to offer promise, it is difficult to assess their merits because, at this stage, no control condition data have been reported. For example, Bauminger (2007) reported promising findings from a study in which children received what was referred to as cognitive-behavioural-ecological social skills training; and, Eack *et al.* (2013) had encouraging findings with adults who received a cognitive rehabilitation intervention called Cognitive Enhancement Therapy. A notable feature of both programmes is that they appear to be somewhat longer and more intensive than other programmes so, in the absence of appropriate control conditions, conclusions regarding the efficacy of these programmes or the mechanisms underlying any positive effects are premature.

Overall, however, the picture that has emerged from more carefully controlled studies of ToM intervention attempts is very similar to that provided by the social skill intervention studies discussed in the previous section. Again we find ourselves unable to provide concrete suggestions about how to improve ToM in ways that will ensure ongoing developmental progress in ToM acquisition and culminate in adaptive social-cognitive functioning in adulthood. Nor are we able to point to the likely effectiveness of interventions directed at adults with either broad or specific ToM deficits. In Chapter 9 we offer some of our own suggestions about how significant progress towards answering such questions might be achieved.

In this and earlier chapters we have also highlighted how the restricted and repetitive interests and sensory hypersensitivities that characterise ASD may interact with ToM deficits to heighten criminal vulnerability. We discuss issues associated with the management of these behaviours in the following sections.

Restricted and Repetitive Interests

The case examples we have reviewed in earlier chapters suggest that the key elements of these behaviours that are potentially problematic from the perspective of contributing to criminal behaviour are excessive adherence to routines, resistance to change and the pursuit of restricted and intense interests. We know that these behaviours often appear to be all-consuming and the diagnostic criteria for ASD point to the potential for any disruption to these activities to produce high levels of duress.

And we have argued in Chapter 5 that, under particular environmental conditions, the relentless pursuit of such activities, or perhaps the intense frustration or even aggression caused by any disruption, may contribute to committing a criminal act. More generally, there has been interest in the design and efficacy of interventions targeting such behaviours, not because of their possible relevance to crime causation but rather because of the widespread belief that their persistence and dominance so limit the individual's socio-environmental interactions that they not only impose major constraints on adaptive social learning and development but they can also undermine family dynamics. Our consideration of such interventions in this book is less detailed than our discussion of ToM interventions because the development and implementation of intervention programmes to assist in the management of problem behaviours, including stereotyped and repetitive behaviours, is a major focus within mainstream clinical psychology; further comprehensive and expert coverage of that extensive literature is widely available (e.g., Rapp and Vollmer 2005a, 2005b).

Moreover, not surprisingly given the prevalence of such behaviours in individuals with ASD (and some other disabilities), programmatic research on interventions for such behaviour problems has also extended to consideration of ASD samples, as reflected in Boyd, McDonough and Bodfish's (2012) recent and wide-ranging review. Given our focus, three major themes to emerge from that review deserve emphasis. First, as is the case throughout the ASD literature, much of the empirical work addresses problem behaviours in child (not adult) samples and in samples with comorbid intellectual disabilities. Moreover, the cases reported have been referred or assigned for treatment and, accordingly, the degree to which they are representative in terms of factors such as the intensity or dominance of the behaviour or interest is unknown. Second, Boyd *et al.* (2012) note the more systematic focus on what are referred to as lower order repetitive behaviours – that is, repetitive or stereotypic behaviours (e.g., self-injurious behaviours) that often demand urgent attention – than on higher order repetitive behaviours. The latter include the intense circumscribed interests or obsessions and the adherence to routines or sameness that we have already discussed at length. Interestingly, it is this latter category of behaviours that some data suggest may – in high-functioning individuals at least – be more likely to persist into adulthood than, for example, some of the stereotyped behaviours (Chowdhury, Benson and Hillier 2010). One inevitable consequence of the combination of the two patterns just described is that the specific behavioural characteristics that have been implicated in crime causation have been relatively ignored in considerations of behaviour management and intervention. Third, evidence for intervention efficacy with ASD samples parallels that observed with other samples and problem behaviours. For example, depending on whether a functional analysis of the problem behaviour permits the identification of potentially useful reinforcers, either antecedent (e.g., discriminative stimuli, calming activities, exercise, enriched environmental conditions) or consequence based (e.g., differential reinforcement of low rates of behaviour or of variability in behaviour), behavioural interventions have proven effective.

Despite the demonstrated promise of behaviourally based intervention programmes for repetitive behaviours, there are other obvious and major unresolved issues. One overarching issue, that was also raised in the Boyd *et al.* (2012) review and parallels one of the major questions we posed regarding ToM training, relates to whether it is possible to do anything that reduces the degree of behavioural inflexibility that characterises the disorder and presumably underpins the restricted and repetitive interests. Although we have great difficulty trying to operationalise what *behavioural flexibility* training might look like, a question that might be more easily answered is whether, for example, systematic intervention programmes targeting restricted and repetitive interests at earlier developmental levels would pave the way for the individuals to develop, over time, a wider array of social and adaptive behaviours. Yet, there are many complexities associated with answering such questions. By trying to reduce an individual's preoccupation with some special interest or activity, might we be undermining activities that provide the individual with a buffer against stressors or anxiety that arise from their daily interactions or offer some important self-validation? And if so, just how much intervention is appropriate? Moreover, the diagnostic criteria advise that interruptions to such activities may produce duress – but they fail to identify exactly how much, for how long or the consequences of any resultant duress. Issues such as these have been discussed in the literature (e.g., Klin *et al.* 2007;

Mercier, Mottron and Belleville 2000; Spiker *et al.* 2012) but, at present, we do not have any satisfactory resolution. In sum, we find ourselves drawing conclusions that are as indecisive as those outlined regarding interventions for ToM deficits.

Sensory Hyper- and Hyposensitivity

Case studies presented in Chapters 5 and 6 suggest that unusual and inappropriate responses to sensory stimuli may sometimes contribute to involvement in criminal activity. Despite the fact that the frequency with which these difficulties lead to crime is likely to be low, the significant and overwhelming impact that sensory issues can have on persons with ASD suggests intervention is required to minimise the distress caused and increase one's socio-environmental opportunities. Crime prevention may be an occasional bonus.

Although substantial numbers of children with ASD receive sensory interventions (Green *et al.* 2006), there is a paucity of research to support the efficacy of the treatments offered. Perhaps this reflects some negativity on the part of practitioners in this area towards implementing evidence-based practice. Dominant forms of treatment have included a combination of directly targeting or challenging the client's senses, often involving sensory integration therapy or sensory-based intervention (cf. Ayres 1979). Strategies for the sensory interventions delivered by occupational therapists typically involve the use of weighted vests, brushing, swinging, being squeezed and other activities (Lang *et al.* 2012). Although sensory integration therapy and sensory-based intervention are the most common interventions, the difference between them is murky, with both involving the use of sensory strategies to influence a child's state of arousal, although the former appears more clinic based and interactive. The published literature indicates problems with the fidelity of interventions (cf. Parham *et al.* 2007), with a variety of practices targeting different sensory modalities (e.g., vestibular, somatosensory and auditory). The target behaviours vary considerably and, if successfully remedied, would make a very impressive list. Behaviours targeted include stereotypical behaviours, self-injurious behaviours, attention, functional outcomes and sensory motor performance (e.g., Davis, Durand and Chan 2011; Devlin, Leader and Healy 2009; Fazlioğlu and Baran 2008; Schaaf *et al.* 2014;

Smith *et al.* 2005; Watling and Dietz 2007). The efficacy of these interventions is difficult to assess due to factors such as inconsistencies in implementation and variability in the duration of treatments. Of the 25 studies included in their comprehensive review, Lang *et al.* (2012) found only three studies reported improvement, eight showed mixed results and the remaining 14 showed no effect. Another frequently used intervention technique is Auditory Integration Therapy, although a review conducted by Sinha *et al.* (2011) again noted insufficient evidence to support its use.

Overall, there is limited support for the efficacy of any of these treatments. A recent review by Case-Smith, Weaver and Fristad (2015) suggests that sensory integration therapy may assist some children with ASD with their sensory processing problems but there is no evidence of positive effects to support the use of sensory-based intervention. Despite suggestions of some low-level improvement among children (cf., Baranek 2002, Case-Smith and Arbesman 2008; Case-Smith *et al.* 2014, Lang *et al.* 2012), the use of these techniques with adults has been largely ignored and there is no evidence to support their efficacy with adult ASD individuals. Moreover, research in this area appears to have eschewed the application of physiological indices of arousal which have the potential to validate whether these sensory-based interventions actually produce the intended impact on arousal states.

While these have been the treatments of choice of occupational therapists, other professions have used behaviour management techniques such as systematic desensitisation and operant behaviour techniques to tackle these sensory issues, following the rich tradition of using behavioural techniques to address the management of challenging behaviours in persons with disabilities. Research using systematic behaviour management techniques shows they can be successful in producing clinically significant gains in intellectual, social, emotional and adaptive functioning (Birnbauer and Leach 1993; Lovaas 1987; McEachin, Smith and Lovaas 1993). In theory, using behaviour management techniques (see, for example, Martin and Pear 2010) such as differential reinforcement of incompatible behaviours (DRI) or of a low rate of behaviour (DRL) to redirect an inappropriate sensory-seeking behaviour to behaviours that are either more functional or socially acceptable has merit. Or, using systematic desensitisation to reduce the anxiety and, ultimately, any undesirable reaction that may be evoked by the sensory stimuli also makes good sense (Lucker 2013). Nevertheless, despite the recent increase in studies examining behavioural intervention in persons with ASD (cf. Matson, Matson and Rivet 2007), few have attempted functional assessments to determine the purpose the behaviour serves or specifically addressed interventions that target sensory issues. It may be that some sensory responses serve a purpose, psychologically, physiologically or behaviourally, and, thus, restraining or modifying that behaviour in some way may lead to more maladaptive behaviours in other areas of functioning. In sum, while these behavioural strategies offer promise for remedying sensory sensitivities in persons with ASD, the impact this may have on other aspects of behaviour is unclear. Research is required to determine the function, if any, the sensitivity and its behavioural corollary serve, how one can remedy the sensory difficulties and, importantly, the impact this remedy may have on other aspects of behaviour.

Intervention Issues for Criminal Justice System Professionals

In Chapter 7 we illustrated how some of the characteristic behaviours of individuals with ASD may shape their interactions with professionals involved in the criminal justice system (e.g., police, lawyers, judiciary) in directions that may be prejudicial to the outcomes of those interactions. Given these possibilities, we briefly consider approaches to intervention that are concerned with enhancing the capacity of criminal justice system professionals to manage interactions with individuals with ASD effectively. We outline the desirable content of such interventions and draw attention to some examples of existing programmes that have been developed to guide individuals with ASD in their interactions with the criminal justice system. We emphasise, however, that we are not aware of any formal empirical evaluations of the efficacy of any of these programmes either from the perspective of (a) enhancing either the knowledge base or the decision making of the criminal justice professionals or (b) altering outcomes for individuals with ASD.

What might such intervention programmes encompass? Leaving aside practical circumstances that may constrain the breadth or delivery of such educational programmes, for any of those sectors of the criminal justice community likely to interact with a suspect, defendant, victim or witness with ASD, it would seem that programmes should focus on (a) recognition of the key symptomatology, (b) an understanding of the deficits associated with the disorder and (c) a sophisticated appreciation of how these deficits might play out during interpersonal interactions and under questioning. For police investigating a crime or perhaps interviewing a suspect or victim, the level of knowledge and understanding expected would obviously exceed that of a juror, as the latter is in a position to be educated *on the spot* by a court-appointed expert or perhaps via judicial instructions. It would also be desirable that this background knowledge includes information about appropriate professional groups (e.g., psychologists or occupational therapists with expertise in the diagnosis and characteristics of ASD) who can provide guidance regarding the disorder and its behavioural consequences.

How might this knowledge be acquired by police, lawyers or judges? Although it might seem desirable that their basic education and training programmes included content on issues associated with dealing with special populations, it seems naive to expect this would happen, or that the content would be retained in the long term. However, incorporation of such material in professional development programmes and online training resources (much like the way in which many occupational health and safety updates occur) does seem feasible. Clearly, major service delivery agencies in the field of ASD also have a role to play in this area in terms of developing educational material and lobbying for its dissemination. Likewise, the latter types of agencies have the responsibility and should have the appropriate contacts to assist in the preparation of individuals with ASD for any possible interactions with the criminal justice system. For example, ensuring that individuals with ASD (and their parents or caregivers) who find themselves interacting with the police or the legal community are sufficiently informed to make their disorder known and to seek formal legal advice is likely to be pivotal in providing optimal management of those interactions.

A number of programmes have been designed for the general purpose of educating criminal justice system professionals regarding the behavioural characteristics of ASD or to provide guidance to individuals with ASD (and their families or carers) about interacting with the justice system. They range from programmes developed by major agencies or organisations in the area of ASD through to programmes developed within specific police jurisdictions. Below are some links to websites that provide just a few examples of programmes that have been developed and are in use in different jurisdictions:

> www.autism.org.uk/working-with/criminal-justice/criminal-justice-system-and-asds.aspx

> www.autism.org.uk/our-services/services-for-people-with-autism/The-autism-alert-card.aspx

> www.justice.gov.uk/youth-justice/toolkits

> www.glasgow.gov.uk/index.aspx?articleid=5884

> www.ottawapolice.ca/en/safety-and-crime-prevention/autism-registry.asp.

We are not aware of formal evaluations of either the usage or the efficacy of such programmes, although we imagine that they are subject to periodic revision in response to informal evaluations or feedback from users of the material.

Chapter 9

>>>>>>>>>>>>>>>>>>>>>>>

FUTURE DIRECTIONS

Sometimes when a particularly nasty crime is committed and it emerges that the perpetrator was a young male, a bit of a loner, quite unusual and perhaps apparently consumed by some obscure interest, explorations of the individual's background quickly lead to media reports suggesting the possibility that the person has an ASD – even when there has been no hint of a formal diagnosis. How such a horrible crime could be committed seems almost inexplicable but, given that ASD is a puzzling disorder, it offers a convenient but inaccurate explanation. This apparent compatibility of crime with disorder is reinforced when more information emerges that highlights the individual's lifetime social inadequacies, the consequential bullying they received at school or, subsequently, their unusual behaviour and interests and so on. Yet, in many of these cases a more considered evaluation of the available information reveals that, regardless of whether the perpetrator had an ASD, there is strong evidence for the presence of some other psychiatric disorder and socio-environmental factors that could quite readily explain their horrible behaviour.

Not surprisingly, therefore, there has been considerable interest in the possibility that people with this disorder, which brings with it significant deficits in social communication skills as well as some obsessive interests and behaviours, may be particularly at risk for engaging in criminal activity. Exploration of this possibility has now occurred across a number of fronts but has been plagued with difficulties. A combination of factors, including very modest sample sizes, various selection biases, dubious measurement techniques and diagnostic confusion has resulted in data sets that are riddled with interpretative problems and thus provide far from definitive answers to the main questions posed in these studies. If, however, we force ourselves to distil a take-home message from the balance of evidence produced by these often problematic studies, it will boil down to (at least in our view) the following. The likelihood of criminal behaviour on the part of individuals with ASD may be no different than for individuals without the disorder. At worst, it may be a bit higher, although the existing data provide no basis for confident estimates. Whether individuals with ASD are over-represented in the commission of particular types of crimes has also been explored and, again, the interpretative problems are such that we don't believe any firm conclusions are justified on the basis of evidence currently available.

Of course, such conclusions about prevalence do not address the issue of how individuals with ASD become involved in crime, nor do they rule out the possibility that there may be some particularly influential mechanisms at work that contribute to such involvement. However, when we closely examined the social, cognitive and behavioural characteristics of people with ASD, a number of factors emerged that we believe are important for understanding how involvement in crime might occur and how their interactions with the justice system might progress. For researchers familiar with the complex multivariate determination of human behaviour, the general tenor of these broad conclusions is unlikely to be particularly surprising. However, for those not scientifically trained, who are perhaps more likely to seek explanations for behaviour in terms of stable and predictable individual difference variables, these conclusions might have come as a surprise.

Perhaps first and foremost, it is clear that for adults with ASD there is enormous variability in terms of behaviour, overall functioning, outcomes and, importantly, the deficits underpinning behaviours and outcomes. Intellectual functioning can extend from exceptionally bright all the way through to the lowest levels of intellectual functioning. People with ASD may have one or more of a variety of comorbid psychiatric conditions, some of which could provide explanations for certain types of criminal behaviour. They may also have experienced a diverse array of socio-environmental conditions, which sometimes appear to have been significant in shaping an individual's wayward behaviour. Moreover, while their diagnosis indicates that they have significant deficits in social-cognitive functioning and are likely to display unusual patterns of behaviours and interests, there is also likely to be enormous individual variation in these areas.

Some individuals will have a pervasive and severe ToM deficit that undermines their ability to use the verbal and nonverbal behaviour of others to discern their intentions, to foresee the broader and potentially adverse consequences of their own behaviour for both themselves and others, to negotiate their way out of difficult and undesirable situations and interactions or to behave in accordance with normative expectations when interacting with the police or the courts. Given an unfortunate alignment of particular adverse environmental or situational conditions, such broad ToM deficits could easily see individuals with ASD drawn naively into criminal behaviour, react inappropriately to the behaviour of others, unable to manage their social interactions in a way that would allow them to extricate themselves from such activity, or behave in a way when interacting with the criminal justice system that is severely prejudicial to the outcome of those interactions. Other individuals may have some more specific but significant ToM deficit that might, under normal circumstances, have few adverse consequences, yet under a particular set of unfortunate circumstances might be a critical determinant of an undesirable outcome. Moreover, some individuals with ASD will also have restricted interests or obsessions that consume them in ways that appear to impede their ability to recognise the unfortunate direction in which a particular course of behaviour may be heading. Further, some may react very badly if pursuit of those interests is interrupted and, again, not foresee the wider ramifications of their reactions.

Compelling examples of the diverse ways in which such deficits may play out given the appropriate situational conditions were provided in the various case studies outlined. This incredible diversity has important implications for understanding the relationship between ASD and crime. The involvement of some individuals with ASD in crime likely has very little, if anything, to do with the presence of ASD. For others, it may be that their particular deficit or range of deficits has made them vulnerable to involvement or inappropriate reactions, made it difficult for them to extricate themselves from problematic situations or increased the likelihood that the consequences of their involvement will be much more negative or serious than would have been the case in the absence of those deficits. A sophisticated understanding of these deficits and their potential implications on the part of the police, lawyers and the courts is absolutely crucial if criminal behaviour is to be understood and culpability and competence assessed appropriately. Moreover, it will underpin the development of robust assessment procedures that can identify the specific deficits leading to the individual's behaviour, as well as intervention paradigms that can prepare individuals with ASD for dealing with many of those complex interactions of everyday life that they are so ill-equipped to handle.

Limitations of Our Current Knowledge Base

In the previous chapters we highlighted various shortcomings in our knowledge base in all of the areas covered. Here we review what we see as the major ones. We identified the lack of any large-scale and comprehensive prospective prevalence study of criminal involvement and ASD. Various gaps in our knowledge about the extent of comorbid psychopathology and ASD, and about the mechanisms by which these comorbid disorders contribute to criminality (either in isolation or in association with ASD), were highlighted. We lamented the absence of a comprehensive developmental theory of ToM that would help in charting expectations regarding ToM in adults, the paucity of empirical evidence on ToM deficits in adults and, similarly, on the precise implications of the level and type of deficit for day-to-day social-cognitive functioning. Also noted were serious limitations in the empirical evidence that is required to clarify the nature, extent and disruptive impact of the restricted or obsessional interests that can consume individuals with ASD. Not surprisingly, therefore, when we discussed approaches to assessment and intervention, we emphasised significant gaps in both areas. It is hard to finalise assessment and intervention protocols when the precise nature and scope of the underlying problem is not known.

In the assessment area, we noted major gaps with respect to:

› differentiating ASD symptomatology

› the availability of comprehensive normative data that allow the objective assessment of ToM deficits

> discriminant validity data that permit links to be drawn between ToM test performance and likely behaviour in day-to-day social contexts that could culminate in criminality

> the availability of the necessary measures, normative reference data and validity data to clarify the patterns and severity of restricted interests that might translate into problematic behaviour.

From the intervention perspective, key shortfalls were identified with respect to what might be the most appropriate focus of any intervention efforts (e.g., global vs. specific ToM deficits), when intervention should occur and parameters of any intervention attempts that would predict maintenance and transfer of skills acquired. Within each of the above areas we identified numerous more specific questions, answers to which would ultimately contribute to understanding the relationship between ASD and criminal behaviour.

Addressing the Research Priorities

The gaps in our knowledge revealed in earlier chapters turn out to be huge, almost dauntingly so. Doubtless, there will be many different views regarding the major priorities and how they should be tackled. Here we offer our perspective on these priorities and, in some cases, suggestions regarding possible approaches to the research.

We start by identifying a couple of areas where we probably would not choose to make our research investment: prospective prevalence studies of criminal involvement by people with ASD and prevalence studies of comorbid psychopathologies associated with ASD. We willingly acknowledge that both can provide invaluable data and could, if done well, address serious weaknesses in the existing literature and guide service delivery resourcing. But as noted when discussing prevalence studies, the necessary scale and complexity of such studies is substantial if the study is to be worthwhile. Moreover, the likely new findings are that individuals with ASD will be involved in crime more or less than non-ASD controls, and comorbid psychopathologies may be represented in ASD samples more or less than the current and generally quite messy data suggest. Such studies will not, however, identify the key mechanisms underpinning the involvement of people with ASD, or with other psychopathology, in criminal activity. In other words, they won't answer the question of which individuals might end up committing a criminal act or why. Nor will they illuminate how and why these comorbidities might arise in people with ASD or how their development might be stifled.

Instead, we see three main priority areas for research. One priority involves the experimental investigation of the mechanisms underlying the involvement of individuals with ASD in criminal activity and in problematic interactions with the criminal justice system. Guided by insights provided by an analysis of consistencies across detailed case studies, we believe that a systematic evaluation of theoretically motivated hypotheses about the causal mechanisms underpinning the behaviour of individuals with ASD in the contexts we have been discussing represents a crucial step in the research process. Thus, for example, we need to formulate clear hypotheses about the likely relationships between the social-cognitive deficits that characterise individuals with ASD and their becoming involved in criminal activity (or being unable to remove themselves from such activity or stop themselves getting in deeper). Then, we need to submit these hypotheses to rigorous experimental tests, a step that will often require considerable imagination in developing laboratory or field tasks or activities where we have control over the key variables while maintaining a reasonable level of external validity. The previous chapters provide pointers to some of the more specific directions such research might take. For example, it might involve experimental demonstrations of how differences in the severity of some specific ToM deficit may shape the likelihood that the individual can be induced into violating some particular behavioural norm or the likelihood that they recognise and decode nonverbal or verbal behaviours of another individual that signal shadiness or dishonesty. Or it might involve a demonstration of varying levels of aggressive responses when restricted interests of different levels of intensity are intterupted, or perhaps investigations of how interviewees' responses to manipulations of literal expressions during a simulated police interview affect observers' judgements of the credibility of the interviewee. This is but a tiny subset of examples and, of course, any of them could be expanded to examine more complex hypothesised interactions between variables. Essentially we are advocating that there should be a sharper focus on understanding the mechanisms or processes underpinning the behaviour of individuals with ASD and a lesser focus on differences at the group level in cognition or behaviour or outcomes between people with ASD and those without.

Another priority, clearly documented in the previous chapter, is the development of robust psychometric instruments that enhance our capacity to predict wayward behaviour and to understand the underlying deficits when such behaviour occurs. The development of assessment instruments appears to proceed at a furious pace in the field of ASD. Yet, this development often has two significant accompanying weaknesses. One is a paucity of normative data, owing to the samples on which the instruments are trialled often being pitifully small and, sometimes, very poorly defined. The other is the absence of detailed validity information. Concurrent validity data correlations with another similar test are common, as are demonstrations of group differences between ASD and non-ASD samples, but more sophisticated measures of criterion-related validity tend to be less common. This is a particular problem in the present context. There is a distinct lack of instruments that are known to discriminate between adults who, for example, can or cannot discriminate when a person is becoming increasingly angry with them, whether a person is leading them into a particularly dodgy venture or is proposing something quite innocent or whether a particular set of actions will or will not have a devastating impact on another person. In other words, desperately needed are assessment devices that not only tap the components and severity of deficits in ToM, or the intensity of an individual's restricted interests and the capacity to withstand interruption, but that also have been validated against independent criteria that attest to their predictive value in the forensic context.

A third priority is the development and evaluation of approaches to intervention that might provide individuals with ASD with some kind of buffer against being led into criminal behaviour or against behaving during interactions with the criminal justice system in ways that have a negative impact on the outcome of those interactions. We highlighted a disturbing array of as yet unanswered questions about issues such as the most appropriate focus, timing, duration and intensity of interventions designed to overcome the problems likely to be associated with ToM deficits or obsessions with narrow interests and to ensure that benefits are secured into adulthood. One major problem in this area is that reasonably sized samples are needed to evaluate programme efficacy meaningfully. Another is that it appears that the intervention efforts will almost certainly need to be lengthy and intensive if meaningful outcome criteria are targeted and maintenance and transfer ensured. We wonder whether it is realistic to believe these objectives can be met given the fragmented way in which intervention studies are conducted and the consequential variations in programme methodology. Indeed, we suspect that, in this area especially, a multi-site coordinated approach to intervention evaluation is needed to provide the resources to ensure adequately defined and powered samples, consistent intervention protocols and the duration and intensity of intervention required to provide a meaningful programme evaluation. In other words, it probably needs a wide-ranging and cooperative approach not unlike that adopted in multi-site replication studies that are currently becoming more prevalent in more basic scientific endeavours.

The challenges are clearly immense if we are to secure a detailed understanding of how people with ASD become involved in (or avoid) crime and create a set of conditions that are likely to guarantee more favourable outcomes. The same applies if we are to ensure that interactions between individuals with ASD and the criminal justice system are not prejudicial to the outcomes experienced by such individuals. Meeting these challenges will, in our view, require research programmes and approaches that focus more sharply on adequately powered and controlled investigations that have the capacity to identify key processes and causal mechanisms, as well as on more robust, systematic and sophisticated approaches to assessment and intervention.

References

Allen, D., Evans, C., Hider, A., Hawkins, S., Peckett, H. and Morgan, H. (2008) 'Offender behaviour in adults with Asperger syndrome.' *Journal of Autism and Developmental Disorders 38*, 4, 748–758.

American Psychiatric Association (APA) (1980) *Diagnostic and Statistical Manual of Mental Disorders* (3rd ed.). Washington, DC: American Psychiatric Publishing.

American Psychiatric Association (APA) (1994) *Diagnostic and Statistical Manual of Mental Disorders* (4th ed.). Washington, DC: American Psychiatric Publishing.

American Psychiatric Association (APA) (2000) *Diagnostic and Statistical Manual of Mental Disorders* (4th ed., text rev.). Washington, DC: American Psychiatric Publishing.

American Psychiatric Association (APA) (2012) *A 09 Autism Spectrum Disorder.* Arlington, VA: Available at http://web.archive.org/web/20120122075158/http://www.dsm5.org/ProposedRevision/Pages/proposedrevision.aspx?rid=94, accessed on 10 February 2015.

American Psychiatric Association (APA) (2013) *Diagnostic and Statistical Manual of Mental Disorders* (5th ed.). Arlington, VA: American Psychiatric Publishing.

Angermeyer, M. C. and Matschinger, H. (1996) 'The effect of violent attacks by schizophrenic persons on the attitude of the public towards the mentally ill.' *Social Science and Medicine 43*, 12, 1721–1728.

Angermeyer, M. C. and Matschinger, H. (2003) 'The stigma of mental illness: Effects of labelling on public attitudes towards people with mental disorder.' *Acta Psychiatrica Scandinavica 108*, 4, 304–309.

Angermeyer, M. C., Dietrich, S., Pott, D. and Matschinger, H. (2005) 'Media consumption and desire for social distance towards people with schizophrenia.' *European Psychiatry 20*, 3, 246–250.

Australian Institute of Health and Welfare (AIHW) (2008) *Australia's Health 2008.* Cat. no. AUS 99. Canberra: AIHW.

Ayres, A. J. (1979) *Sensory Integration and the Child.* Los Angeles, CA: Western Psychological Services.

Bachorowski, J. and Owren, M. J. (1995) 'Vocal expressions of emotion: Acoustic properties of speech are associated with emotional intensity and content.' *Psychological Science 6*, 4, 219–225.

Ballaban-Gil, K., Rapin, I., Tuchman, R. and Shinnar, S. (1996) 'Longitudinal examination of the behavioral, language, and social changes in a population of adolescents and young adults with autistic disorder.' *Pediatric Neurology 15*, 3, 217–223.

Banse, R. and Scherer, K. R. (1996) 'Acoustic profiles in vocal emotion expression.' *Journal of Personality and Social Psychology 70*, 3, 614–636.

Baranek, G. T. (2002) 'Efficacy of sensory and motor interventions for children with autism.' *Journal of Autism and Developmental Disorders 32*, 5, 397–422.

Baron-Cohen, S. (1988) 'An assessment of violence in a young man with Asperger's syndrome.' *Journal of Child Psychology and Psychiatry 29*, 3, 351–360.

Baron-Cohen, S. (1995) *Mindblindness: An Essay on Autism and Theory of Mind.* Boston, MA: MIT Press/Bradford.

Baron-Cohen, S. (2001) 'Theory of mind and autism: A review.' *Special Issue of the International Review of Mental Retardation 23*, 169–184.

Baron-Cohen, S. (2008) 'Theories of the autistic mind.' *The Psychologist 21*, 2, 112–116.

Baron-Cohen, S. and Wheelwright, S. (1999) 'Obsessions in children with autism or Asperger syndrome: Content analysis in terms of core domains of cognition.' *The British Journal of Psychiatry 175*, 484–490.

Baron-Cohen, S., Leslie, A. M. and Frith, U. (1985) 'Does the autistic child have a "theory of mind"?' *Cognition 21*, 1, 37–46.

Baron-Cohen, S., Jolliffe, T., Mortimore, C. and Robertson, M. (1997) 'Another advanced test of theory of mind: Evidence from very high functioning adults with autism or Asperger syndrome.' *Journal of Child Psychology and Psychiatry 38*, 7, 813–822.

Baron-Cohen, S., Wheelwright, S., Hill, J., Raste, Y. and Plumb, I. (2001a) 'The "Reading the Mind in the Eyes" test revised version: A study with normal adults, and adults with Asperger syndrome or high-functioning autism.' *Journal of Child Psychology and Psychiatry 42*, 2, 241–251.

Baron-Cohen, S., Wheelwright, S., Skinner, R., Martin, J. and Clubley, E. (2001b) 'The autism spectrum quotient (AQ): Evidence from Asperger syndrome/high-functioning autism, males and females, scientists and mathematicians.' *Journal of Autism and Developmental Disorders 31*, 1, 5–17.

Barry-Walsh, J. B. and Mullen, P. E. (2004) 'Forensic aspects of Asperger's syndrome.' *Journal of Forensic Psychiatry and Psychology 15*, 1, 96–107.

Bauminger, N. (2007) 'Brief report: Individual social-multi-modal intervention for HFASD.' *Journal of Autism and Developmental Disorders 37*, 8, 1593–1604.

Begeer, S., Gevers, C., Clifford, P., Verhoeve, M., *et al.* (2011) 'Theory of mind training in children with autism: A randomized controlled trial.' *Journal of Autism and Developmental Disorders 41*, 8, 997–1006.

Berney, T. (2004) 'Asperger syndrome from childhood into adulthood.' *Advances in Psychiatric Treatment 10*, 5, 341–351.

Birnbauer, J. S. and Leach, D. J. (1993) 'The Murdoch early intervention program after 2 years.' *Behaviour Change 10*, 2, 63–74.

Blackshaw, A. J., Kinderman, P., Hare, D. J. and Hatton, C. (2001) 'Theory of mind, causal attribution and paranoia in Asperger syndrome.' *Autism 5*, 2, 147–163.

Boden, J. M., Fergusson, D M. and Horword, L. J. (2012). 'Alcohol misuse and violent behavior: Findings from a 30-year longitudinal study.' *Drug and Alcohol Dependence, 122*, 1–2, 135–141.

Bodfish, J. W., Symons, F. J., Parker, D. E. and Lewis, M. H. (2000) 'Varieties of repetitive behaviour in autism: Comparisons to mental retardation.' *Journal of Autism and Developmental Disorders 30*, 3, 237–243.

Bollingmo, G., Wessel, E., Eilertsen, D. E. and Magnussen, S. (2008) 'Credibility of the emotional witness: A study of ratings by police investigators.' *Psychology, Crime and Law 14*, 1, 29–40.

Bollingmo, G., Wessel, E., Sandvold, Y., Eilertsen, D. E. and Magnussen, S. (2009) 'The effect of biased and non-biased information on judgments of witness credibility.' *Psychology, Crime and Law 15*, 1, 61–71.

Bowler, D. M. (1992) '"Theory of Mind" in Asperger's Syndrome.' *Journal of Child Psychology and Psychiatry 33*, 5, 877–893.

Boyd, B. A., McDonough, S. G. and Bodfish, J. W. (2012) 'Evidence-based behavioral interventions for repetitive behaviors in autism.' *Journal of Autism and Developmental Disorders 42*, 6, 1236–1248.

Brennan, P. A., Mednick, S. A. and Hodgins, S. (2000) 'Major mental disorders and criminal violence in a Danish birth cohort.' *Archives of General Psychiatry 57*, 5, 494–500.

Brugha, T. S., McManus, S., Bankart, J., Scott, F., *et al.* (2011) 'Epidemiology of autism spectrum disorders in adults in the community in England.' *Archives of General Psychiatry 68*, 5, 459–466.

Butler, R. C. and Gillis, J. M. (2011) 'The impact of labels and behaviors on the stigmatization of adults with Asperger's Disorder.' *Journal of Autism and Developmental Disorders 41*, 6, 741–749.

Cahill, B. S., Coolidge, F. L., Segal, D. L., Klebe, K. J., Marle, P. D. and Overmann, K. A. (2012) 'Prevalence of ADHD and its subtypes in male and female adult prison inmates.' *Behavioral Sciences and the Law 30*, 2, 154–166.

Cappadocia, M. C., Weiss, J. A. and Pepler, D. (2012) 'Bullying experiences among children and youth with autism spectrum disorders.' *Journal of Autism and Developmental Disorders 42*, 2, 266–277.

Case-Smith, J. and Arbesman, M. (2008) 'Evidence-based review of interventions for autism used in or of relevance to occupational therapy.' *American Journal of Occupational Therapy 62*, 4, 416–429.

Case-Smith, J., Weaver, L. L. and Fristad, M. A. (2015) 'A systematic review of sensory processing interventions for children with autism spectrum disorders.' *Autism, 19*, 2, 133–148.

Cederlund, M., Hagberg, B., Billstedt, E., Gillberg, I. C. and Gillberg, C. (2008) 'Asperger syndrome and autism: A comparative longitudinal follow-up study more than 5 years after original diagnosis.' *Journal of Autism and Developmental Disorders 38*, 1, 72–85.

Celani, G., Battacchi, M. W. and Arcidiacono, L. (1999) 'The understanding of the emotional meaning of facial expressions in people with autism.' *Journal of Autism and Developmental Disorders 29*, 1, 57–66.

Chae, P. K., Jung, H. O. and Noh, K. S. (2001) 'Attention deficit hyperactivity disorder in Korean juvenile delinquents.' *Adolescence 36*, 144, 707–725.

Chakrabarti, S. and Fombonne, E. (2001) 'Pervasive developmental disorders in preschool children.' *JAMA 285*, 24, 3093–3099.

Cheely, C. A., Carpenter, L. A., Letourneau, E. J., Nicholas, J. S., Charles, J. and King, L. B. (2011) 'The prevalence of youth with autism spectrum disorders in the criminal justice system.' *Journal of Autism and Developmental Disorders 42*, 9, 1856–1862.

Chen, P. S., Chen, S. J., Yang, Y. K., Yeh, T. L., Chen, C. C. and Lo, H. Y. (2003) 'Asperger's disorder: A case report of repeated stealing and the collecting behaviours of an adolescent patient.' *Acta Psychiatrica Scandinavica 107*, 1, 73–76.

Chevallier, C., Kohls, G., Troiani, V., Brodkin, E. S. and Schultz, R. T. (2012) 'The social motivation theory of autism.' *Trends in Cognitive Sciences, 16*, 4, 231–239.

Chowdhury, M., Benson, B. A. and Hillier, A. (2010) 'Changes in restricted repetitive behaviors with age: A study of high-functioning adults with autism spectrum disorders.' *Research in Autism Spectrum Disorders 4*, 2, 210–216.

Clarke, D. E., Narrow, W. E., Regier, D. A., Kuramoto, S. J., *et al.* (2013) 'DSM-5 field trials in the United States and Canada, Part I: Study design, sampling strategy, implementation, and analytic approaches.' *American Journal of Psychiatry 170*, 1, 43–58.

Cohen, D.J., Paul, R. and Volkmar, F. R. (1986) 'Issues in the classification of pervasive and other developmental disorders: toward DSM-IV.' *Journal of the American Academy of Child and Adolescent Psychiatry 25*, 2, 213–220.

Coid, J. W., Ullrich, S., Kallis, C., Keers, R., *et al.* (2013) 'The relationship between delusions and violence: Findings from the east London first episode psychosis study.' *JAMA Psychiatry 70*, 5, 465–471.

Colledge, E. and Blair, R. J. R. (2001) 'The relationship in children between the inattention and impulsivity components of attention deficit and hyperactivity disorder and psychopathic tendencies.' *Personality and Individual Differences 30*, 7, 1175–1187.

Cook, R., Brewer, R., Shah, P. and Bird, G. (2013) 'Alexithymia, not autism, predicts poor recognition of emotional expressions.' *Psychological Science 24*, 723–732.

Cooper, S. A., Mohamed, W. N. and Collacott, R. A. (1993) 'Possible Asperger's syndrome in a mentally handicapped transvestite offender.' *Journal of Intellectual Disability Research 37*, 2, 189–194.

Copeland, W. E., Miller-Johnson, S., Keeler, G., Angold, A. and Costello, E. J. (2007) 'Childhood psychiatric disorders and young adult crime: A prospective, population-based study.' *The American Journal of Psychiatry 164*, 11, 1668–1675.

Costello, E. J., Mustillo, S., Erkanli, A., Keeler, G. and Angold, A. (2003) 'Prevalence and development of psychiatric disorders in childhood and adolescence.' *Archives of General Psychiatry 60*, 8, 837–844.

Davis, T. N., Durand, S. and Chan, J. M. (2011) 'The effects of a brushing procedure on stereotypical behavior.' *Research in Autism Spectrum Disorders 5*, 3, 1053–1058.

Deb, S. and Prasad, K. B. (1994) 'The prevalence of autistic disorder among children with a learning disability.' *The British Journal of Psychiatry 165*, 3, 395–399.

DeMyer, M. K., Barton, S., DeMyer, W. E., Norton, J. A., Allen, J. and Steele, R. (1973) 'Prognosis in autism: A follow-up study.' *Journal of Autism and Childhood Schizophrenia 3*, 3, 199–246.

Devlin, S., Leader, G. and Healy, O. (2009) 'Comparison of behavioral intervention and sensory-integration therapy in the treatment of self-injurious behavior.' *Research in Autism Spectrum Disorders 3*, 1, 223–231.

Dickson, K., Emerson, E. and Hatton, C. (2005) 'Self-reported anti-social behaviour: Prevalence and risk factors amongst adolescents with and without intellectual disability.' *Journal of Intellectual Disability Research 49*, 2, 820–826.

Dziobek, I., Fleck, S., Kalbe, E., Rogers, K., *et al.* (2006) 'Introducing MASC: A movie for the assessment of social cognition.' *Journal of Autism and Developmental Disorders 36*, 5, 623–636.

Eack, S. M., Greenwald, D. P., Hogarty, S. S., Bahorik, A. L., *et al.* (2013) 'Cognitive enhancement therapy for adults with Autism Spectrum Disorder: Results of an 18-month feasibility study.' *Journal of Autism and Developmental Disorders 43*, 12, 2866–2877.

Eaves, L. C. and Ho, H. H. (2008) 'Young adult outcome of autism spectrum disorders.' *Journal of Autism and Developmental Disorders 38*, 4, 739–747.

Edwards, T. L., Watkins, E. E., Lotfizadeh, A. D. and Poling, A. (2012) 'Intervention research to benefit people with autism: How old are the participants?' *Research in Autism Spectrum Disorders 6*, 3, 996–999.

Eltman, F. and Goldman, A. (2013) 'AP: Lawyer says teenage NY terror suspect autistic.' *Yahoo News*, 11 July 2013. Available at http://news.yahoo.com/ap-lawyer-says-teenage-ny-terror-suspect-autistic-230906466.html, accessed on 10 February 2015.

Eme, R. F. (2009) 'Attention-deficit/hyperactivity disorder and correctional health care.' *Journal of Correctional Health Care 15*, 1, 5–18.

Emerson, E. and Hatton, C. (2007) 'Mental health of children and adolescents with intellectual disabilities in Britain.' *The British Journal of Psychiatry 191*, 6, 493–499.

Enayati, J., Grann, M., Lubbe, S. and Fazel, S. (2008) 'Psychiatric morbidity in arsonists referred for forensic psychiatric assessment in Sweden.' *Journal of Forensic Psychiatry and Psychology 19*, 2, 139–147.

Eronen, M., Hakola, P. and Tiihonen, J. (1996) 'Mental disorders and homicidal behavior in Finland.' *Archives of General Psychiatry 53*, 6, 497–501.

Esbensen, A. J., Seltzer, M. M., Lam, K. S. and Bodfish, J. W. (2009) 'Age-related differences in restricted repetitive behaviors in autism spectrum disorders.' *Journal of Autism and Developmental Disorders 39*, 1, 57–66.

Eyestone, L. L. and Howell, R. J. (1994) 'An epidemiological study of attention-deficit hyperactivity disorder and major depression in a male prison population.' *Journal of the American Academy of Psychiatry and the Law 22*, 2, 181–193.

Farley, M. A., McMahon, W. M., Fombonne, E., Jenson, W. R., *et al.* (2009) 'Twenty-year outcome for individuals with autism and average or near-average cognitive abilities.' *Autism Research 2*, 2, 109–118.

Farrant, A., Blades, M. and Boucher, J. (1998) 'Source monitoring by children with autism.' *Journal of Autism and Developmental Disorders 28*, 1, 43–50.

Fazel, M., Långström, N., Grann, M. and Fazel, S. (2008) 'Psychopathology in adolescent and young adult criminal offenders (15–21 years) in Sweden.' *Social Psychiatry and Psychiatric Epidemiology 43*, 4, 319–324.

Fazlioğlu, Y. and Baran, G. (2008) 'A sensory integration therapy program on sensory problems for children with autism.' *Perceptual and Motor Skills 106*, 2, 415–422.

Fazio, R. L., Pietz, C. A. and Denney, R. L. (2012) 'An estimate of the prevalence of Austism-Spectrum disorders in an incarcerated population.' *Open Access Journal of Forensic Psychology*, 69–80.

Feldman, R. S. and Chesley, R. B. (1984) 'Who is lying, who is not: An attributional analysis of the effects of nonverbal behavior on judgements of defendant believability.' *Behavioral Sciences and the Law 2*, 4, 451–461.

Fergusson, D. M., Boden, J. M. and Horwood, J. (2010) 'Classification of behavior disorders in adolescence: Scaling methods, predictive validity, and gender differences.' *Journal of Abnormal Psychology 119*, 4, 699–712.

Finn, M. A. and Stalans, L. J. (1995) 'Police referrals to shelters and mental health treatment: Examining their decisions in domestic assault cases.' *Crime and Delinquency 41*, 4, 467–480.

First, M. B., Gibbon, M., Spitzer, R. L., Williams, J. B. W. *et al.* (1997) *Structured Clinical Interview for DSM-IV Axis II Personality Disorders. (SCID-II).* Washington, D.C.: American Psychiatric Press, Inc.

First, M. B., Spitzer, R. L., Gibbon, M. and Williams, J. B. W. (2002) *Structured Clinical Interview for DSM-IV-TR Axis I Disorders, Research Version, Patient Edition. (SCID-I/P).* New York: Biometrics Research.

Fischer, M., Barkley, R. A., Smallish, L. and Fletcher, K. (2002) 'Young adult follow-up of hyperactive children: Self-reported psychiatric disorders, comorbidity, and the role of childhood conduct problems and teen CD.' *Journal of Abnormal Child Psychology 30,* 5, 463–475.

Fisher, N. and Happé, F. (2005) 'A training study of theory of mind and executive function in children with autistic spectrum disorders.' *Journal of Autism and Developmental Disorders 35,* 6, 757–771.

Fisher, R. P. and Geiselman, R. E. (1992) *Memory-Enhancing Techniques For Investigative Interviewing: The Cognitive Interview.* Springfield: Charles C. Thomas.

Fiske, S. T. and Taylor, S. E. (2013) *Social Cognition: From Brains to Culture.* Sage.

Fletcher-Watson, S., McConnell, F., Manola, E. and McConachie, H. (2014) 'Intervention Based on the Theory of Mind Cognitive Model for Autism Spectrum Disorder (ASD)'. Cochrane database of systematic reviews. Available at http://onlinelibrary.wiley.com/doi/10.1002/14651858.CD008785.pub2/full, accessed on 2 April 2015.

Fodor, J. A. (1983) *The Modularity of Mind: An Essay on Faculty Psychology.* Cambridge, MA: MIT Press.

Fombonne, E. (2001) 'Epidemiological Investigations for Autism and Pervasive Developmental Disorders.' In C. Lord (ed.) *Educating Children with Autism.* Washington, DC: National Academy of Sciences Press.

Frith, U. (1989) *Autism: Explaining the Enigma.* Oxford: Basil Blackwell.

Frith, U. (2004) 'Emanuel Miller lecture: Confusions and controversies about Asperger syndrome.' *Journal of Child Psychology and Psychiatry 45,* 4, 672–686.

Frith, U. and Happé, F. (1999) 'Theory of mind and self consciousness: What is it like to be autistic?' *Mind and Language 14,* 1, 82–89.

Fukunaga, R. and Lysaker, P. (2013) 'Criminal history in schizophrenia: Associations with substance use and disorganized symptoms.' *The Journal of Forensic Psychiatry and Psychology 24,* 3, 293–308.

Gaffney, A., Jones, W., Sweeney, J. and Payne, J. (2010) *Drug Use Monitoring in Australia: 2008 Annual Report on Drug Use Among Police Detainees.* Canberra: Australian Institute of Criminology.

Gantman, A., Kapp, S. K., Orenski, K. and Laugeson, E. A. (2012) 'Social skills training for young adults with high-functioning autism spectrum disorders: A randomized controlled pilot study.' *Journal of Autism and Developmental Disorders 42,* 6, 1094–1103.

Ghaziuddin, M. and Mountain-Kimchi, K. (2004) 'Defining the intellectual profile of Asperger syndrome: Comparison with high-functioning autism.' *Journal of Autism and Developmental Disorders 34,* 3, 279–284.

Ghaziuddin, M., Weidmer-Mikhail, E. and Ghaziuddin, N. (1998) 'Comorbidity of Asperger syndrome: A preliminary report.' *Journal of Intellectual Disability Research 42,* 4, 279–283.

Gibbons, F. X. and Kassin, S. M. (1982) 'Behavioral expectations of retarded and nonretarded children.' *Journal of Applied Developmental Psychology 3,* 2, 85–104.

Gillberg, C. and Steffenburg, S. (1987) 'Outcome and prognostic factors in infantile autism and similar conditions: A population-based study of 46 cases followed through puberty.' *Journal of Autism and Developmental Disorders 17*, 2, 273–287.

Giora, R., Gazal, O., Goldstein, I., Fein, O. and Stringaris, R. (2012) 'Salience and context: Interpretation of metaphorical and literal language by young adults diagnosed with Asperger's Syndrome.' *Metaphor and Symbol 27*, 1, 22–54.

Golan, O. and Baron-Cohen, S. (2006) 'Systemizing empathy: Teaching adults with Asperger syndrome or high-functioning autism to recognize complex emotions using interactive multimedia.' *Development and Psychopathology 18*, 2, 591–617.

Golan, O., Baron-Cohen, S., Hill, J. J. and Golan, Y. (2006) 'The "Reading the Mind in Films" task: Complex emotion recognition in adults with and without autism spectrum conditions.' *Social Neuroscience 1*, 2, 111–123.

Golan, O., Baron-Cohen, S., Hill, J. J. and Rutherford, M. D. (2007) 'The "Reading the Mind in the Voice" test-revised: A study of complex emotion recognition in adults with and without autism spectrum condition.' *Journal of Autism and Developmental Disorders 37*, 6, 1096–1106.

Gottlieb, J. (1975) 'Attitudes toward retarded children: Effects of labeling and behavioral aggressiveness.' *Journal of Educational Psychology 67*, 4, 581–585.

Granhag, P. A. and Vrij, A. (2005) 'Deception Detection.' In N. Brewer and K. D. Williams (eds), *Psychology and Law: An Empirical Perspective* (pp.43–92). New York: Guilford.

Greaves-Lord, K., Eussen, M. J. M., Verhulst, F., Minderaa, R., *et al.* (2013) 'Empirically based phenotypic profiles of children with pervasive developmental disorders: Interpretation in the light of the DSM-5.' *Journal of Autism and Developmental Disorders 43*, 8, 1784–1797.

Green, V. A., Sigafoos, J., Pituch, K. A., Itchon, J., O'Reilly, M. and Lancioni, G. E. (2006) 'Assessing behavioral flexibility in individuals with developmental disabilities.' *Focus on Autism and Other Developmental Disabilities 21*, 4, 230–236.

Gregory, C., Lough, S., Stone, V., Erzinclioglu, S., *et al.* (2002) 'Theory of mind in patients with frontal variant frontotemporal dementia and Alzheimer's disease: Theoretical and practical implications.' *Brain 125*, 4, 752–764.

Gresham, F. M. and Elliott, S. N. (1990) *Social Skills Rating System: Manual.* Circle Pines, MN: American Guidance Service.

Griffin-Shelley, E. (2010) 'An Asperger's adolescent sex addict, sex offender: A case study.' *Sexual Addiction and Compulsivity 17*, 1, 46–64.

Gross, T. F. (2004) 'The perception of four basic emotions in human and nonhuman faces by children with autism and other developmental disabilities.' *Journal of Abnormal Child Psychology 32*, 5, 469–480.

Gunter, T. D., Arndt, S., Riggins-Caspers, K., Wenman, G. and Cadoret, R. J. (2006) 'Adult outcomes of attention deficit hyperactivity disorder and conduct disorder: Are the risks independent or additive?' *Annals of Clinical Psychiatry 18*, 4, 233–237.

Hadwin, J., Baron-Cohen, S., Howlin, P. and Hill, K. (1997) 'Does teaching theory of mind have an effect on the ability to develop conversation in children with autism?' *Journal of Autism and Developmental Disorders 27*, 5, 519–537.

Happé, F. G. E. (1994) 'An advanced test of theory of mind: Understanding of story characters' thoughts and feelings by able autistic, mentally handicapped, and normal children and adults.' *Journal of Autism and Developmental Disorders 24*, 2, 129–154.

Hare, D. J., Gould, J., Mills, R. and Wing, L. (1999) *A Preliminary Study of Individuals with Autistic Spectrum Disorders in Three Special Hospitals in England.* London: National Autistic Society.

Hartley, S. L. and Sikora, D. M. (2010) 'Detecting Autism Spectrum Disorder in children with intellectual disability: Which DSM-IV-TR criteria are most useful?' *Focus on Autism and Other Developmental Disabilities 25,* 2, 85–97.

Heavey, L., Phillips, W., Baron-Cohen, S. and Rutter, M. (2000) 'The awkward moments test: A naturalistic measure of social understanding in autism.' *Journal of Autism and Developmental Disorders 30,* 3, 225–236.

Hill, K. M. (2012) 'The prevalence of youth with disabilities among older youth in out-of-home placement: An analysis of state administrative data.' *Child Welfare 91,* 4, 61–84.

Hobson, R. P. (1986a) 'The autistic child's appraisal of expressions of emotion.' *Journal of Child Psychology and Psychiatry 27,* 3, 321–342.

Hobson, R. P. (1986b) 'The autistic child's appraisal of expressions of emotion: A further study.' *Journal of Child Psychology and Psychiatry 27,* 5, 671–680.

Hobson, R. P., Ouston, J. and Lee, A. (1988) 'What's in a face? The case of autism.' *British Journal of Psychology 79,* 4, 441–453.

Hodgins, S., Lapalme, M. and Toupin, J. (1999) 'Criminal activities and substance use of patients with major affective disorders and schizophrenia: A two-year follow up.' *Journal of Affective Disorders 55,* 2–3, 187–202.

Hofvander, B., Delorme, R., Chaste, P., Nydén, A., *et al.* (2009) 'Psychiatric and psychosocial problems in adults with normal-intelligence autism spectrum disorders.' *BMC Psychiatry 9,* 1, 35.

Howlin, P. (2004) *Autism: Preparing for Adulthood* (2nd ed.). London: Routledge.

Howlin, P., Goode, S., Hutton, J. and Rutter, M. (2004) 'Adult outcome for children with autism.' *Journal of Child Psychology and Psychiatry 45,* 2, 212–229.

Huerta, M., Bishop, S. L., Duncan, A., Hus, V. and Lord, C. (2012) 'Application of DSM-5 criteria for autism spectrum disorder to three samples of children with DSM-IV diagnoses of pervasive developmental disorders.' *The American Journal of Psychiatry 169,* 10, 1056–1064.

Hurley, P. J. and Eme, R. (2008) *ADHD and the Criminal Justice System: Spinning Out of Control.* Charleston, SC: BookSurge.

Jansen, L. M. C., Gispen-de Wied, C. C., van der Gaag, R. J., Ten Hove, F., *et al.* (2000) 'Unresponsiveness to psychosocial stress in a subgroup of autistic-like children, multiple complex developmental disorder.' *Psychoneuroendocrinology 25,* 8, 753–764.

Jehle, A., Miller, M. K. and Kemmelmeier, M. (2009) 'The influence of accounts and remorse on mock jurors' judgments of offenders.' *Law and Human Behavior 33,* 5, 393–404.

Jolliffe, T. and Baron-Cohen, S. (1999) 'The strange stories test: A replication with high functioning adults with Autism or Asperger Syndrome.' *Journal of Autism and Developmental Disorders 29,* 5, 395–406.

Jones, A. P., Happé, F. G., Gilbert, F., Burnett, S. and Viding, E. (2010) 'Feeling, caring, knowing: Different types of empathy deficit in boys with psychopathic tendencies and autism spectrum disorder.' *Journal of Child Psychology and Psychiatry 51,* 11, 1188–1197.

Joshi, G., Wozniak, J., Petty, C., Martelon, M., *et al.* (2013) 'Psychiatric comorbidity and functioning in a clinically referred population of adults with autism spectrum disorders: A comparative study.' *Journal of Autism and Developmental Disorders 43,* 6, 1314–1325.

Kanner, L. (1943) 'Autistic disturbances of affective contact.' *Nervous Child 2,* 3, 217–250.

Katz, N. and Zemishlany, Z. (2006) 'Criminal responsibility in Asperger's syndrome.' *The Israel Journal of Psychiatry and Related Sciences 43*, 3, 166–173.

Kaufmann, G., Drevland, G. C. B., Wessel, E., Overskeid, G. and Magnussen, S. (2003) 'The importance of being earnest: Displayed emotions and witness credibility.' *Applied Cognitive Psychology 17*, 1, 21–34.

Kessler, R. C., Adler, L., Barkley, R., Biederman, J., *et al.* (2006) 'The prevalence and correlates of adult ADHD in the United States: Results from the national comorbidity survey replication.' *The American Journal of Psychiatry 163*, 4, 716–723.

Kibbie, K. S. (2012) 'Maleficent or mindblind: Questioning the role of Asperger's in quant hedge fund malfeasance and modeling disasters.' *American Criminal Law Review 49*, 367–402.

Kim, J. A., Szatmari, P., Bryson, S. E., Streiner, D. L. and Wilson, F. J. (2000) 'The prevalence of anxiety and mood problems among children with autism and Asperger syndrome.' *Autism 4*, 2, 117–132.

Kleinman, J., Marciano, P. L. and Ault, R. L. (2001) 'Advanced theory of mind in high functioning adults with autism.' *Journal of Autism and Developmental Disorders 31*, 1, 29–36.

Klin, A. (2006) 'Autism and asperger syndrome: An overview.' *Revista Brasileira de Psiquiatria 28*, 1, S3–S11.

Klin, A., Danovitch, J. H., Merz, A. B., and Volkmar, F. R. (2007) 'Circumscribed interests in higher functioning individuals with autism spectrum disorders: An exploratory study.' *Research and Practice for Persons with Severe Disabilities 32*, 2, 89–100.

Kobayashi, R., Murata, T. and Yoshinaga, K. (1992) 'A follow-up study of 201 children with autism in Kyushu and Yamaguchi areas, Japan.' *Journal of Autism and Developmental Disorders 22*, 3, 395–411.

Kolvin, I. (1971) 'Studies in the childhood psychoses: I. Diagnostic criteria and classification.' *The British Journal of Psychiatry 118*, 381–384.

Kuhn, E. S. and Laird, R. D. (2013) 'Parent and peer restrictions of opportunities attenuate the link between low self-control and antisocial behavior.' *Social Development 22*, 4, 813–830.

Kumagami, T. and Matsuura, N. (2009) 'Prevalence of pervasive developmental disorder in juvenile court cases in Japan.' *Journal of Forensic Psychiatry and Psychology 20*, 6, 974–987.

Lang, R., O'Reilly, N., Healy, O., Rispoli, M., *et al.* (2012) 'Sensory integration therapy for autism spectrum disorders: A systematic review.' *Research in Autism Spectrum Disorders 6*, 3, 1004–1018.

Långström, N., Grann, M., Ruchkin, V., Sjöstedt, G. and Fazel, S. (2009) 'Risk factors for violent offending in Autism Spectrum Disorder: A national study of hospitalized individuals.' *Journal of Interpersonal Violence 24*, 8, 1358–1370.

Laugeson, E. A., Frankel, F., Mogil, C. and Dillon, A. R. (2009) 'Parent-assisted social skills training to improve friendships in teens with autism spectrum disorders.' *Journal of Autism and Developmental Disorders 39*, 4, 596–606.

Leary, M. R., Kowalski, R. M., Smith, L. and Phillips, S. (2003) 'Teasing, rejection, and violence: Case studies of the school shootings.' *Aggressive Behavior 29*, 3, 202–214.

Leekam, S. R., Prior, M. R. and Uljarevic, M. (2011) 'Restricted and repetitive behaviors in autism spectrum disorders: A review of research in the last decade.' *Psychological Bulletin 137*, 4, 562.

Lewis, M. (2010) *The Big Short: Inside the Doomsday Machine.* New York: W. W. Norton and Company.

Leyfer, O. T., Folstein, S. E., Bacalman, S., Davis, N. O., *et al.* (2006) 'Comorbid psychiatric disorders in children with autism: Interview development and rates of disorders.' *Journal for Autism and Developmental Disorders 36*, 7, 849–861.

Lind, S. E. and Bowler, D. (2008) 'Episodic memory and autonoetic consciousness in autistic spectrum disorders: The roles of self-awareness, representational abilities and temporal cognition.' In J. Boucher and D. Bowler (eds) *Memory in Autism: Theory and Evidence* (pp.166–187). New York: Cambridge University Press.

Lindqvist, P. and Allebeck, P. (1990) 'Schizophrenia and crime. A longitudinal follow-up of 644 schizophrenics in Stockholm.' *British Journal of Psychiatry 157*, 3, 345–350.

Link, B. G., Cullen, F. T., Frank, J. and Wozniak, J. F. (1987) 'The social rejection of former mental patients: Understanding why labels matter.' *American Journal of Sociology 92*, 6, 1461–1500.

Link, B. G., Phelan, J. C., Bresnahan, M., Stueve, A. and Pescosolido, B. A. (1999) 'Public conceptions of mental illness: Labels, causes, dangerousness, and social distance.' *American Journal of Public Health 89*, 9, 1328–1333.

Lopata, C., Thomeer, M. L., Volker, M. A., Toomey, J. A., *et al.* (2010) 'RCT of a manualized social treatment for high-functioning autism spectrum disorders.' *Journal of Autism and Developmental Disorders 40*, 11, 1297–1310.

Lord, C. and Hopkins, J. M. (1986) 'The social behavior of autistic children with younger and same-age nonhandicapped peers.' *Journal of Autism and Developmental Disorders 16*, 3, 249–262.

Lord, C., Petkova, E., Hus, V., Gan, W., *et al.* (2012a) 'A multisite study of the clinical diagnosis of different autism spectrum disorders.' *Archives of General Psychiatry 69*, 3, 306–313.

Lord, C., Rutter, M., DiLavore, P. C., Risi, S., Gotham, K. and Bishop, S. L. (2012b) *Autism Diagnostic Observation Schedule* (2nd ed., ADOS-2). Torrence, CA: Western Psychological Services.

Lovaas, O. I. (1987) 'Behavioral treatment and normal educational and intellectual functioning in young autistic children.' *Journal of Consulting and Clinical Psychology 55*, 1, 3–9.

Lovibond, S. H. and Lovibond, P. F. (1995) *Manual for the Depression Anxiety Stress Scales* (2nd ed.). Sydney: Psychology Foundation.

LoVullo, S. V. and Matson, J. L. (2009) 'Comorbid psychopathology in adults with autism spectrum disorders and intellectual disabilities.' *Research in Developmental Disabilities 30*, 6, 1288–1296.

Lucker, J. R. (2013) 'Auditory hypersensitivity in children with autism spectrum disorders.' *Focus on Autism and Other Developmental Disabilities 28*, 3, 184–191.

Lugnegård, T., Hallerbäck, M. U. and Gillberg, C. (2011) 'Psychiatric comorbidity in young adults with a clinical diagnosis of Asperger syndrome.' *Research in Developmental Disabilities 32*, 5, 1910–1917.

Lundström, S., Forsman, M., Larsson, H., Kerekes, N., *et al.* (2014) 'Childhood neurodevelopmental disorders and violent criminality: A sibling control study.' *Journal of Autism and Developmental Disorders 44*, 11, 2707–2716.

Luteijn, E. F., Jackson, S. E., Volkmar, F. and Minderaa, R. (1998) 'Brief report: The development of the Children's Social Behavior Questionnaire: Preliminary data.' *Journal of Autism and Developmental Disorders 28*, 6, 559–565.

Magiati, I., Tay, X. W. and Howlin, P. (2012) 'Early comprehensive behaviorally based interventions for children with autism spectrum disorders: A summary of findings from recent reviews and meta-analyses.' *Neuropsychiatry 2*, 6, 543–570.

Mandell, D. S., Lawer, L. J., Branch, K., Bridkin, E. S., *et al.* (2012) 'Prevalence and correlates of autism in a state psychiatric hospital.' *Autism 16*, 6, 557–567.

Maras, K. L. and Bowler, D. M. (2014) 'Eyewitness testimony in autism spectrum disorder: A review.' *Journal of Autism and Developmental Disorders 42*, 1–16.

Martin, G. L. and Pear, J. (2010) '*Behavior Modification: What it is and How to Do it* (9th ed.). Boston, MA: Pearson Education/Allyn and Bacon.

Martin, I. and McDonald, S. (2004) 'An exploration of causes of non-literal language problems in individuals with Asperger syndrome.' *Journal of Autism and Developmental Disorders 34*, 3, 311–328.

Matson, J. L., Matson, M. L. and Rivet, T. T. (2007) 'Social-skills treatments for children with autism spectrum disorders: An overview.' *Behavior Modification 31*, 5, 682–707.

Mattila, M.-L., Kielinen, M., Linna, S.-L., Jussila, K., *et al.* (2011) 'Autism spectrum disorders according to DSM-IV-TR and comparison with DSM-5 draft criteria: An epidemiological study.' *Journal of the American Academy of Child and Adolescent Psychiatry 50*, 6, 583–592.

McDonald, S., Flanagan, S. and Rollins, J. (2011) *The Awareness of Social Inference Test (Revised).* Sydney Australia: Pearson Clinical Assessment.

McEachin, J. J., Smith, T. and Lovaas, O. I. (1993) 'Long-term outcome for children with autism who received early intensive behavioral treatment.' *American Journal of Mental Retardation 97*, 359–359.

McPartland, J. C., Reichow, B. and Volkmar, F. R. (2012) 'Sensitivity and specificity of proposed DSM-5 diagnostic criteria for autism spectrum disorder.' *Journal of the American Academy of Child and Adolescent Psychiatry 51*, 4, 368–383.

Mercier, C., Mottron, L. and Belleville, S. (2000) 'A psychosocial study on restricted interest in high-functioning persons with pervasive developmental disorders.' *Autism 4*, 4, 406–425.

Modestin, J., Hug, A. and Ammann, R. (1997) 'Criminal behavior in males with affective disorders.' *Journal of Affective Disorders 42*, 1, 29–38.

Monahan, J. (1983) 'The Prediction of Violent Behavior: Developments in Psychology and Law.' In C. J. Scheirer and B. L. Hammonds (eds) *Psychology and the Law.* Washington, DC: American Psychological Association.

Mordre, M., Groholt, B., Kjelsberg, E., Sandstad, B. and Myhre, A. M. (2011) 'The impact of ADHD and conduct disorder in childhood on adult delinquency: A 30 years follow-up study using official crime records.' *BMC Psychiatry 11*, 1, 57.

Moss, S., Prosser, H., Costello, H., Simpson, N., *et al.* (1998) 'Reliability and validity of the PAS-ADD checklist for detecting psychiatric disorders in adults with intellectual disability.' *Journal of Intellectual Disability Research 42*, 2, 173–183.

Mouridsen, S. E., Rich, B., Isager, T. and Nedergaard, N. J. (2008) 'Pervasive developmental disorders and criminal behavior: A case control study.' *International Journal of Offender Therapy and Comparative Criminology 52*, 2, 196–205.

Mullen, P. E. (2006) 'Schizophrenia and violence: From correlations to preventative strategies.' *Advances in Psychiatric Treatment 12*, 4, 239–248.

Munesue, T., Ono, Y., Mutoh, K., Shimoda, K., Nakatani, H. and Kikuchi, M. (2008) 'High prevalence of bipolar disorder comorbidity in adolescents and young adults with high functioning autism spectrum disorder: A preliminary study of 44 outpatients.' *Journal of Affective Disorders 111*, 2–3, 170–175.

Munkner, R., Haastrup, S., Joergensen, T. and Kramp, P. (2003) 'The temporal relationship between schizophrenia and crime.' *Social Psychiatry and Psychiatric Epidemiology 38*, 7, 347–353.

Murphy, D. E (2001), 'Judge, clearly not amused, sentences a subway impostor.' *The New York Times*, 30 March.

Murphy, G., Macdonald, S., Hall, S. and Oliver, C. (2000) 'Aggression and the termination of 'rituals': A new variant of the escape function for challenging behavior?' *Research in Developmental Disabilities 21*, 1, 43–59.

Murray, J., Irving, B., Farrington, D. P., Colman, I. and Bloxsom, C. A. J. (2010) 'Very early predictors of conduct problems and crime: Results from a national cohort study.' *Journal of Child Psychology and Psychiatry 51*, 11, 1198–1207.

Murrie, D. C., Warren, J. I., Kristiansson, M. and Dietz, P. E. (2002) 'Asperger's syndrome in forensic settings.' *International Journal of Forensic Mental Health 1*, 1, 59–70.

Myers, F. (2004) *On the Borderline? People with Learning Disabilities and/or Autistic Spectrum Disorders in Secure, Forensic and other Specialist Settings.* Edinburgh: Scottish Executive Social Research.

Newman, S. S. and Ghaziuddin, M. (2008) 'Violent crime in Asperger syndrome: The role of psychiatric comorbidity.' *Journal of Autism and Developmental Disorders 38*, 10, 1848–1852.

Nuske, H. J., Vivanti, G. and Dissanayake, C. (2013) 'Are emotion impairments unique to, universal, or specific in Autism spectrum disorder? A comprehensive review.' *Cognition and Emotion 27*, 6, 1042–1061.

Oakley, C., Hynes, F. and Clark, T. (2009) 'Mood disorders and violence: A new focus.' *Advances in Psychiatric Treatment 15*, 4, 263–270.

Odgers, D. L., Moffitt, T. E., Broadbent, J. M., Dickson, *et al.* (2008) 'Female and male antisocial trajectories: From childhood origins to adult outcomes.' *Developmental Psychopathology 20*, 2, 673–716.

Ozonoff, S., South, M. and Miller, J. N. (2000) 'DSM-IV-defined Asperger syndrome: Cognitive, behavioral and early history differentiation from high-functioning autism.' *Autism 4*, 1, 29–46.

Parham, L. D., Cohn, E. S., Spitzer, S., Koomar, J. A. *et al.* (2007). 'Fidelity in sensory integration research.' *American Journal of Occupational Therapy 61*, 2, 216–227.

Paul, R., Augustyn, A., Klin, A. and Volkmar, F. R. (2005) 'Perception and production of prosody by speakers with autism spectrum disorders.' *Journal of Autism and Developmental Disorders 35*, 2, 205–220.

Payne, J. and Gaffney, A. (2012) *How Much Crime is Drug Or Alcohol Related?: Self-reported Attributions of Police Detainees (Trends and Issues in Crime and Criminal Justice No. 439), Trends and Issues in Crime and Criminal Justice.* Canberra: Australian Institute of Criminology.

Paynter, J. and Peterson, C. C. (2013) 'Further evidence of benefits of thought-bubble training for theory of mind development in children with autism spectrum disorders.' *Research in Autism Spectrum Disorders 7*, 2, 344–348.

Pelphrey, K. A., Sasson, N. J., Reznick, J., Paul, G., Goldman, B. D. and Piven, J. (2002) 'Visual scanning of faces in autism.' *Journal of Autism and Developmental Disorders 32*, 4, 249–261.

Penn, D. L., Kohlmaier, R. J. and Corrigan, P. W. (2000) 'Interpersonal factors contributing to the stigma of schizophrenia: Social skills, perceived attractiveness, and symptoms.' *Schizophrenia Research 45*, 1, 37–45.

Polanczyk, G., de Lima, M. S., Horta, B. L., Biederman, J. and Rohde, L. A. (2007) 'The worldwide prevalence of ADHD: A systematic review and metaregression analysis.' *American Journal of Psychiatry 164*, 6, 942–948.

Ponnet, K., Buysse, A., Roeyers, H. and De Clercq, A. (2008) 'Mind-reading in young adults with ASD: Does structure matter?' *Journal of Autism and Developmental Disorders 38*, 5, 905–918.

Ponnet, K. S., Roeyers, H., Buysse, A., De Clercq, A. and van Der Heyden, E. (2004) 'Advanced mind-reading in adults with Asperger syndrome.' *Autism 8*, 3, 249–266.

Powell, M. B., Fisher, R. P. and Wright, R. (2005) 'Investigative interviewing.' In N. Brewer and K. D. Williams (eds), *Psychology and Law: An Empirical Perspective* (pp.11–42). New York: Guilford.

Premack, D. and Woodruff, G. (1978) 'Does the chimpanzee have a theory of mind?' *Behavioral and Brain Sciences 1*, 4, 515–526.

Pryor, B. and Buchanan, R. W. (1984) 'The effects of a defendant's demeanour on juror perceptions of credibility and guilt.' *Journal of Communication 34*, 3, 92–99.

Radomsky, A. S. and Rachman, S. (1999) 'Memory bias in obsessive-compulsive disorder (OCD).' *Behaviour Research and Therapy 37*, 7, 605–618.

Rao, P. A., Beidel, D. C. and Murray, M. J. (2008) 'Social skills interventions for children with Asperger's syndrome or high-functioning autism: A review and recommendations.' *Journal of Autism and Developmental Disorders 38*, 2, 353–361.

Rapoport, J., Chavez, A., Greenstein, D., Addington, A. and Gogtay, N. (2009) 'Autism spectrum disorders and childhood-onset schizophrenia: Clinical and biological contributions to a relation revisited.' *Journal of the American Academy of Child and Adolescent Psychiatry 48*, 1, 10–18.

Rapp, J. T. and Vollmer, T. R. (2005a) 'Stereotypy I: A review of behavioral assessment and treatment.' *Research in Developmental Disabilities 26*, 6, 527–547.

Rapp, J. T. and Vollmer, T. R. (2005b) 'Stereotypy II: A review of neurobiological interpretations and suggestions for an integration with behavioral methods.' *Research in Developmental Disabilities 26*, 6, 548–564.

Regier, D. A., Narrow, W. E., Clarke, D. E., Kraemer, H. C., *et al.* (2013) 'DSM-5 field trials in the United States and Canada, Part II: Test-retest reliability of selected categorical diagnoses.' *American Journal of Psychiatry 170*, 1, 59–70.

Rey, J. M., Morris-Yates, A., Singh, M., Andrews, G. and Stewart, G. W. (1995) 'Continuities between psychiatric disorders in adolescents and personality disorders in young adults.' *American Journal of Psychiatry 152*, 6, 895–900.

Ritvo, R. A., Ritvo, E. R., Guthrie, D., Ritvo, M. J., *et al.* (2011) 'The Ritvo autism Asperger diagnostic scale-revised (RA ADS-R): A scale to assist the diagnosis of autism spectrum disorder in adults: An international validation study.' *Journal of Autism and Developmental Disorders 41*, 8, 1076–1089.

Robinson, L., Spencer, M. D., Thomson, L. D. G., Stanfield, A. C., *et al.* (2012) 'Evaluation of a screening instrument for Autism Spectrum Disorders in prisoners.' *PloS One 7*, 5, e36078.

Roeyers, H., Buysse, A., Ponnet, K. and Pichal, B. (2001) 'Advancing advanced mind reading tests: Empathic accuracy in adults with a pervasive developmental disorder.' *Journal of Child Psychology and Psychiatry 42*, 2, 271–278.

Rogers, K., Dziobek, I., Hassenstab, J., Wolf, O. T. and Convit, A. (2007) 'Who cares? Revisiting empathy in Asperger syndrome.' *Journal of Autism and Developmental Disorders 37*, 4, 709–715.

Rogers, S. J., Hepburn, S. and Wehner, E. (2003) 'Parent reports of sensory symptoms in toddlers with autism and those with other developmental disorders.' *Journal of Autism and Developmental Disorders 33*, 6, 631–642.

Rose, M. R., Nadler, J. and Clark, J. (2006) 'Appropriately upset? Emotion norms and perceptions of crime victims.' *Law and Human Behavior 30*, 2, 203–219.

Rösler, M., Retz, W., Retz-Junginger, P., Hensch, G., Schneider, M. and Supprian, T. (2004) 'Prevalence of attention deficit-/hyperactivity disorder (ADHD) and comorbid disorders in young male prison inmates.' *European Archives of Psychiatry and Clinical Neuroscience 254*, 6, 365–371.

Rowe, R., Costello, E. J., Angold, A., Copeland, W. E. and Maughan, B. (2010) 'Developmental pathways in oppositional defiant disorder and conduct disorder.' *Journal of Abnormal Psychology 119*, 4, 726–738.

Rutter, M., Bailey, A., Lord, C. and Berument, S. K. (2003) *Social Communication Questionnaire.* Los Angeles, CA: Western Psychological Services.

Rutter, M., Le Couteur, A. and Lord, C. (2003) *Autism Diagnostic Interview-Revised.* Los Angeles, CA: Western Psychological Services.

Salekin, R. T., Ogloff, J. R. P., McFarland, C. and Rogers, R. (1995) 'Influencing jurors' perceptions of guilt: Expression of emotionality during testimony.' *Behavioral Sciences and the Law 13*, 2, 293–305.

Salvatore, C. and Taniguchi, T. A. (2012) 'Do social bonds matter for emerging adults?' *Deviant Behavior 33*, 9, 738–756.

Samuels, J., Bienvenu, O. J., Cullen, B., Costa Jr, P. T., Eaton, W. W. and Nestadt, G. (2004) 'Personality dimensions and criminal arrest.' *Comprehensive Psychiatry 45*, 4, 275–280.

Santosh, P. J. and Mijovic, A. (2006) 'Does pervasive developmental disorder protect children and adolescents against drug and alcohol use?' *European Child and Adolescent Psychiatry 15*, 4, 183–188.

Schaaf, R. C., Benevides, T., Mailloux, Z., Faller, P., *et al.* (2014) 'An intervention for sensory difficulties in children with autism: A randomized trial.' *Journal of Autism and Developmental Disorders 44*, 7, 1493–1506.

Schaaf, R. C., Toth-Cohen, S., Johnson, S. L., Outten, G. and Benevides, T. W. (2011) 'The everyday routines of families of children with autism: examining the impact of sensory processing difficulties on the family.' *Autism, 15*, 3, 373–389.

Scholl, B. J. and Leslie, A. M. (1999) 'Modularity, development and 'theory of mind'. *Mind and Language 14*, 1, 131–153.

Schopler, E., Reichler, R., DeVellis, R., and Dally, K. (1980) 'Toward objective classification of childhood autism: Childhood Autism Rating Scale (CARS).' *Journal of Autism and Developmental Disorders 10*, 1, 91–103.

Schwartz-Watts, D. M. (2005) 'Asperger's disorder and murder.' *Journal of the American Academy of Psychiatry and the Law Online 33*, 3, 390–393.

Scragg, P. and Shah, A. (1994) 'Prevalence of Asperger's syndrome in a secure hospital.' *British Journal of Psychiatry 165*, 5, 679–682.

Seltzer, M. M., Krauss, M. W., Shattuck, P. T., Orsmond, G., Swe, A. and Lord, C. (2003) 'The symptoms of autism spectrum disorders in adolescence and adulthood.' *Journal of Autism and Developmental Disorders 33*, 6, 565–581.

Shattuck, P. T., Seltzer, M. M., Greenberg, J. S., Orsmond, G. I., *et al.* (2007) 'Change in autism symptoms and maladaptive behaviors in adolescents and adults with an autism spectrum disorder.' *Journal of Autism and Developmental Disorders 37*, 9, 1735–1747.

Sibley, M. H., Pelham, W. E., Molina, B. S. G., Gnagy, E. M., *et al.* (2011) 'The delinquency outcomes of boys with ADHD with and without comorbidity.' *Journal of Abnormal Child Psychology 39*, 1, 21–32.

Simonoff, E., Pickles, A., Charman, T., Chandler, S., Loucas, T. and Baird, G. (2008) 'Psychiatric disorders in children with autism spectrum disorders: Prevalence, comorbidity, and associated factors in a population-derived sample.' *Journal of the American Academy of Child and Adolescent Psychiatry 47*, 8, 921–929.

Sinha, Y., Silove, N., Hayen, A. and Williams, K. (2011). 'Auditory integration training and other sound therapies for autsim spectrum disorders (ASD) (Review).' *Cochrane Database of Systematic Reviews, 12*, 1–46.

Siponmaa, L., Kristiansson, M., Jonson, C., Nydén, A. and Gillberg, C. (2001) 'Juvenile and young adult mentally disordered offenders: The role of child neuropsychiatric disorders.' *Journal of the American Academy of Psychiatry and the Law 29*, 4, 420–426.

Sizoo, B., van den Brink, W., Koeter, M., van Eenige, M. G., van Wijngaarden-Cremers, P. and van der Gaag, R. J. (2010) 'Treatment seeking adults with autism or ADHD and co-morbid substance use disorder: Prevalence, risk factors and functional disability.' *Drug and Alcohol Dependence 107*, 1, 44–50.

Smith, S. A., Press, B., Koenig, K. P. and Kinnealey, M. (2005) 'Effects of sensory integration intervention on self-stimulating and self-injurious behaviors.' *American Journal of Occupational Therapy 59*, 4, 418–425.

Sourander, A., Elonheimo, H., Niemela, S., Nuutila, A., *et al.* (2006) 'Childhood predictors of male criminality: A prospective population-based follow-up study from age 8 to late adolescence.' *Journal of the American Academy of Child and Adolescent Psychiatry 45*, 5, 578–586.

Spek, A. A., Scholte, E. M. and van Berckelaer-Onnes, I. A. (2010) 'Theory of mind in adults with HFA and Asperger syndrome.' *Journal of Autism and Developmental Disorders 40*, 3, 280–289.

Spiker, M. A., Lin, C. E., van Dyke, M. and Wood, J. J. (2012) 'Restricted interests and anxiety in children with autism.' *Autism 16*, 3, 306–320.

Spotorno, N. and Noveck, I. A. (2014) 'When is irony effortful?' *Journal of Experimental Psychology: General 143*, 4, 1649–1665.

Steadman, H. J. (1981) 'Critically reassessing the accuracy of public perceptions of the dangerousness of the mentally ill.' *Journal of Health and Social Behavior 22*, 3, 310–316.

Stephens, S. and Day, D. M. (2013) 'Distinguishing among weapons offenders, drug offenders, and weapons and drug offenders based on childhood predictors and adolescent correlates.' *Criminal Behaviour and Mental Health 23*, 3, 177–190.

Stone, D. L. and Colella, A. (1996) 'A model of factors affecting the treatment of disabled individuals in organizations.' *The Academy of Management Review 21*, 2, 352–401.

Stone, V. E. and Gerrans, P. (2006) 'What's domain-specific about theory of mind?' *Social Neuroscience 1*, 3–4, 309–319.

Stone, V. E., Baron-Cohen, S. and Knight, R. T. (1998) 'Frontal lobe contributions to theory of mind.' *Journal of Cognitive Neuroscience 10*, 5, 640–656.

Swanson, J. W., Holzer, C. E., Ganju, V. K. and Jonu, R. T. (1990) 'Violence and psychiatric disorder in the community: Evidence from the epidemiological catchment area surveys.' *Hospital and Community Psychiatry 41*, 761–770.

Tani, M., Kanai, C., Ota, H., Yamada, T., *et al.* (2012) 'Mental and behavioral symptoms of persons with Asperger's syndrome: Relationships with social isolation and handicaps.' *Research in Autism Spectrum Disorders 6*, 2, 907–912.

Tantam, D., Monaghan, L., Nicholson, H. and Stirling, J. (1989) 'Autistic children's ability to interpret faces: A research note.' *Journal of Child Psychology and Psychiatry 30*, 4, 623–630.

Tata, P. R., Leibowitz, J. A., Prunty, M. J., Cameron, M. and Pickering, A. D. (1996) 'Attentional bias in obsessional compulsive disorder.' *Behaviour Research and Therapy 34*, 1, 53–60.

Taylor, E. and Sonuga-Barke, E. (2008) 'Disorders of Attention and Activity.' In M. Rutter *et al.* (eds) *Rutter's Child and Adolescent Psychiatry* (5th ed.). Malden, MA: Blackwell Publishing.

Taylor, P. J. and Gunn, J. (1984) 'Violence and psychosis I: Risk of violence among psychotic men.' *British Medical Journal 288*, 6435, 1945–1949.

Teplin, L. A., Abram, K. M., McClelland, G. M., Dulcan, M. K. and Mericle, A. A. (2002) 'Psychiatric disorders in youth in juvenile detention.' *JAMA Psychiatry 59*, 12, 1133–1143.

Thapar, A., Harrington, R. and McGuffin, P. (2001) 'Examining the comorbidity of ADHD related behaviours and conduct problems using a twin study design.' *The British Journal of Psychiatry 179*, 3, 224–229.

Thomeer, M. L., Lopata, C., Volker, M. A., Toomey, J. A., *et al.* (2012) 'Randomized clinical trial replication of psychosocial treatment for children with high-functioning autism spectrum disorders.' *Psychology in the Schools 49*, 10, 942–954.

Tietz, J. (2002) 'The boy who loved transit.' *Harper's Magazine 304*, 43.

Tiihonen, J., Isohanni, M., Räsänen, P., Koiranen, M. and Moring, J. (1997) 'Specific major mental disorders and criminality: A 26-year prospective study of the 1966 northern Finland birth cohort.' *American Journal of Psychiatry 154*, 6, 840–845.

Tyrer, P., Gunderson, J., Lyons, M. and Tohen, M. (1997) 'Special feature: Extent of comorbidity between mental state and personality disorders.' *Journal of Personality Disorders 11*, 3, 242–259.

Vachon, D. D., Lynam, D. R. and Johnson, J. A. (2014) 'The (non)relation between empathy and aggression: Surprising results from a meta-analysis.' *Psychological Bulletin 140*, 3, 751–773.

van de Cruys, S., Evers, K., van der Hallen, R., van Eylen, L. *et al.* (2014). 'Precise minds in uncertain worlds: Predictive coding in autism. *Psychological Review 121*, 4, 649–675.

van der Gaag, R. J., Caplan, R., van Engeland, H., Loman, F. and Buitelaar, J. K. (2005) 'A controlled study of formal thought disorder in children with autism and multiple complex developmental disorders.' *Journal of Child and Adolescent Psychopharmacology 15*, 3, 465–476.

Veale, D., Freeston, M., Krebs, G., Heyman, I. and Salkovskis, P. (2009) 'Risk assessment and management in obsessive-compulsive disorder.' *Advances in Psychiatric Treatment 15*, 5, 332–343.

Vogel, M. and Messner, S. F. (2011) 'Social correlates of delinquency for youth in need of mental health services: Examining the scope conditions of criminological theories.' *Justice Quarterly 29*, 4, 546–572.

von Polier, G. G., Vloet, T. D. and Herpertz-Dahlmann, B. (2012) 'ADHD and delinquency: A developmental perspective.' *Behavioral Sciences and the Law 30*, 2, 121–139.

Vreugdenhil, C., Doreleijers, T. A. H., Vermeiren, R., Wouters, L. F. J. M. and van den Brink, W. (2004) 'Psychiatric disorders in a representative sample of incarcerated boys in The Netherlands.' *Journal of the American Academy of Child and Adolescent Psychiatry 43*, 1, 97–104.

Wallace, B. (2012) 'Autism spectrum: Are you on it?' *New York Magazine*, 12 May 2014.

Wallace, C., Mullen, P. E. and Burgess, P. (2004) 'Criminal offending in schizophrenia over a 25-year period marked by deinstitutionalization and increasing prevalence of comorbid substance use disorders.' *American Journal of Psychiatry 161*, 4, 716–727.

Walsh, E., Buchanan, A. and Fahy, T. (2002) 'Violence schizophrenia: Examining the evidence.' *The British Journal of Psychiatry 180*, 6, 490–495.

Wareham, J. and Boots, D. P. (2012) 'The link between mental health problems and youth violence in adolescence.' *Criminal Justice and Behavior 39*, 8, 1003–1024.

Watling, R. L. and Dietz, J. (2007) 'Immediate effect of Ayres's sensory integration-based occupational therapy intervention on children with autism spectrum disorders.' *American Journal of Occupational Therapy 61*, 5, 574–583.

Watson, A. C., Corrigan, P. W. and Ottati, V. (2004a) 'Police officers' attitudes toward and decisions about persons with mental illness.' *Psychiatric Services 55*, 1, 49–53.

Watson, A. C., Otey, E., Westbrook, A. L., Gardner, A. L., *et al.* (2004b) 'Changing middle schoolers' attitudes about mental illness through education.' *Schizophrenia Bulletin 30*, 3, 563–572.

Wellman, H. M., Cross, D. and Watson, J. (2001) 'Meta-analysis of theory-of-mind development: The truth about false belief.' *Child Development 72*, 3, 655–684.

Wessel, E., Drevland, G. C., Eilertsen, D. E. and Magnussen, S. (2006) 'Credibility of the emotional witness: A study of ratings by court judges.' *Law and Human Behavior, 30*, 2, 221–230.

Wessely, S. (1998) 'The Camberwell study of crime and schizophrenia.' *Social Psychiatry and Psychiatric Epidemiology 33*, 1, S24–S28.

White, S. W., Keonig, K. and Scahill, L. (2007) 'Social skills development in children with autism spectrum disorders: A review of the intervention research.' *Journal of Autism and Developmental Disorders 37*, 10, 1858–1868.

White, S. W., Kreiser, N. L., Pugliese, C. and Scarpa, A. (2012) 'Social anxiety mediates the effect of autism spectrum disorder characteristics on hostility in young adults.' *Autism 16*, 5, 453–464.

Willcutt, E. G. (2012) 'The prevalence of DSM-IV attention-deficit/hyperactivity disorder: A meta-analytic review.' *Neurotherapeutics 9*, 3, 490–499.

Williams, K. D. (2009) 'Ostracism: A Temporal Need-Threat Model.' In M. P. Zanna (ed.) *Advances in Experimental Social Psychology*. San Diego, CA: Elsevier Academic Press.

Williams, K. D. and Nida, S. A. (2011) 'Ostracism: Consequences and coping.' *Current Directions in Psychological Science 20*, 2, 71–75.

Wimmer, H. and Perner, J. (1983) 'Beliefs about beliefs: Representation and constraining function of wrong beliefs in young children's understanding of deception.' *Cognition 13*, 1, 103–128.

Wing, L. (1981) 'Asperger's syndrome: A clinical account.' *Psychological Medicine 11*, 1, 115–129.

Wing, L. and Gould, J. (1979) 'Severe impairments of social interaction and associated abnormalities in children: Epidemiology and classification.' *Journal of Autism and Developmental Disorders 9*, 1, 11–29.

Wolke, D., Copeland, W. E., Angold, A. and Costello, J. (2013) 'Impact of bullying in childhood on adult health, wealth, crime, and social outcomes.' *Psychological Science 24*, 10, 1958–1970.

Woodbury-Smith, M. R., Clare, C. H., Holland, A. J. and Kearns, A. (2006) 'High functioning autistic spectrum disorders, offending and other law-breaking: Findings from a community sample.' *The Journal of Forensic Psychiatry and Psychology 17*, 1, 108–120.

World Health Organization (1994) 'F84 pervasive developmental disorders.' In *International Statistical Classification of Diseases and Related Health Problems* (10th ed.). Geneva: World Health Organization. Available at http://apps.who.int/classifications/icd10/browse/2010/en#/F84, accessed on 10 February 2015.

Wright, A., Jorm, A. F. and Mackinnon, A. J. (2011) 'Labeling of mental disorders and stigma in young people.' *Social Science and Medicine 73*, 4, 498–506.

Yirmiya, N., Sigman, M. D., Kasari, C. and Mundy, P. (1992) 'Empathy and cognition in high-functioning children with autism.' *Child Development 63*, 1, 150–160.

Young, R. L. and Posselt, M. (2012) 'Using the transporters DVD as a learning tool for children with autism spectrum disorders (ASD).' *Journal of Autism and Developmental Disorders 42*, 6, 984–991.

Young, R. L. and Rodi, M. L. (2014) 'Redefining autism spectrum disorder using DSM-5: The implications of the proposed DSM-5 criteria for autism spectrum disorders.' *Journal of Autism and Developmental Disorders 44*, 4, 758–765.

Young, S. and Gudjonsson, G. H. (2006) 'ADHD symptomatology and its relationship with emotional, social and delinquency problems.' *Psychology, Crime and Law 12*, 5, 463–471.

Young, S., Gudjonsson, G., Ball, S. and Lam, J. (2003) 'Attention deficit hyperactivity disorder (ADHD) in personality disordered offenders and the association with disruptive behavioural problems.' *The Journal of Forensic Psychiatry and Psychology 14*, 3, 491–505.

Zablotsky, B., Bradshaw, C. P., Anderson, C. and Law, P. (2012) 'Involvement in bullying among children with autism spectrum disorders: Parents' perspectives on the influence of school factors.' *Behavioral Disorders 37*, 3, 179–191.

Zaki, J. (2014). 'Empathy: A motivated account.' *Psychological Bulletin, 140*, 6, 1608–1647.

Zalla, T., Sav, A. M., Stopin, A., Ahade, S. and Leboyer, M. (2009) 'Faux pas detection and intentional action in Asperger Syndrome. A replication on a French sample.' *Journal of Autism and Developmental Disorders 39*, 2, 373–382.

Subject Index

Author Index

Pages 15, 6

15